# FOREIGN AFFAIRS

**Special Collection**

## CRISIS AND RESPONSE

# Introduction

*Gideon Rose*

The project of European integration has always been a dream spurred by a nightmare. To escape the continent's volatile, bloody past, the argument ran, European countries needed to bind themselves together and forge a harmonious common future.

In fits and starts, to varying degrees on varying issues, this project has managed to achieve extraordinary success over the past seven decades, enabling Europe to reach levels of peace and prosperity at which previous generations could only have marveled. But the endeavor has always been more popular with elites than with the masses, has lurched from crisis to crisis, and has struggled to deal with the differences that keep Europe's disparate parts from forming a seamless whole.

*Foreign Affairs* has been covering the effort closely from the beginning, and as the Greek crisis comes to a head, we've decided to pull together highlights of our analysis of the quest for economic union in particular. This collection provides an unparalleled look at the past, present, and future of Europe's common currency, showcasing more than two dozen of the world's leading experts on European economics and politics to help you better understand the story behind the headlines. From the earliest days of the European Economic Community, to the formation of the European Union, to the introduction of the euro, to the trauma of the recent financial crisis and the debate over Grexit, the articles trace all the major issues from all significant perspectives.

The current turmoil has not come out of the blue, nor is it the fault of any one party alone. Greece should not have been allowed into the eurozone, because it was so far away from meeting the

*A man cycles by anti-EU graffiti in Athens, Greece June 28, 2015. (Alkis Konstantinidis / Reuters)*

appropriate criteria. Once in, it should not have spent far beyond its means, running a Third World state in a First World area. The banks should not have lent so much to Greece, and once they did so, they should have been forced to accept the adverse consequences of their own bad bets. European leaders should have dealt with the crisis earlier and then should have recognized that their supposed remedies were making matters worse rather than better. And in recent months, Greek leaders should not have played their hand so badly.

The issue now is not just what will happen with Greece but how whatever happens with Greece will affect the future of the broader multigenerational project of European economic integration—in other words, whether the current night terrors will end the dream for good. Like everybody else, we will be watching closely; we offer this collection to explain how and why things got to this point and to suggest where they might go next.

# Europe's Progress Toward Economic Integration

*Willard L. Thorp*

In 1949 Paul Hoffman said to the Council of the O.E.E.C.: "The people and the Congress of the United States, and, I am sure, a great majority of the people of Europe have instinctively felt that economic integration is essential if there is to be an end to Europe's recurring economic crises." He was certainly right in stressing the "instinctive" source of the conclusion, for this put the matter in the realm of feeling, implying an unreasoned background and the absence of any strict definition. The various discussions of economic integration show a common agreement as to the general direction in which Europe should go but also provide an uncommon confusion of terminology (coöperation, coördination, integration, unification) and wide disagreement as to who is to go on which route, how far, and to what specific goal.

"Europe" did not become an important proper noun in American economic foreign policy until General Marshall on June 5, 1947, suggested that United States assistance would no longer be given on a piecemeal basis but rather in relation to a joint program, "agreed to by a number, if not all European nations." When the Marshall Plan was enacted, the preamble to the Act included these words: "Mindful of

WILLARD L. THORP, Professor of Economics, Amherst College; Assistant Secretary of State for Economic Affairs and member of U.S. delegations at many international conferences, 1946–52; author of "Trade, Aid or What?" and other works on economic topics the advantages which the United States has enjoyed through the existence of a large domestic market with no internal trade barriers," it shall be the policy to encourage "that economic coöperation in Europe which is essential for lasting peace and prosperity." This certainly was a comfortably vague statement.

The position of the European countries was equally unimpeachable and general. And the early reports of the Economic Coöperation Administration are full of phrases such as "maximum benefit for Europe as a whole," "total economic effort of the European nations" and "total European economy." The European Recovery Program therefore focused attention on Europe as such, but there is no evidence that it was to be more than a joint program and coöperative venture.

The advocates of a united Europe were not content to let the matter rest at this point. The effort to write something stronger into the original Marshall Plan legislation had been turned down as implying interference. However, in April 1949, the revised Act included a new declaration: "It is further declared to be the policy of the people of the United States to encourage the unification of Europe." (The House words "and federation" were deleted in conference.) When Senator Fulbright proposed as an amendment the insertion of "political" before "unification," Senator Connally summarily stated that "The committee considered this amendment very carefully, and was almost unanimously against either undertaking to coerce Europe or to pay Europe to achieve union," and the amendment was voted down, 67 to 15. As to the final result, a later report by the Senate Committee on Foreign Relations was guilty of an understatement when it said, "There is some doubt as to the meaning, whether this language refers to political federation, economic federation, or both."

While the Congress was limiting itself to the encouragement of some sort of unification, a much more vigorous position was taken by the E.C.A. Administrator, Mr. Hoffman. On October 31, 1949, he addressed the Council for Economic Coöperation in Paris and outlined two tasks to be performed; first, to balance Europe's dollar accounts, and second, the building of an expanding economy in Western Europe through economic integration. The substance of such integration would be the formation of a single large market within which quantitative restrictions on the movements of goods, monetary barriers to the flow of payments and, eventually, all tariffs are permanently swept away. . . . The creation of a permanent, freely trading area, comprising 270,000,000 consumers in Western Europe, would have a multitude of helpful consequences. It would accelerate the development of large-scale, low-cost production industries. It would make the effective use of all resources easier, the stifling of healthy competition more difficult.

In developing the theme further, he stressed the need for a substantial measure of coördination of national fiscal and monetary policies, necessary adjustments of exchange rates, means of cushioning temporary disturbances, and the resolution of conflicting commercial policies and practices. At least, here is some real content, although the definition in terms of a specific program still is not very exact.

Another important statement on the subject was made by General Eisenhower on July 3, 1951, before the English-Speaking Union in London. There can be no doubt as to the direction of his argument, although again the concept is not entirely clear. The attack is on "patchwork territorial fences," which foster localized interest, pyramid costs, bar the efficient division of labor and resources, and promote distrust. The plea is for "unity," "a United Europe," "integration of Western Europe," "a workable European federation" and "a similar integration" to that of the British Commonwealth and the United States. "Once united, the farms and factories of France and Belgium, the foundries of Germany, the rich farmlands of Holland and Denmark, the skilled labor of Italy, will produce miracles for the common good."

This position was restated by President Eisenhower on January 20, 1953, in his inaugural address: "In Europe, we ask that enlightened and inspired leaders of the Western nations strive with renewed vigor to make the unity of their peoples a reality." Three weeks later, Secretary Dulles, returning from his first flying trip abroad as Secretary of State, said that, "It has been clear for some time that the biggest single postwar task would be to end the disunity in Europe which makes for weakness and war." Although not explicitly stated, his interest clearly lay in avoiding the division of Europe "into rival national camps." His report was concerned primarily with the European Defense Community, although he pointed to the Schuman Plan as an outstanding example of accomplishment.

There can be no doubt about the strong American interest in European integration, but it also has had European support. Many European statesmen have actively endorsed the notion, although they often put more emphasis on the obstacles. Many of the most enthusiastic supporters do so for political reasons, usually related to the problem of Germany and her relations with the West. On the other hand, many have stressed the economic importance of a unified Europe. Europe, they say, is cut up into small pieces and national boundaries create major obstacles to the flow back and forth of economic goods, labor and capital. The result is that resources are not used effectively, trade is restricted, competition is limited and economic growth is hampered. The structure of each little economy is forced into an unspecialized and inefficient pattern. In the absence of economic expansion, class conflicts are sharpened, and monetary policies are limited to the narrow base of each country's resources. Economic aggression, retaliation and international distrust result.

The confusion in terminology obscures the significance of recent developments. From the economist's point of view, it is not difficult to describe economic integration in terms of the ideal. The fundamental purpose of economic policy is to develop and utilize resources so that they will produce the maximum supply of goods and services, and to distribute the economic product so that the effective demand for it is best satisfied. The maximum satisfaction of wants can be achieved when there is the freest flow of resources and products, when arbitrary interference with economic forces is at a minimum. In a large country like the United States, this objective is fairly well achieved because there is a single market: labor and capital can move about freely, the economies of large-scale operation can be achieved, and products produced over a wide area can be marketed over a similarly wide area. There are no currency problems since the dollar is legal tender everywhere and commercial and legal procedures are fairly well standardized. The forces of competition can work over a whole continent and provide that dynamic element which leads to higher productivity.

The same state of affairs would certainly be achieved for Europe if a single government replaced the governments of the separate Western European countries, but few indeed have ever argued for such a drastic step. A much larger group of advocates talks of federation, but disagrees as to the essential area that should be federated and the amount of authority to be transferred to the central government. Neither single government nor federation has appeared. More than five years have passed since Congress stated the American position in one sentence and Paul Hoffman outlined the economic argument in more detail. In both cases, it was clear that the proponents believed that a substantial amount of economic integration could take place even without political unification. How much progress has been made since then?

## THE FIRST TEST: THE FLOW OF TRADE

A phrase which recurs again and again in discussions of economic integration is that of "the common market." The first test of whether progress has been made, then, is the degree of the reduction of trade barriers in Europe and the expansion of trade. The immediate postwar period found the European countries not only impeding trade by tariff barriers but directly cutting down their imports by quota restrictions. They were all in difficulties over the balance of payments as the result of the heavy demand for imported goods, the shortage of goods for export, the reduction in invisible earnings, the loss of foreign assets and the increase in foreign liabilities. Imports had to be limited to the foreign purchasing power available (plus assistance) and this was done by import controls.

At first, efforts to resume trade took the form of bilateral agreements, with more or less equal commitments on each side to buy and sell in increased amounts, thus not adding to each other's trade deficit. Obviously, this was a very limited approach and only the establishment of the European Payments Union made possible multilateral settlements whereby a country might use its surpluses with one country to offset deficits with another. At the same time, the O.E.E.C. embarked on a program of trade liberalization whereby the various member countries simultaneously undertook to remove quota restrictions against each other. There have been times when countries felt their reserves were threatened and have backslid. But in June 1954, the average degree of liberalization achieved was about 80 percent; Austria and France had freed more than 50 percent of their trade, while Germany, Italy, the Netherlands, Portugal, Sweden and Switzerland had freed more than 90 percent.

This is real progress, of course, but the quota restrictions that remain are important, and from time to time countries have had to suspend liberalization (the United Kingdom in November 1951 and France in February 1952). Also, it should be noted that liberalization of trade in agricultural produce lags behind that in raw materials and even manufactured goods. Furthermore, the liberalization program does not relate to trade on government account, and this has increased substantially since before the war.

Quotas are largely a postwar phenomenon. Although they were adopted originally for reasons of balance-of-payments, they also provide protection for domestic industries. The substantial residue still present is therefore net loss when compared with the earlier European trade picture; but the situation is decidedly better than it was in the immediate postwar years.

It is difficult to evaluate the argument sometimes heard that reduction of barriers to intra-European trade will increase competition within the area, that this will lead to increased productivity, and that this greater production will act to strengthen European sales in markets outside the European area. This seems to be a series of propositions containing many "leakages," so that the premise does not necessarily lead to the conclusion. It is not clear that increase in productivity requires such a large market, except for a few products involving very large-scale production. (The argument was first put forward by an automobile manufacturer.) Competition may come from outside, or may take place in the outside markets where a small country would certainly have to sell to obtain foreign exchange. And differences in productivity can be more than offset by the level of foreign exchange rates. In fact, it is easy to postulate that a preferred market within Europe might reduce some of the pressure to venture into other areas, or to argue that competition is a cultural habit and not much related to whether the area involved is large or small. Despite these caveats, most economists would agree that removing barriers will tend to lower rather than increase costs. It is clear that the E.P.U. and the program to liberalize trade made possible a considerable expansion in intra-European trade, and this is certainly to be desired.

The O.E.E.C. focused its attack on quantitative restrictions for four reasons. First, their economic effect is likely to be greater than that of a tariff. Tariffs add a fixed amount to the cost of delivering the goods to the importing customer, but there is no limit to the amount of goods which can flow over the barrier. Quotas, however, establish a limit in terms of quantities and the effect on price is limited only by the elasticity of the demand. Second, quotas may be used for discrimination among competing countries, while tariffs, at least so long as the most-favored-nation clause applies, do not inject an artificial selection among foreign producers. Third, quota restrictions are the latest in date of the various types of international barriers and have the least vested interest behind them. Finally, tariffs are more clearly in the domain of GATT—the General Agreement on Tariffs and Trade— and international organizations have an undue respect for the "no trespassing" rule.

The measurement of tariff levels is certain to be an unsatisfactory undertaking. However, estimates published by GATT indicate that European tariffs rose substantially from 1925 to 1939 and that the trend has been downward since 1947 as a result of multilateral negotiations at Geneva, Annecy and Torquay. While Scandinavian tariffs were lower in 1952 than in 1925, those of the United Kingdom and other countries of Western Europe were higher. The prospect is not bright for further reductions by the method of reciprocal concessions, because some countries already have very low tariffs and therefore cannot reciprocate. GATT has been considering proportional reductions as a possible road to further progress, but no agreement on principle or method has yet been reached. Thus in regard to tariffs as well as quotas the situation is worse than in the inter-war period but better than during the early post-war years, with further improvement appearing to be increasingly difficult.

If one dares to draw generalizations from statistical aggregates, it may be noted that the records show that the value of export trade by the O.E.E.C. countries has increased each year since the war, and, with the exception of 1950, each year since 1948 has seen the value of their exports to each other expand more rapidly than exports to other areas. The percentage of intra-O.E.E.C. exports to total exports during the first six months of 1954 was slightly higher than the prewar level (50.6 compared with 50.4). Since imports from outside the area are related to the amount of external aid, and since this has been diminishing, imports from sources within the area have increased more rapidly since 1948 than imports from other countries. There does not appear to be any appreciable difference in price behavior for export trade within the area and to countries outside it, so the percentage changes in value of exports reflect changes in volume of trade. However, prices of goods from outside the area have risen relatively more from prewar levels than prices of goods traded within the area, so the increased ratio of imports within the organization to total imports (44.1 compared with 39.3) probably understates the changing source of imports.

Two conclusions can be drawn from this record. In the first place, since imports and exports in intra-O.E.E.C. trade must be approximately equal, imports from outside the area have not increased as rapidly as have exports to the outer area. Secondly, trade among the countries which are members of the organization has shown a substantial gain during the postwar period; and they have increased their trading with each other more than with the rest of the world. It might also be added that the volume of intra--O.E.E.C. trade has increased more rapidly than the rate of production, when measured either against the prewar situation or since 1948. These figures would tend to support the conclusion that the European countries constitute slightly more of a common market today than before the war, and substantially more than in the early postwar years.

## THE FLOW OF LABOR AND CAPITAL

But the notion of a common market does not relate solely to the purchase and sale of commodities. It also involves the flow of the mobile factors of production, labor and capital. In the days when there was substantial migration to the United States and other areas, this safety valve tended to equalize labor differences in Europe. During the inter-war period, restrictions on the international movement of peoples developed rapidly. Doors were closed overseas, and licensing requirements for permission to work, encouraged by labor unions and professional organizations, hampered the foreigner's opportunity in Europe.

Since the war, the situation has remained largely frozen because of the shortages of goods and houses, the fear of a flood of refugees, the implications of higher birth rates, and, finally, the commitment of governments to maintain full employment. To be sure, exceptions have been made—as in France, where it is estimated that there has been a total gross immigration of 500,000 between 1946 and 1952, and in the case of coal miners into Belgium and Great Britain and of foreign seasonal workers into Switzerland. One consequence of the establishment of Benelux is that workers can move freely among the three countries, although they do not seem to have done so in any appreciable numbers. Nevertheless, it is probably true that the boundaries are as tightly closed as before against intra-European migration as a means of achieving more efficient utilization of Europe's labor supply. Certainly, there has been no significant increase in labor mobility.

The entire international long-term capital market has been inactive since the early thirties. Furthermore, the postwar period has been one in which the need for capital within each country, plus the obligations of a number of them toward overseas territories, was so great as to make any redistribution of capital funds among the European countries quite unlikely. It is difficult to get a pooling if it merely means shifting capital from the country where the shortage is least severe to one where it is greater.

Actually, the O.E.E.C. was never able to develop a "plan for Europe." A limited attempt was made to achieve some rationalization in certain strategic areas by setting up technical committees in iron, steel and oil. The member countries informed the committees of projects for expansion, reconstruction or modernization in these sectors of industry. The committees reviewed the projects and in the light of the total European picture reported back to the country and to the E.C.A. It is said that in certain cases programs were revised or adjusted, and that the accumulated information made it possible to consider implications for raw materials, power and the like.

But the nearest to a coördination in the use of capital has come through United States aid. This flow was consciously directed to the different countries with an eye to their need for foreign finance. However, this element in the picture is sharply diminishing. In general, it can be said that the supply of capital in each country is related primarily to its own savings (including enforced savings through taxes) and that each country allocates its investment resources largely within its own boundaries. Thus separate national needs and planning tend to limit greatly the efficient allocation of capital in Western Europe as a whole.

Another element in the disintegration of Europe which reached back to the prewar era was the breakdown of the international monetary machinery. The thirties saw devaluations and related variations in foreign exchange levels. In the immediate postwar years nearly all currencies were inconvertible and international payments were largely on a bilateral basis. Short-term adjustments were made through limited inter-government credits.

Although American assistance improved the situation somewhat, the chief agency for putting intra-European settlements on a multilateral basis was the European Payments Union, established in 1950. Not only did this device provide for the clearing of surpluses and debits among its members but it also provided for the extension of credit within certain limits. Thus, each country could operate on the basis of its economic position toward all the others instead of being concerned over each bilateral balance. The E.P.U. is of course important beyond the European countries involved; it probably handles the settlements of some 50 percent of the payments arising from world trade.

The basic Payments Union agreement itself makes clear that it was not designed to be the first step toward a single currency for Europe, but rather that it would be a transitional system intended to facilitate a return to complete multilateralism in trade and to the general convertibility of currencies. It has achieved its initial purpose of bringing about a substantial degree of convertibility for the currencies of its member countries with each other. However, while convertibility within a regional system is helpful to the members, problems remain because of surpluses or deficits with countries outside the area. The monetary machinery will never work smoothly if the basic economic relationships do not permit general multilateral trade and, with it, the convertibility of currencies.

One of the most important contributions made by O.E.E.C. and E.P.U. is in convincing the members that they have an important interest in each other's business. Thus it has come to be accepted that the economic situation of any member of E.P.U. is subject to detailed examination by a competent group representing the organization. From time to time, the 18 member governments submit to an extremely detailed examination of their economic and financial positions and policies—once closely guarded secrets. These examinations often serve to bring to light repercussions which such policies may have on the economies of other countries. The international organization seems to have no inhibitions about making recommendations concerning the internal financial and economic policies of its members (except direct suggestions as to exchange rates). At this point, something new has been added—a real degree of coöperation among the countries of Western Europe in monetary and fiscal policy.

## FORMS OF PARTIAL INTEGRATION

In examining the progress which has been made toward European integration, one must also note certain forms of partial integration, the first being the effort to develop customs unions or other special forms of coöperation by smaller groups of countries. In his Paris speech, Mr. Hoffman had stressed the desirability of such arrangements, and in the renewal of the E.C.A. legislation in 1949 much was made of their promise. However, in spite of brave statements of intent, unstinting work by technical experts and frequent meetings by ministers, Benelux stands out as the only case where the negotiations have led to practical results. The French and Italian Governments signed a customs union treaty but it failed of ratification. The Scandinavian countries began the consideration of a customs union in 1947, but ended by listing the problems which could not be overcome. (To be sure, they did amalgamate their separate air lines.) A project involving both trade and payments to include the Benelux countries, France, Italy and possibly Germany (known by the charming name of Finebel or the less euphonious Fritalux), was dropped since its objectives largely duplicated those of E.P.U. Negotiations between Greece and Turkey appear to be in a stalemate.

The decision to establish an economic union of Belgium, the Netherlands and Luxembourg was made in 1943. Five years later, customs duties among them were abolished and a common tariff against fourth countries was adopted. (Benelux has negotiated in

GATT as a unit.) The elimination of tariffs at the time was largely symbolic, since it was not until the middle of 1949 that internal quantitative restrictions on trade were abolished, with some very important exceptions. Benelux is of course a relative success in the absence of progress elsewhere, but it does suggest that substantial difficulties are inherent in economic union. The Benelux Governments have declared that their hope to achieve the free movement of goods and resources makes necessary a close coördination of internal financial, monetary and economic policies as well as joint external economic policies, and that they have not yet succeeded in bringing them into line, though this is their immediate objective.

Various less ambitious arrangements have been made among other nations, perhaps the most important of which involved the United Kingdom and the Scandinavian countries in the payments field (Uniscan). Signed early in 1950, this agreement provided for a limited freeing of some types of capital transfers and service items and the unlimited acceptability of sterling within the area. The recent announcement that France and Germany would endeavor to coöperate more closely on certain matters of common economic interest in trade and investment is as yet only an agreement between heads of governments. How it will be carried out remains to be seen.

There is little encouraging to report in the way of partial integration by geographical sub-groups, but the idea of putting sectors of the economies of several nations under a supranational authority—as in the European Coal and Steel Community—is a recent major experiment. Many supporters of the Coal and Steel Community—the Schuman Plan—feel that it suggests the route to be followed for real European integration. It is too early to be able to judge its effectiveness as an instrument of integration, but it has broken down many barriers within the area of the six countries involved; the intra-community trade in coal has already increased while coal imports into the area have fallen. No notable change in pattern for steel is yet visible. The fact that the Authority has substantial funds from its regular revenue and from a United States

Willard L. Thorp

loan gives it the opportunity to apply new capital on the basis of over-all economic criteria rather than according to separate national compartments.

The Schuman Plan clearly is an integrating force in Europe. In fact, the chief problem of its future is whether or not it can operate on a common market basis alongside national behavior in other economic categories. If wage, tax or credit policies differ widely among the members, then the common market for coal and steel will be subject to tremendous strains. On the other hand, it will itself exert a pull toward compatible policies. Undoubtedly, the common defense effort will contribute to such a harmonization. Perhaps the single patent office as envisaged by the Council of Europe is also worthy of note as a development in a highly specialized area. At present, however, no other suggestion for sector integration, as, for example, that of a "green pool" to integrate European agriculture, seems to be under serious consideration.

## V. CONDITIONS OF FURTHER PROGRESS

By the usual indicators, great economic progress has been made in Europe during the last five years. But progress in the direction of integration has not been so notable, despite apparent European enthusiasm and strong American support. Evidently there are many forces besides social and political inertia which give national boundaries persistent importance, many vested interests which prefer the security of a protected market to the strains of external competition.

It has always been recognized that one obstacle to integration would be the different levels of economic wealth and resources of the various countries. Other differences are also important. A quite complete economic integration would be much easier to achieve if all the countries involved either had totalitarian governments or a minimum of government intervention in their economies. But the fact that they vary so widely in the extent to which governments participate in economic life and take responsibility for it makes unification particularly difficult. Under these circumstances, it has been much easier to arrange joint adventures rather than an unlimited partnership.

As to the likelihood of further progress, three changing factors need examination. The first is that so much economic progress has been made. There is obviously a relationship between the economic pressures under which a country finds itself and its willingness to take revolutionary steps. When there are shortages of raw materials and capital and when the international machinery falters, a small country is likely to be in special trouble. The larger the country, the more its recovery is in its own hands, so to speak, and the less it is at the mercy of the external world. Under such circumstances, size looks very attractive.

Today the economic pressures have eased. The European economies have made a strong recovery. The index for industrial production for O.E.E.C. countries was at 80 in 1948, 100 in 1950, 116 in 1953, and 125 in the second quarter of 1954. Intra-European trade has expanded even more. Measured in volume, it rose from an index of 59 in 1948 to 100 in 1950, 120 in 1953, and 140 in the second quarter of 1954. Rearmament expenditure seems to have reached a plateau. Inflation has been brought under control and reserves are much greater. In other words, the painful postwar economic strains and stresses are relaxing. The countries of Western Europe have more leeway to coöperate in their programs and policies; but by the same token they are less likely to take revolutionary steps, such as a more formal unification of Europe would involve.

Nor is economic pressure the only force which has diminished. The Gray Report (November 1950) stated that rapid progress toward Western European integration was of great immediate significance as an essential element in improving national morale and fears for the future on the Continent. The last three years have seen this picture change also. To be sure, there is continued interest in the joint effort of common defense—an active force for integration. Since a strong defense must rest upon a strong economic base, the interest in economic progress will continue, but it no longer holds the center of the stage and the direct pressures for extraordinary measures of economic integration have somewhat subsided.

The second development of some importance is the growing awareness of the fact that there are limitations on the regional approach. The economist does not think in regional terms; to him, geography is important only as it affects shipping costs and creates a problem of the appropriate location of economic activity. The ideal economic goal is to have or approximate a common market for the world rather than merely for some region. The larger the unit, the better.

The substantial economic progress which has been made in Europe since the end of the war has without doubt been the result of the efforts of the individual countries, plus United States aid, plus the coöperative effort created within the O.E.E.C. However, the problem of Europe is not merely one of its internal economy but of its relationship with the rest of the world. Trade, payments, investments, raw materials are all matters which reach beyond the borders of Europe. Intra-European convertibility still leaves the dollar problem unsolved. Lower trade barriers within Europe are no solution to the expansion of trade with other areas. To be sure, it can be argued that if economic integration of Europe improves its productivity, its competitive position in the United States and in third markets will be strengthened. But barriers outside Europe can also interfere with European progress.

One basic issue is whether or not such a regional preference system works against an even wider multilateralism. Obviously, a system which lowers barriers within the area but raises them against the rest of the world has just this effect. There clearly are economic gains in a system that lowers internal barriers while keeping the outside barriers unchanged. But even so, there are disadvantages if it diverts attention from the wider goal or means the establishment of new structural patterns which do not represent the best allocation of resources within a wider area.

Nor is the principle that barriers will not be raised against outside areas always easy to maintain. How can one judge the action of the

United Kingdom in 1951 when it increased restrictions against both the United States and the E.P.U. area, maintaining the discrimination established under the European liberalization scheme? Particularly relevant is the case of Belgium when for some time it had been a persistent creditor in the Payments Union in excess of its quota. The program which was followed for several years over United States protest was that Belgium should place additional restrictions against the importation of United States goods as a means of encouraging purchasing power to be diverted to European suppliers, thus helping to correct her intra-European payments position. The good neighbor policy within the European economy came into direct conflict with that of a good neighbor in the world economy.

Many of the objectives of European integration can be accomplished by actions on a smaller scale than the European continent, or require action on a greater scale. Premier Mendès-France is not waiting for the unification of Europe, but has said that he hopes to stimulate French industry by opening the doors to foreign competition. In the monetary field, interest is centered largely on a wider extension of convertibility. Perhaps the best source for further economic progress lies in the directions laid out by the early postwar planners. Regionalism provides only the next best solution.

The third special point to be noted is that many people supported economic integration chiefly as a means to political unification, and their interest has now turned to other areas of international coöperation. Senator Vandenberg said in 1949: "This drive for self-help and mutual aid is not only economic. Already it envisions coöperation for security, and it is political in its ultimate aspiration. Here stems the ultimate United States of Europe or its effective equivalent." Senator Fulbright said it more simply: "The E.R.P. will prove to have been a colossal failure, unless political unity is achieved in Europe."

Clearly, the economic objective has not proved sufficient to bring about actual unification, although considerable economic integration has been achieved. However, the desire for greater European unity now has another driving force in the new Western

European Union. In fact, Chancellor Adenauer and President Eisenhower in a joint statement declared that when the decisions taken at London and Paris become effective, "the road towards a strong and united Europe will have been paved." It is likely that, as distinct from the steps contemplated in 1949 when everything seemed to stem from economic interest, further progress toward actual unification will depend upon the strength of other unifying forces. It is likely that, as in the case of the O.E.E.C., the Western European Union and NATO will provide the unity of action needed in their particular fields. Again, the problem is dealt with by a joint adventure rather than a full partnership.

## A TREND ESTABLISHED

After this mixed report on European developments, how can one summarize the situation? If one uses the word "integration" in the dynamic sense of a process rather than a goal, then it is clear that many factors are contributing to the integration of Europe, although the goal of the common market and all the rest is still far away. The trend seems toward a gradual lowering of trade barriers. The monetary situation is less and less a positive obstacle. The Schuman Plan represents a major experiment. Some of the lesser geographical groupings have some promise of achieving closer economic relationships.

However, the decided improvement in the European economic situation has made economic necessity less a rallying-point for those who seek unification, and the reduced amount of American economic aid has weakened one strong centripetal force. But if the drive toward integration of the European economy itself seems less persistent, other integrating forces are at work. The defense community will represent an important factor, even though the machinery of supply in the new program does not appear to promise as much centralization as did the E.D.C. proposal. The political community seems to be gathering strength and the Council of Europe concerns itself from time to time with problems in the economic field. Finally, to the extent that the broader world economy achieves relaxation in trade barriers, increased currency convertibility and a more orderly capital market, this will contribute to the strength of the European economic community.

Perhaps the most important element of all is the fact that certain institutions and habits have been formed within the European community. Government representatives have come to realize that the actions of any one country may seriously affect others, and new forms of inter-governmental consultation have developed. In a world where economic life is so greatly affected by government actions of one kind or another, this new intimacy is of major importance. If European integration is still far away from the ideal goal which might be achieved under political unification, at least developments in the last five years have checked the disintegration of Western Europe into autarchic economic islands and set the trend firmly in the direction of a joint effort to deal with common problems.

# New Opportunities and New Challenges

*Valery Giscard d'Estaing*

The past-including my past-is over. The prophet Isaiah wrote: "Forget the former things. Do not dwell on the past. See, I am doing a new thing. Now it springs up. Do you not perceive it?" At every moment of life, at every moment of activity, one should mostly envisage the future, and that is the reason for the title of these lectures.

In my comments on the world economic situation, I will cover three points. The first will be the conditions for a lasting economic recovery; the second, my view on the phased march toward a new Bretton Woods; and the third, a joint assessment of the structural aspects of the crisis.

## II

The Williamsburg Summit provided an opportunity to mark the end of the world economic crisis we have lived through since 1973. Mutual undertakings should have carried a clear signal to all actors on the economic scene. The opportunity was not seized.

I do not want to minimize the results of the Williamsburg Summit. For instance, the joint statement on arms control and security, in the present context of relations between the Soviet Union and the West, was a significant collective step, with three major components:

- The confirmation by the three European countries concerned that they will proceed with the deployment of Euromissiles starting at the end of this year unless a now improbable agreement on current INF negotiations takes place before; the electoral results since then in the United Kingdom and Italy have given additional weight to this commitment;

- The explicit exclusion of the French and British nuclear forces from INF negotiations, which was necessary since some imprudent steps had led the Soviet Union to insist on their inclusion and cast some doubts on the attitude of Western countries; to be sure, the proposal by the U.S.S.R. after the Williamsburg Summit to impose a freeze on existing nuclear forces, including European ones, shows that this fundamental question, which is addressed in my third Lecture of this series, remains most unfortunately outstanding;

- The reference to the indivisibility of security, to be approached on a global basis, conveys to Japan and indirectly to the People's Republic of China, recently neglected by the United States and European countries, the most welcome indication that any agreement on a new equilibrium of forces in Europe will not be to the detriment of the much needed equilibrium of forces in Asia.

But, as far as the economic recovery is concerned, the Williamsburg communiqué, through its vague references to the commitment to reduce structural budget deficits and to "pursue appropriate monetary and budgetary policies that will be conducive to low inflation, reduced interest rates, higher investment, and greater employment opportunities," does not reflect any resolute collective leadership in the management of the world economy. And public opinion, whatever was the wording of the conclusion, intuitively but clearly perceived that there was neither a strong political will nor a personal commitment to enforce the resolutions.

In my judgment, the Williamsburg Summit should have led to three precise mutual undertakings: the United States and Canada committing themselves to action aiming at a decline in interest rates; Japan committing itself to an opening of its economy; and the European countries committing themselves to a greater convergence of their respective economic and financial policies. These undertakings, supplemented by a strong and binding commitment to fight protectionism and to open a dialogue on energy prices with oil-producing countries, would have sent clear signals. Since they did not occur, there is a need to have a fresh look at the world economic recovery, after the Williamsburg Summit and in light of its shortcomings.

Indeed, there are greater indications that a steady recovery is currently under way in the United States, confirming a judgment already made in April. Industrial production has grown since November 1982 by more than eight percentage points, recovering more than two-thirds of the losses registered from July 1981 to November 1982. The latest figures available on the rate of capacity utilization, on orders of durable goods, and more broadly on advanced indicators confirm this trend. After increases, in real terms, at annual rates of more than 2.5 and eight percent respectively in the first two quarters of 1983, the GNP (gross national product) will undoubtedly register additional substantial gains during the second half of the year, and might well, as projected by the Organization for Economic Cooperation and Development (OECD), grow at a yearly rate somewhere between five and six percent at the end of the year. But will this recovery be durable and sustained and sufficiently widespread to cope with the employment problems which are plaguing our societies?

As far as the components of demand in the United States are concerned, there are some positive elements, such as the relatively low level of inventories and household indebtedness and the positive evolution of real wages, but at the same time, the high level of real interest rates, which presently stand at five percent against a historical level of two percent, and the present dollar exchange rate act as deterrents to exports and to productive investments.

Factors other than real interest rates, such as consumer demand, fiscal incentives and profitability, are important determinants for business investment, but a significant decline in nominal interest rates is awaited by markets as a signal of a sustained recovery. This issue is linked to the question of the U.S. budget deficit in a manner clearly summarized by Martin Feldstein: "If the Government continues to borrow 5 or 6 percent of the gross national product to finance its budget deficits, the real interest rate must remain high in order to squeeze private borrowers down to the limited amount of funds that remain . . . . Real long-term interest rates must be reduced by convincing evidence that the budget deficit in future years will be declining rapidly."1 In the absence of any precise commitment by the United States in Williamsburg, I personally do not see how the present deadlock, under which the President wants a rapid increase of military expenditure, the Congress wants to protect social expenditure, and nobody wants seriously to increase taxes, could be overcome before the November 1984 election. It means that high real interest rates and a high real exchange value of the dollar, even if it is slightly reduced, might persist, thus hindering recovery forces presently at play.

But more fundamentally there is a risk that the international diffusion of the U.S. recovery will not take place according to usual patterns, which might in due course hurt the U.S. economy itself, even if it is less dependent than other industrialized countries on export developments. Traditionally a U.S. recovery has fueled exports of developing countries, increasing their orders of equipment goods from countries such as Japan, Germany and France, and the interdependence between European countries has led to a diffusion in Europe of these expansionary forces, thereby sustaining the world recovery.

This time, and due to the international debt crisis, developing countries will not be in a position to benefit fully from the U.S. recovery. They have undertaken major adjustment programs, which implies that their growth will most probably not exceed two percent in 1983 against an average growth of five to six percent in the past 15 years. Demand for equipment goods from oil-producing countries will fall substantially, as already indicated by Saudi

Arabia, while real economic growth in East European countries, which averaged eight percent in the early 1970s and four percent from 1975 through 1980, should continue to be negative in 1983 after a contraction of two percent in 1981 and one percent in 1982. Therefore, the industrial countries have to count more on themselves than in the past to assure a lasting recovery. And the signs in industrial countries other than the United States are only moderately encouraging.

At present, the Japanese economy grows at a rate of about three percent, quite modest by its past standards, but the permanent competitiveness of its industry means that it would undoubtedly be in a position to be a full participant in a broad recovery of industrial countries. Thus the key issue is the problem of recovery in Western Europe-at a time when high real interest rates are hurting European countries, probably even more than the U.S. economy, since financial techniques developed in the U.S. markets to alleviate some of the effects of high interest rates (such as the widespread use of variable interest rates and of futures markets) have not yet materialized in the European financial markets.

To be sure, there are some positive signs in Germany and in the United Kingdom. But there is no example in the past of a sustained recovery in Europe without a mutually reinforcing expansion both in Germany and France, two major countries with intense mutual trade relations. Such a coordinated expansion is probably out of reach in present circumstances. After a most unfortunate countercyclical policy in 1981 and 1982, France is engaged in a much needed adjustment program, with an uncertain timetable and an unconvincing overall determination to implement it, in view of the political contradictions of its present government majority. It is unlikely that it will be able to play a positive role in contributing to the present phase of recovery.

After the missed opportunity of Williamsburg, there is therefore a need for a collective discipline to be agreed upon between European countries, a matter on which the meager results of the Stuttgart EEC Summit in June cast evident doubts. However, the campaign for the next European parliamentary election, to be held in June 1984, offers an opportunity to impose on governments this much-needed sense of action. I launched the elections to the European Assembly by direct ballot; in my judgment, even if other internal political consequences might have to be derived from their results in some individual countries, they should fundamentally be used to give popular support to undertakings and policies for Europe as a whole.

As far as the 1984 elections are concerned, the major issues are the unification of the fundamental economic sectors, the impulse to be given to common policies, and the joint problems of defense and political unity of the continent which I address in my second Lecture. At the same time, I would propose that a clear mandate for a coordinated strategy aiming at economic recovery be given to the European Council, which I launched at the same time as the direct elections to the European Assembly; in my view they were the two pillars of future progress toward European unity.

The components of this strategy will have to be assessed in due time in view of the most recent developments in individual economies, but the overall aim is already clear. Countries suffering major imbalances would have to cut further their public expenditures while giving the proper incentive to the productive sector. Countries having mastered their price and balance-of-payments developments would at the same time give some additional impulses to their ongoing recovery. The coordinated strategy launched in mid-1984 would aim at having, at the end of that year, when the U.S. recovery forces might begin to dissipate, an ongoing collective recovery in Europe sustaining a worldwide expansion. At the same time, at the next summit of the major industrialized countries, the European participating countries, as a complementary element to their own action, will have to convince their partners of the need to take mutual reinforcing actions along the lines aptly described by Anthony Solomon and George de Menil in their excellent report on economic summitry or by Helmut Schmidt's prescriptions, which I basically support.2

During the same time, progress should be made toward addressing international monetary problems, and notably debt problems, in order to broaden to the world economy as a whole the recovery in industrial countries.

## III

The Williamsburg Summit ended with an ambiguous reference to an international monetary conference, stating in its final declaration: "We have invited Ministers of Finance, in consultation with the Managing Director of the IMF, to define the conditions for improving the international monetary system and to consider the part which might in due course be played in this process by a high level international monetary conference." As I see it, early strong movement toward a conference is not likely, especially in view of some of the comments publicly offered by U.S. authorities after the Williamsburg Summit. Since procedures should not come before substance, I had advocated, before the summit, a strategy of gradual steps-what I have called "a phased march" toward a new Bretton Woods. This gradual approach remains in my judgment appropriate, but special emphasis should be put in the coming months on initiatives to be taken at the European level as a contribution, or an alternative, to a wider international monetary agreement.

The first step would be to strengthen the role of the ECU (European currency unit) and the EMS (European monetary system), for three mutually reinforcing reasons. A strong European pillar is an indispensable component of any lasting international monetary system. It could provide for Europe an alternative if it appeared that no collective agreement could be reached at the world level. The promotion of the EMS is the best way for Europeans to induce the American authorities to assess better the international role of the dollar, as was demonstrated in 1978–79 when the launching of the EMS led the U.S. government to initiate a comprehensive program to bolster the value of its currency, at a time when relative positions were the reverse of the present ones.

The decisions to be taken to strengthen the EMS are well known: an extension to all European currencies, including the pound sterling; a consolidation and a broadening of existing credit facilities; more automatic intervention on exchange markets; and a wider utilization of the ECU which should become gradually a freely usable monetary instrument and an intervention currency. It implies, above all, a greater convergence in the economic policies of individual countries, since no system of stable exchange rates can function between countries with such differences in inflation rates and monetary aggregate developments. A collective discipline in Europe is at the same time a condition for a lasting economic recovery and for a viable international monetary system. The passage to the second phase of the EMS will therefore be a part of the coordinated economic strategy I will propose for the European elections in mid-1984.

The second step would then be to implement a "target zones" system between the ECU, the dollar and the yen. It would start with wider margins than in the EMS, but these margins would be reduced gradually. Since exchange rates are largely determined by domestic monetary developments, it would require mutually agreed monetary targets. Coordinated interventions by central banks would operate in support of this action.

It is self-evident that interventions cannot assure by themselves the stability of nominal exchange rates if they are not supported by effective economic policies, notably domestic monetary policies, aiming at a stability of real exchange rates. But interventions can avoid unjustified short-term deviations from basic trends and in addition can induce stabilizing forces on exchange markets. In the absence of interventions, speculative placements can shift from one currency to another on the basis of relative nominal interest rates, with a limited risk of seeing potential gains offset by an adverse move of exchange rates. The threat of intervention could induce more caution, through, for instance, a larger use of relative real interest rates or of covered interest rates, and therefore limit the impact of destabilizing capital movements.

After the effective functioning of this target zones system over two or three years-through what I have called a progressive "coagulation" of the system-the time would be ripe to address in a conference the question of the stabilization of monetary relations within a "World Monetary System" (WMS), which should place great weight on the need for stable, while adjustable, exchange rates.

In my judgment, these steps and the ultimate goal to return to a system of stable exchange rates should have been announced in Williamsburg. At a time when we see the end of the energy crisis, whose positive effects on prices and employment should mirror the negative effects of the two oil shocks of 1973–74 and 1979–80, a collective commitment to return to a stable international monetary system would have sent the clear signal that the world economic crisis was over, thus liberating economic initiatives to themselves contribute to the fulfillment of the prediction.

Since this has not proven possible and probably would not prove so before some years, let us take an approach based first on a joint European initiative, but without losing sight of what should be the ultimate goal.

The second major problem for which steps in the direction of a solution should gradually take place is the debt problem. In 1982, the fragility of the system, under which during the last 20 years international bank claims were increasing at an annual rate of 25 percent, was exposed by a series of major financial and political events: the debt crisis in Eastern Europe, in the wake of the Polish crisis; the debt crisis of Latin America, in the wake of the Falklands War; and bank failures in Europe and the United States contributing to the disruption of international financial markets.

These difficulties were related to a conjunction of events: a worldwide recession, a sharp fall in commodities prices, and high interest rates due to excessive reliance on monetary policies. But they also indicated more fundamental problems: a weakness in the structure of developing countries' debt with a pronounced trend toward shorter maturities, which implied great vulnerability to a shift in the attitude of commercial banks; an excessive reliance on the interbank market, highly sensitive to confidence factors; a problem of funding for nondollar-based banks, with the marked reduction in the OPEC surplus.

Under the far-sighted and decisive leadership of the Managing Director of the International Monetary Fund, it has been possible to overcome these crises in 1982 by an appropriate mix of adjustment policies, new financing by the Fund and the Bank for International Settlements, and additional commitments by commercial banks. Prompt action by all countries on the IMF quota increases is a vital element of this ongoing process, based on wider use of the Fund's resources. In addition, unexpected developments or difficulties in the implementation of adjustment programs (as exemplified by the Brazilian case) might well lead to renewed problems, and we should build upon the experience of 1982 to define a more systematic approach. Severe adjustment was obviously needed, but it cannot be a permanent solution for countries facing major development challenges.

The solutions are complex, since the indispensable confidence of lenders, most notably bankers, has to be maintained. This is why I do not believe in schemes based on massive refunding or on mandatory transfers of existing claims to a new international organization. Such a "political" approach ignores several basic factors, notably the very diverse situations of the borrowing countries, and the need to demonstrate their ability to restore in the future an adequate economic balance. One should think rather of mechanisms assuring a more rapid access to short-term liquidity provided by the BIS and the IMF, and of a market for bank claims with some participation by central banks, starting with the weakest element, which is the interbank market. In addition, a system of partial guarantees by multilateral institutions, acting in support of sound economic programs, might be contemplated.

There is a need to avoid past excesses in lending and at the same time to maintain an adequate flow of financing. Clearly, specific measures to proceed with the resumption of a reasonable growth of international credit cannot be determined only through the public representatives or through the private lenders, but require a joint approach and review. Hence my proposal to set up a small but representative international commission, including government officials and private lenders from different countries, and representatives from borrowing countries and multilateral institutions, to make concrete proposals on the handling of debt problems.

Developing countries are severely adjusting their economies, and their people need to know that their efforts will be fruitful. The annual meeting of the IMF and the World Bank should provide an opportunity to display a collective endeavor both to give adequate resources to multilateral institutions and to address more lastingly the problems of developing countries.

If it were possible to launch action in the direction of stability of exchange rates through a European initiative, and to give an adequate answer to the debt problem, major steps would have been taken in the direction of a new Bretton Woods conference which should be the end and the culmination of such a cooperative process.

## IV

While the conditions for a sustained economic recovery in the world and the possible steps in the direction of a new Bretton Woods conference are for obvious reasons the most widely discussed topics in international economic circles, they should not make us lose sight of the long-term and fundamental problems which are confronting us. Clearly their solution will emerge from the collective evolution of our diversified countries and not from official prescriptions. But there is a need to have a fresh look, in view of the most recent developments, at the key elements of long-term growth and prosperity in the world: population and employment; natural resources and energy; new technology and capital formation in the framework of expansion of international trade.

I intend to come back to the fundamental problem of employment, which has economic, social and cultural dimensions, when addressing the challenges facing our democracies. At this stage I will offer only some preliminary remarks on what could be the scope of a joint assessment of issues that the world is collectively facing: the structural aspects of the crisis.

Natural resources and energy. The availability of natural resources is a major component in long-term growth. It has been one of the merits of the Club of Rome, and the Meadows study, even if many of their fears were probably unfounded, that they introduced into the public debate and into public policies the associated questions of natural resources and of environmental values. It is an area where additional progress is needed to reconcile the desire of producing countries to get predictability and profitability for the prices of their products and the desire of importing countries to protect the role of market forces. Discussions are under way at the EEC level with the coming renewal of the Lomé Convention with associated countries, and discussions are still going on at the world level on the Common Fund, and I do not want at this stage to do more than to stress their importance.

The focus on energy issues is an example of the contribution of international cooperation through the summit process as has, again, been lucidly described in the Council on Foreign Relations report.

After the first oil shock, the United States maintained a perverse policy of control of domestic oil prices which implied a subsidy given by domestic producers to oil imports, a blended price for consumers lower than the world level and an associated overconsumption, and an absence of incentive for exploration and drilling. The undertaking by the U.S. President at the 1978 Bonn Summit to decontrol oil prices, an undertaking fulfilled by President Carter in 1979 under a timetable later accelerated by President Reagan, has made major contributions to a better world energy balance: a resumption of oil production and exploration in the United States; a decline by five percent in the energy/GNP ratio in the United States; a decline by one-third in U.S. oil imports. After the second oil shock the coordinated answer given by the 1979 Tokyo Summit, with undertakings on maximum oil imports, was also an important contribution; we have now a manageable world energy situation where demand is compatible for several years with the present level of OPEC productive capacity.

But the breathing space thus obtained should not be used for complacency. We have to build on a sound basis our long-term dialogue with oil-producing countries. But we have, as well, to maintain our efforts to reduce our dependence on oil imports, since the medium-term political vulnerability of the Middle East remains and there is still a long-term need to shift from an oil-dominated energy picture to a more diversified one. This means that consumers should not get wrong signals from market prices (which raises in some countries the question of additional taxation), that all producer prices and notably the price of natural gas in the United States should reflect world prices, that obstacles to the development of coal production and nuclear energy should be removed, and that adequate financial incentives should be given to long-term projects such as synthetic fuels and solar energy.

*Innovation, capital formation and trade flows.* The second fundamental element for which some joint approach is needed is the problem of innovation and capital formation in the framework of increasing trade and capital flows.

To be sure, high-technology industries will not directly solve our problem of employment. According to a Data Resources, Inc. study on the U.S. economy, high-technology industries will see their output more than doubled in the next 15 years (against an increase by about one-third for manufacturing), but in view of their small share and their rapid productivity growth, jobs in these industries will stand at only four million against more than 20 million in the rest of manufacturing and more than 50 million in trade and services.

But they will provide a large demand for highly qualified jobs, consistent with the projected educational level of our young people, contribute to a higher rate of productivity growth, which is the key to living standards, and leave room for a decline in traditional industries where jobs in industrial countries are displaced by the exports of newly industrialized countries.

On this, I must add, because I do not want to be misunderstood, that it is very important for our countries to keep a very broad base of industrial production. The idea of a general evolution toward services or high-technology activities, in isolation from other industries, would be a historical mistake. We need to keep on our soil, your soil, the soil of Western Europe, a large part of the industrial ability to produce general industrial goods. It is not by direct public support that we can solve this problem, but certainly the general environment, the tax policy, the credit policy must be adequate to this goal, which is to keep a diversified, living industrial sector.

Neither can an adequate promotion of high-technology industries depend on undue government interference. We all have in mind examples of state-owned industries where the unpredictability of future financial resources, the absence of adequate reaction to market signals, and the lack of incentives through competition have combined to hamper technological developments. Governments should confine themselves to maintaining an adequate economic environment based on competition, to granting adequate incentives to industry-based research, and to financing fundamental research and seeing to it that its results are readily available to private industry.

But nevertheless, in view of the magnitude of the challenge and the need for international cooperation, I see merits in the idea of some general discussion of major technological problems between summit countries, provided it does not pave the way for a bureaucratic approach to problems which belong to the industry itself. Clearly our market economies and our Western world still have the technological leadership and the aptitude to promote it.

The promotion of technology will imply additional financial requirements on top of those required by traditional manufacturing, housing, and infrastructure, and those required by a forceful energy program. Associated with this, there should therefore be an effort in each industrial country to promote saving, through price stability, an adequate tax structure, and competition between financial intermediaries, and to channel a large part of it toward risk capital and industry financing.

If we succeed in such an endeavor, we will be in a better position to address the difficult question of trade. It is self-evident that the international division of labor benefits all of us and that the key for the development of many developing countries is access to major markets for their products. At the same time, in a period of low growth and rising unemployment, governments in industrial countries are not able to master the everlasting demands for protectionist measures. We all know of examples in the United States, in Europe and in Japan of such moves which under different names, notably self-imposed restrictions, have the same adverse effects on trade, growth and future employment. And, most unfortunately, in spite of the Williamsburg pledge, recent actions such as the quotas imposed on European specialty steels by the U.S. government show that protectionist forces remain very much alive.

A sustained recovery is clearly the fundamental condition for a resumption of trade liberalization which has shown and will show how it can amplify growth and spread its benefits all over the world. If a broadly-based recovery is well under way in 1984, the time might be ripe to launch internationally an initiative on trade which will complement the initiative on technology. It is too early to define it more precisely, but it could include additional access to industrial markets for LDCs' goods, the abandonment of some projects in industries with long-term excess capacity such as the steel industry, and the refining and petrochemical industry, and the promotion of exports of capital goods through adequate financing schemes. If we have been able to resist protectionism during the crisis, it would be a major failure if we were not able to overcome it when the crisis is receding.

Let it be my hope that more convergence between European countries may lay the groundwork for new European initiatives to address jointly with other major countries these long-term issues on which our future depends.

## CURRENT PROBLEMS IN INTERNATIONAL RELATIONS

My topic in this second Lecture will be international relations, mainly in the light of transatlantic relations between the United

States and its Western European partners. Most of the economic questions I dealt with in my first Lecture play, of course, an important role in these relations. But they are only part of a global picture in which ideology, politics, strategy considerations, and reactions of public opinion are also of utmost importance. Therefore, transatlantic relations need to be considered in the broader context of the competition between two geopolitical systems, the Western liberal democracies and the Eastern entity led by the U.S.S.R., two systems which have entered a new period of tension, this time mainly concentrated on Europe.

There is a trend in the United States today toward focusing less exclusively on Europe and showing more interest or concern about other areas, such as Asia or Central America. This might be partly the result of the drift of your society in the direction of the West Coast and the South. But it occurs at a time when the Soviet Union concentrates its efforts on Western Europe. In Western Europe, there are new trends which might be dangerous for our common interests-the pacifist and neutralist movement in Germany (which Chancellor Kohl's victory should not obscure), in the Netherlands, in Scandinavia, and even in France, which has shown more response to pacifism recently than in earlier periods. Also, there is a different approach in analyzing the Soviet situation and the growth of a certain anti-American feeling. All these elements indicate that it is time to think about a common attitude toward East-West relations, about a shared responsibility in North-South relations, and about new initiatives for Western Europe in order to achieve a better balance in our Western world.

## II

The process of détente, which started around 1970, has now been practically interrupted. It was based on a balance of forces and a certain understanding of common interests which have nowadays been reduced. Everybody has become conscious, or should have, of the Soviet military threat, which is now permanent and diversified. But we are also aware of the economic weakness of the Eastern countries and of the contempt of the leaders of the U.S.S.R. for human rights. At the time of Helsinki, now eight years ago, we could expect that our continent could obtain security, foster development and progress in standards of living by commercial and technological exchange, and achieve serious progress in human rights, freedom of information, and free movement of people. Some results were achieved in the following years. But at this point in time, this evolution has deviated from its course. Today, Western Europe's security is jeopardized, East-West trade is hampered, and the eastern part of our continent is a zone which some of its nationals want to leave, whereas our part of the world is a zone where foreign migrant workers long to stay. Obviously, the main objective of the U.S.S.R. is again Europe, after various Third World undertakings, with uncertain success.

What the Soviet Union would like to achieve is not a military invasion and occupation of Western Europe, but what is called, in an inappropriate term, and an inelegant term, "Finlandization" of Western Europe. It is inappropriate because the Finns resent it very strongly since they are trying to keep their own personality and independence. The word "Finlandization" is something which deeply hurts them, and which is certainly not the proper one to characterize the inability to resist any military, or even political, blackmail. But the desire of the Soviet Union to create such an inability, using various leverages such as inter-German relationships, is a reality.

It is strange that so many Europeans do not have a clear perception of this present menace and express more fear of the arms which will protect them tomorrow than of the arms that threaten them today. For some Europeans, the American military presence and strategic deterrence, which appeared yesterday as a safety to our security, are now labeled "risk." People want peace without effort, not understanding what is at stake. The fact that modern armament, mainly nuclear devices, has become an area reserved to specialists may have diluted the traditional link between the people and their defense or their army. European masses seem sometimes less concerned with their defense and to be putting emphasis on other values. Everyone knows the expression, "Besser Rot als Tot" ("Better Red than Dead"), which was used by some German youth and older people too. Our common preoccupation, therefore, has to be: should Europe be defended? Can it be defended? And does it want to be defended?

It is obvious that Europe has to be defended, and in the present situation, to reach the desirable high level of security, we cannot stop or lessen our efforts to achieve a modern and strong defense. This is a reason why we approve your efforts to work toward this vital objective, even if the cost is high. We do also have to stress our political will, to do what we can for the protection of our continent. And I would like the European countries to speak with one voice on this matter of the utmost importance. I was, for instance, very disappointed that the European countries were not able to answer the questions raised by President Reagan or by Vice President Bush, in February of this year, when they said that they were ready to study any proposal or suggestion concerning the deployment, made by the European countries themselves. I think it was a historical occasion that the European countries let slip away.

In this perspective, the progressive deployment of the Euromissiles is an undeniable element of our security and of a balanced situation in Europe. But let's not forget that the rationale of this armament effort is to realize a true balance of forces and not to stress the search for superiority. We should, therefore, maintain our concern for security and keep our armament effort on the borderline of negotiability with the other party. In the field of Euromissiles, it means that the confirmed will for their deployment, which has been adequately expressed in April by Mrs. Thatcher and Chancellor Helmut Kohl in London, should be combined with a phased program of implementation and an affirmation of the possibility for the U.S.S.R. to enter a negotiation at different steps.

This is a complicated technical problem, but I will insist on two points. First, negotiability, which is at the core of discussions about arms control. Clearly, we should not eliminate any option if this option is needed, solely because the Soviets declare it nonnegotiable. But, on the other hand, when a proposition is presented as being open to negotiation, a precise evaluation of the negotiability value is necessary. For instance, I personally think that the most recent proposal, to have another single level of deployment on both sides announced or chosen before the deployment, has a very weak value of negotiability.

It seems to me very important when you speak of negotiability to transfer the possibility of negotiation from what I will call the "ante-period" to the "post-period" of deployment. At the moment there is still the idea that there could be useful negotiations before the deployment. There is not a single chance to succeed there. In fact, insisting on this possibility reduces the credibility of the negotiations. So the move, the change, is to show that first there will be deployment, because now the conditions not to have it will certainly never be met, but after the start of deployment, then the will to negotiate will go on, taking into account the further phases of deployment.

My second point is the very important question of the treatment of independent European nuclear forces. In SALT I and SALT II, it was decided that the British and French strategic forces were not to be included in SALT discussions. In 1979 and 1980, when there was the discussion on the deployment of the Pershing II and cruise missiles, I refrained from taking a public stand because I thought it was impossible for us to take part in a decision which did not concern us because we are not among the deploying countries-and at the same time to affirm that our nuclear forces should be kept out of the negotiations. So my view was to support privately, with the American President, the British Prime Minister and the German Chancellor, the decision for deployment and to tell them we would take parallel steps, such as the development of a new French missile, the S3, which will parallel the deployment of the Pershing. Recently, this position has been changed, and there was an official French expression of support for the deployment. The response by the Soviet Union was predictable: the inclusion of the French and British strategic forces in the negotiation.

This is unacceptable to us for a simple reason. Our nuclear system is intended for two purposes: one, to be used with the allied system in case of a general confrontation, but the other purpose is to be able to match a direct threat by the Soviet Union to ourselves-blackmail, or pressure, or a threat-by the ability to inflict upon them a very damaging strike. So, we cannot enter into negotiations in which our nuclear system will be reduced just to match the intermediate missiles of the U.S.S.R. Because if there was a confrontation, or a threat by the Soviet Union, it would be a threat by all the strategic missiles of the U.S.S.R. They will not say: we will use only the SS-20. They will use all their systems to frighten us. So, we must have an evaluation of our strength which is not calculated only by the medium-range missiles, but by the whole strategic Soviet system. Thus, we have to stress that it is impossible for the French system to be included in the INF negotiations. For the immediate future, we should have to keep the level of our deterrence at at least the present level, and it is only in the case of a significant reduction in the global strategic level of the U.S.S.R. that we could enter into a negotiation. It is an area where developments in recent months have brought at the same time some plusses, with the Williamsburg Declaration recognizing the special character of independent nuclear forces, and some minuses, with the Soviet proposal to freeze such forces; it will remain a major concern for all those attached to a strong and independent Europe, within the Atlantic Alliance.

Whatever our common determination is, we certainly cannot give up hope of a better and more relaxed future for East-West relations in Europe. So the present necessities should not prevent us from expecting that détente might be revived one day, when necessary changes have occurred in the minds of the new Soviet leadership. But in the Western world, there remains an important divergence between those who favor economic and financial pressures in order to bring the communist system to its collapse, and those who think that this policy has proven an illusion in the past, that the Russian people will react to it by sticking closer to its leadership, whatever the hardship might be, and that a change in the regime, which is of course one of our objectives, can only be the result of a slow, long-term and complex evolution.

It is a fact that if we are at this time vulnerable in terms of security, Eastern Europe remains extremely vulnerable in terms of its economy and way of life. Western Europe is more than ever attractive for the various countries of the eastern part of our continent, both for the peoples who long for better living conditions and more freedom-and who have shown this dramatically, for instance, in Poland-and also for the governments which expect much from our technology and from our production to palliate the shortcomings of their centrally-planned economies. Our European agriculture produces enough to feed our own people, and in addition, much of the population of these countries where collectivism has proved unable to provide enough appropriate food. Therefore, I do not think that we should be shy in demonstrating our superiority in this domain, especially as the East European market might be an important element in the recovery of our own economies.

In the recent past, there has been excess in lending. There is now excess in the opposite direction. Of course, we must discuss a common approach to limit energy dependence and to control technological transfers more effectively, which are justified aims. We should also study a reasonable policy for granting new credits under proper terms to these countries, which already have heavy debt burdens and are in the process of severe adjustments, in several cases under IMF programs. We should, using our financial leverage, encourage the trends toward economic reforms, which should bring more decentralization, more openness, and more market forces into largely closed systems.

Our recognized goal-which might seem very illusory to some of you, but my experience with Poland and with Hungary has given me some demonstration of the contrary-should be to increase our economic attraction for Eastern Europe, to create an effect of economic Finlandization. Instead of being only afraid of the military and political pressure coming from the East, we should have a symmetrical pressure coming from the West through a rather sophisticated and complicated policy increasing our economic attraction and, perhaps, presence. Finally, we should also remain firm on human rights, while maintaining a balance between the necessarily discreet diplomatic handling of some individual cases and the need to stress the global problem by public criticism and political discussions.

## III

In the mid-1970s, there was some hope of seeing the relations between the developing countries and the industrialized world start on a new base and of obtaining positive results in pursuing the North-South dialogue, which we started in Paris in 1975. Today we are, on the contrary, faced with a blocked situation. There is certainly a need to find a more pragmatic approach to a problem which remains one of the most dramatic of our time and where the capacity of the Western world to respond to the needs of the South and to contribute better to the realization of its potential is challenged. The communist system has already shown its inability to adapt its programs to the conditions which prevail in developing countries. Let our imagination, our will, and our much more flexible system demonstrate that the liberal world can cope with the problem in an efficient way.

The developing countries appear generally as a unity, even if the nonaligned movement cannot hide political differences and even conflicts among its members. It is not our purpose to challenge this apparent unity of the Third World, but let us make some distinctions for analytical reasons.

The first group is the group of oil-producing countries. They are facing a completely new situation, which will have, if it endures, long-lasting effects not only on the world energy market and on our economies, but also on their own development and on their participation in the various financial circuits. More than ever, the Middle East oil sources remain vulnerable, mainly because of political factors which could have a serious impact on our regular supply. The world economy has been and still is under the destabilizing effects of the erratic movement of oil prices, of the debt problems of some of the most important oil exporters, including those in Latin America, and of the drastic change in the reserve situation of some of the major countries. It seems to me that the time has come for a new dialogue with these countries. This feeling is shared by Helmut Schmidt, who declared recently that "when the heads of governments of the industrial world talk to each other at top level, they should envisage follow-up talks at top level with the major oil-producing countries, too."3 In Rome I had made some proposals toward achieving some kind of long-term assessment of oil prices, which could be in the common interest of all of us. Without prejudging the exact content of this dialogue with the oil producers, there is a need to open it without delay, to review the energy situation, oil prices and their economic consequences which should be a mutual concern.

I do believe in the superiority of dialogue over an attitude of open conflict. You remember that, in the winter of 1973–74, there was the beginning of a confrontation between the oil-producing countries and the consuming countries, with measures of retaliation and some threats against them. It was a possible way, but I did not believe in it because among the oil-producing countries you have many friends of the West. So to enter into a confrontation would have been very dangerous, because we could have destabilized one or two of our potential friends in the area.

For instance, it is fair to say that in the last years the Saudi leaders have had a moderating influence on the energy prices. They avoided an excess in prices and they avoided also the collapse of the market, so they had a responsible attitude. And I thought that jointly we could try to encourage some of the rational or pragmatic attitudes and discourage some of the excesses.

I am always trying to put myself in the place of others. For instance, when I thought of another head of state, I always tried to imagine where he lived and to understand his feelings, which is always very difficult. The developing countries are absolutely convinced that we do not care about their problems and that we are just showing polite interest to avoid aggressive attitudes on their behalf, but that we are not really interested in proposing or enforcing solutions. And indeed, we are giving a very clear demonstration of this: when the price of oil was moving up, all the Western leaders were saying that the price of oil was a question of mutual concern calling for consultation. But now when the price is moving down, we say that it is not a concern for anyone. We are waiting for the decrease in the price of oil, which is cutting incomes in oil-producing countries, stopping their investments, hampering some of their financial resources. So, if we want to convey a feeling of world responsibility, since we asked to discuss the consequences of the increase, we should propose discussing the consequences of the decrease. This does not mean that we should look for a joint unified price-the market forces will come into play-but we should review long-term prospects for alternative sources and try to envisage what the global energy picture could be in the future.

As far as the newly industrialized countries are concerned, most of them being located in Asia and Latin America, they will benefit the most from a world economic recovery, provided they find outlets for their production. The combined efforts made by industrialized countries in the field of new technologies and trade should find useful applications there. Some of these newly industrialized countries have to face a major debt problem, and we should now build upon the experience of 1982 to define a more systematic approach, such as the one I proposed in my first Lecture. It is certainly necessary to handle the debt problem in a coordinated way, both to give these countries some relief in the debt servicing and to maintain an adequate capital flow. The World Bank and the International Monetary Fund should be involved in this effort, while multilateral guarantees could be sought for private lending and direct investments; a specific effort should be made on energy projects.

For some low-income countries, there is a fundamental need to increase official development aid, which is the only regular reliable source of financing most of these countries can count on. In recent years, the world economic crisis has heavily affected these countries, the prices of their commodities, the cost of their energy supply, the volume of foreign aid and investment. Some of them are in a most dramatic situation, for instance in Africa, where climatic circumstances have added to their difficulties. I think that in the common effort to share in order to help these countries overcome this crisis, the United States should have a more positive attitude, in better accordance with your possibilities, with your tradition and with your philosophy. Low-income countries are forgotten in the world of today, since their economic importance is limited. But they will be the test of our ability to cope with situations which are not directly linked with our personal interests.

These new efforts in favor of the low-income countries should be coordinated, as we started to do when we created, at my suggestion, the Coordinated Action for Development in Africa (CADA). We need to address jointly some of the fundamental issues: basic needs, food and agriculture; population policy; stabilization of prices of commodities and compensation for shortfalls in export earnings; and diversification of the economic base. For instance, it is a historical mistake for the European countries and for the United States not to embark on a large program of development in Africa, which would not be very costly and which would probably change the balance for this continent for decades to come.

## IV

Let me now speak of a new start in the construction of Europe, as a balancing factor for the Western world.

European elections to be held in 1984 will be the next and best occasion for European leaders, parties and people to express themselves and to show their capacity to give Europe such a new start. It is true that the faith of the Fathers of Europe has vanished and that the European Community has evolved into a bureaucratic institution with too much bureaucracy and too little imagination. During the last five years of the 1970s there were a number of achievements and an effective impulse was given to the existence of a political Europe by the setting up of the periodic European Councils. But later, in 1979–80, we entered a pre-election period, and no significant progress has been made during the last three years.

So I agree with some statements and I share the disillusioned view of Europe's absence today. It is probably one of the periods in recent history in which European countries are most silent and give least impulse to new proposals or new achievements for the Western world. But I think the time will come for a new start, which would consist in seeking more unification of the fundamental economic sectors, giving impulse to existing common policies, and taking a new approach to the joint problems of defense and political unity of the continent.

I remind you of the statement which was made in 1972 by the Paris Conference of the European heads of state, which declared that 1980 would be the final year for the union of Europe. We are now in 1983 and are still without any significant move toward unification, as demonstrated by the limited results of the European Summit in Stuttgart, where Chancellor Kohl was unable to get adequate backing for his European initiative, modest as it was. In various fundamental economic sectors, like energy, transportation, communications and telecommunications, and financial services, I suggest that we should tend toward large unified European markets where private operators could compete freely. It would need serious measures of deregulation-the United States and the United Kingdom have been taking some in recent years.

In the field of energy, we could think, for instance, of a closer integration of electric grids, the establishment of gas and oil transportation networks considered in the perspective of the global market, the joint development of major projects, like exploitation of the North Sea gas reserves, and common objectives for energy imports.

To give a new impulse also to already existing common policies and define new ones, let us have a review of the Common Agricultural Policy, where real unification should be sought. My proposal would be that, in the future, the level of prices should be indifferent to exchange rates. We should accept that our national economy, when we devaluate, or when we reevaluate, supports the cost of the change. It is a technical point, but it is a fragmentation of the market if every time we change an exchange-rate parity in Europe we restore for agricultural products a tariff barrier, the so-called "monetary compensatory amounts." We should also give consideration to a policy for Mediterranean products, now that the Common Market has to envisage the membership of Spain and Portugal. And we should also better affirm the legitimacy of our policy with a clear and far-reaching debate and discussion with our American partners.

In the field of research and technology, we should consider funding projects and joint endeavors by and between industrial firms, especially in the domain of biotechnology, where Europe has the capacity to develop into a major partner for American and Japanese research and industry. We should also, which is more complicated, devote effort to establishing a coherent common social attitude with a view toward harmonizing labor legislation, and to addressing jointly the most difficult sectoral and regional employment problems.

Finally, the time has come for a new approach to our problems of defense and political unity, to which I would have devoted a large part of my time in the last two years if I had been reelected. I thought that it was too early before to do so for various reasons, but I thought that the time was ripe now to envisage the possibility, the risks, and the challenge of some initiative for European defense. In 1975, Germany and France decided to build a tank-a Franco-German tank-which would have been unique and built half and half by France and Germany, and I regret to have seen this project recently cancelled. Because a closer integration in the field of armaments could have probably led to joint projects and to more interchangeability of equipment.

Some European countries, France and Italy for the moment, are already cooperating in the emergency peacekeeping forces in

Beirut. Why could we not think, for example, of setting up jointly with the other Europeans and, notably, the British, who have some parallel activities in Lebanon, a European rapid deployment force-the ERDF-with a permanent staff and coordinated logistics, which could be used for peacekeeping purposes and for emergencies without having to call for separate European countries to act. And of course we should have an altogether fresh look at nuclear strategies-and it is one of my regrets-I've mentioned this before-that the beginning of this year was not used to make a counterproposal, a suggestion, to the American Administration, concerning the way to deploy in Europe the new intermediate missiles.

In the parliamentary field, which will be more exposed during the next year because of the perspective of the 1984 elections to the European Parliament, why not establish a new mechanism for reaching better harmonization among European legislations? At the moment there is the question of the role and the responsibilities of this Parliament, and there is a conflict between the executive branch and the parliamentary branch over drawing the line, but why not set up a kind of legislative shuttle between the national parliaments and the European Parliament, to progressively create a harmonization and then some unification of the legislation in sensitive fields? Finally, we should also think about other measures which would strengthen the political powers of the Community-for instance, by progressively changing the rules which require unanimity for all important decisions; and by progressively giving room for normal votes by qualified or single majorities; and by having a new thought about the presidency of the Community, which is now a rotating responsibility with little impact on international life. There are ways which could be suggested to change the importance and the efficiency of this presidency.

I really believe we should give Europe a new start in order to react to three potential threats which have developed in recent months: West German neutralism-not the neutralism of all Germany, but forces of neutralism in Germany; the French tendency to protectionism; and British particularism. And if we could embark on a significant move it would be a major contribution to a better balance of power and to a closer understanding in transatlantic relations, which are really the pillars of world equilibrium.

## RECENT TRENDS IN EUROPEAN DEMOCRACIES

This last Lecture refers to recent trends in European democracies. It will be, I suppose, a new and somewhat disturbing approach to the political problems for some of you, but I think that the way to envisage those problems is really fundamental for the future of politics.

All our democracies share common goals and common features, but at the same time each of them has its own particular characteristics. I will not, therefore, address the recent evolution of U.S. society, but focus on European democracies. To be sure, recent developments in Europe must appear to a U.S. observer as contradictory and puzzling. For instance, conflicting electoral results in recent months, with the victory of the left in Spain and Portugal and its defeat or retreat in Germany and Austria; contrasting economic policies between EEC countries leading to periodic gatherings of their finance ministers to adjust their exchange rates accordingly; contradictions among crosscurrents in the same country. The various temptations of neutralism, terrorism or anarchy are often present. But the overall commitment to a common European vision of modern democracy-a new "Weltanschauung"-finally prevails. It is this new vision of European democracy that I would like to discuss with you under three headings: the challenge of intense cultural and social change; a new dimension in political leadership; a new approach to long-term problems.

## II

In recent years, a fragmentation of the traditional society has taken place in Europe. There is, at the same time, a quest for new individual liberties and for reference to the past, what you have called here the "Roots" phenomenon. The young are bringing into the public debate the new themes of environment, human rights, and truth and morality in public life. The citizen who traditionally had only two dimensions-his work and his multigeneration family-is more and more part of a diversified network of associations or groups through which he develops his aspirations for travel, culture and information. New structures have appeared with the rapid evolution of our educational systems and the emergence of new types of family relations. Women are playing an ever-growing role in the work force and in the political debate. An awareness of problems throughout the world and of international tensions is present in day-to-day decisions.

But, when one looks at the various tendencies present in different measure across the borders of Europe, four fundamental trends emerge. First, a move toward autonomy and informality. The quest for personal expression is now one of the most powerful currents, and the rejection of authority and social constraints is still a very important force that has emerged in the last decade. But what is curious to note is that in the last three or four years, one detects a more open attitude, rejecting the most radical stance and accepting some kind of modernized leadership.

A second feature is a move toward intuition and emotion, with the decline of rationalism or moralism, and more broadly of ideologies in general. To be more specific, a political campaign in Europe cannot be won now through rationalism or the quality of argument. It is through emotions, through a more intuitive approach, which was used, for instance, in the last French presidential campaign. At the same time, introspection, femininity, a sense of the potentialities of time act as substitutes for former rigid ideologies.

Third, there is a move toward a new modernity, which started with the rejection of a society dominated by consumption, or a society manipulated by the media and advertising, and which is evolving now in the direction of a new realism.

And the last feature, which is very curious-all this is based on long studies and not on my personal judgment-is a move toward complexity and uncertainty, which is the recognition of the integrated world to which all societies belong.

These fundamental movements have been supplemented by technological changes in the gathering and the transmission of information. The modern media (TV, cable TV, satellites, individual computers, video tapes) add to our societies the new dimensions of instant information, permanent dialogue and added selectivity in choices.

I would like to give you some figures showing how these new trends affect a country like France. Between, for instance, 1974 and 1981-my presidential term-the change in certain aspects of French society has been dramatic and not at all in the political field. For instance, in 1981, 17 percent of the persons interviewed, which corresponds overall to 8.5 million people, expressed the view that they were more sexually liberated now than seven years before. Another example, in the same period in which there was dissatisfaction with the crisis, ten percent of the population, that is, about five million people, expressed the view that they were more satisfied with their lives on the job than they were seven years ago.

So the reactions of the population are very different from what one expects. And also, this evolution is faster in the segment of the population in which one probably would suppose that the evolution would be slower. For instance, in this period, the fastest evolution was for the French people having only a primary education; for the industrial workers, for the retired people, for the men between 50 and 64 years, and for women. On the other hand, this evolution was slower for the students, the executive people, and the people less than 20 years old. For instance, the need for personal expression increased by ten percent in the working class and fifteen percent among farmers.

To understand these changes is to understand the very structure of the society. French society is a society in which the extremes are moving faster than the middle, and they are moving toward the middle-toward the behavior, the attitude, the cultural position of the middle. So we are not at all a radicalizing society; we are a society with a deep movement of convergence.

## III

These new dimensions of the citizen (better informed, more educated, and with greater aspirations to the full recognition of his
individual rights and individual expression) have to be taken into
account by the political leadership in its three main functions,
which are for me the three functions of modern statesmen: to listen, to decide and to communicate.

First, to listen. The very nature of democracy, and its unchal-
lengeable superiority, is having the final decision in the hands of
the citizen who, at election time, indicates if and when he feels that
his message has been sufficiently listened to. To listen is not easy.
The amount of information received by political leaders is increasingly vast and it is necessary to discriminate between that which
carries fundamental messages and that which is transitory and
contradictory-more noise than information. The intervention of
the media and the wide use of polls allow citizens to participate in
a kind of direct referendum-a kind of Swiss referendum-on every
type of subject and without a proper institutional channel. Hence,
the tendency toward excessive personalization of power, abrupt
changes in policy formulation or implementation, and temptations
to bypass the whole institutional system through demonstrations-
for instance, the marches for peace-or even their perversion by direct action, like terrorism. Thus, the ability to listen to the ongoing
change might well become the fundamental characteristic of political leadership in modern democracies.

The second function is to decide. Decision is the essence of political leadership and the major difference between political leaders
and intellectual leaders, whom I highly respect and praise, and who
analyze or judge. A leader is a mechanism built to decide, and all
that he receives is at the end translated into a very simple act,
which is to say "yes" or "no." We are watching what I would call
"democracy in real time"-this is a use of the language of computers-
under which now, through the media, the event, the reaction to the
event, the decision-making process, the decisions, the reactions
to the decisions of various groups, are simultaneously transmitted

to the citizen and assessed by him. It might well be that our present democratic practices are not fully consistent with this evolution. At a time when society has to be conducted with flexibility, by a series of mutually reinforcing impulses given without delay, the discontinuities which are inherent in the election process might appear to the historians of the future as an anomaly. Hence the need, perceived in many European countries but without significant success up to now, to try to engage in a bipartisan dialogue where long-term issues are collectively assessed, while the final decisions clearly lie in the hands of the elected political leadership.

And the third function is to communicate. The political leader has finally to be able to communicate, which means to deliver his own message not only to a small group of other politicians or intermediaries or experts but now to each individual citizen at his home. This function is in itself complex, diversified, frustrating and evolutionary. It will dominate the procedures of selection of political leaders, who will become increasingly judged according to a dual standard, with different criteria: the ability to conduct the society through permanent changes and also the ability to communicate to the citizen the goals to be reached and the path to be followed to reach these goals. Communication for a political leader is not only a question of words to be transmitted but also of acts and decisions which are perceived as symbols of the direction in which our societies have to engage themselves.

It is, I think, a very important and historical change. Henry Kissinger said, or wrote, that the leaders of the world are less and less selected according to their ability to govern; they are selected by other criteria. And we must admit these two dimensions of the political leader. We must not fight against it-it is a fact-and in the past there were such situations. For instance, in the far away past, a leader usually was required to have two abilities: military ability and governmental ability-Caesar, Alexander, Napoleon. A modern leader must have two abilities: an ability to govern and an ability to communicate. And an ability to govern will not be recognized in modern times without the ability to communicate.

And if we accept this, then each one must prepare himself for it by an adequate training and preoccupation. The risk is that the second criterion will one day surpass the first one and that people will be mainly judged for their ability to communicate. This was expressed by some articles in the American press which I read recently. I don't think we will go to such extremes; these extremes existed always. It is a problem to fight against a demagogue, but our societies will probably respond to this by the multiplication of the communications networks and probably through a diversified structure of communications. It will be perhaps less easy to be judged on your ability to communicate just through one single medium, which is for the moment mainly, of course, image.

## IV

These new trends in European democracies-deep change in the society, deep need for communication-should lead to a new approach to the long-term problems that our societies are jointly facing.

1. **The need to focus more on long-term issues.** During the last ten years of what we called the "crisis"-which is a code name for a number of interrelated changes in technology, behavior, energy consumption and production patterns, international relations, and domestic and external monetary developments-profound changes have occurred in private enterprise management. I will just mention these because you know them, often more than I do: new types of decision-making based more on discussion and openness; an accent put on reducing vulnerability to random events, which implies ability to change a strategy rapidly; the dismissal of five-year planning, in view of growing uncertainties, and an accent put, on the one hand, on the short term (revolving plans for two or three years) plus, on the other, an in-depth consideration of a few salient long-term strategic issues over a ten- or twenty-year horizon. Through these changes the market economies and the private enterprises have continued to demonstrate their superiority over centrally-planned economies.

But, curiously, the same changes have not taken place in the conduct of economic affairs of governments, which rely basically on the same instruments, on the same methods, and on the same procedures as ten years ago. In my judgment, progress should be made in three directions:

- To achieve more stability and more predictability. For instance, the lags, the delay, in monetary and fiscal policies, have had countercyclical effects, which suggests that additional caution is necessary in using these instruments. We should rely more on medium-term monetary targets and on predictable fiscal policies, while strengthening, by deregulation, market forces, with their built-in stabilizing effects.
- To introduce into these policies a greater degree of adaptability. In fiscal policy there might be a case for giving the executive some added flexibility in adjusting tax rates to the current economic situation. In monetary matters, international cooperation on interest rates and exchange rate management-combined with some fixed references-would provide a more predictable framework while allowing at the same time rapid changes. And finally, as far as incomes are concerned, there might be lessons to be learned from the German experience with what they call "concerted action," which links the adjustment of wages to the global economic outlook.
- To develop a long-term strategy. There is a need for governments to focus more and more on long-term issues which have been neglected in all our countries, like, for instance, social security, employment trends, education, and research and technology. Of course, the absence-the total absence-of short-term rewards and the importance of short-term pressures explains everywhere the political indifference or desire not to be too directly involved in these difficult issues. Hence, a need to build a new type of dialogue, if possible

bipartisan, with the direct involvement of the citizen himself. And I must say that in this field probably the United States is in advance vis-à-vis European countries. You had, for instance, the important discussion about retirement age, which is one of the major issues of our social equilibrium of the ten years to come, and you gave some indication of the consensus finally starting to emerge. But up to now in Europe we have not been able to reach such a consensus-or even to study deeply such an issue.

**2. The problem of employment.** To exemplify what I mean, I will deal with the most fundamental long-term issue, which is employment. Employment is still the major challenge of Western societies and will remain so.

More than 32 million people are presently out of work in Western industrial countries and even if OECD countries were to get back to a real growth rate of three percent, unemployment would not drop in the next few years. Clearly a sustained worldwide recovery is the key answer, but at the same time there should be a renewed effort to assess better the link between growth and employment. Since 1973 real GDP (Gross Domestic Product) in the United States and in the four major EEC countries (France, Germany, Italy and the United Kingdom) has grown at the same yearly rate of about 2.2 percent. But associated with this there was a yearly increase of employment of about two percent in the United States (which implies the creation of 18 million new jobs from 1973 to 1981, a result modestly impaired by a new reduction of one million in 1982) against a stagnant employment in the EEC (yearly increase of about 0.2 percent). Stagnant employment makes problems of unemployment still more acute since workers who have lost their jobs may stay unemployed for a long time and young people may never find jobs. Long-term unemployment (more than six months) is several times higher in Europe than in the United States, and the share of youth unemployment in total unemployment has risen steadily since 1973.

To a large extent, this contrasting situation reflects development in labor costs. From 1973 to 1980, output per worker in the United States rose one percent annually, and real compensation rose 1.8 percent annually, while in the EEC the corresponding figures were 2.7 percent and 4.1 percent. Faced with a rapid increase in labor costs, declining productivity growth and rising oil prices, European firms have seen their profitability squeezed. They have closed their marginal plants and invested in capital-intensive techniques contributing to employment stagnation.

There is no easy answer to this fundamental problem, since ultimately one cannot envisage sustained growth if the purchasing power of the employed population is not growing steadily. There is therefore a need to reduce the non-wage component of labor costs, which means probably a stabilization of social benefits associated with a broad reform of social security systems in Europe, with a view to reducing the share of contributions based on wages. There is, at the same time, a need to learn from America's success in developing part-time employment, which represents 15 percent of your working force against 8 percent in my country, France.

Finally, the associated long-term problems of employment and the viability of social security systems, and notably of retirement schemes, should be addressed adequately. There are lessons for Europe to draw from the Japanese experience with an ever-increasing level of education of the working force, which might well imply extending to 18 years the mandatory education period, and from the U.S. experience, which gives flexibility in the selection by individuals of their age of retirement.

Employment will be largely determined in the future by social and cultural attitudes toward part-time work, retirement and education and therefore should not be addressed only in economic terms but in the broader context of the overall evolution of our societies.

Demography is both fundamental and predictable, while employment is the yardstick against which our ability to run free societies will be measured in the years to come. But if the data and the stakes are well-known, the possible solutions remain largely unknown. They should reflect national priorities and traditions, but I think that a better exchange of experiences, and a bipartisan dialogue in each individual country, is clearly needed.

I have already mentioned other issues, such as natural resources, innovation and capital formation as examples of the long-term problems to which the leaders should address themselves. If they do, they will gain nothing in political terms, since probably the intellectual horizon of the people does not go beyond a few months. By evaluation, by research, it appears that for the average Frenchman, the intellectual horizon is probably three months. What will happen beyond three months is not a direct concern for him. And when one is a leader, one ignores the next three months-one is living in a perspective of between a year and a half and ten years. A year and a half because any decisions you take will not normally have a result before that, in the economic, monetary or fiscal field. And if you embark on a new, major development-nuclear energy, a new weapon, a new technology-you know that the result will only come in a period which could be estimated between five and ten years. So there is a built-in discrepancy of point of view between the leaders and the voters, and it is an inherent responsibility of the leaders to address themselves to these long-term issues.

## V

The general conclusion of these three lectures is left open for you as listeners-and now as readers. But I will suggest this. There was, before the crisis, a gradual evolution in international relations: growing interdependence and complementarity between industrial countries, détente in East-West relations-with, however, weaknesses (indifference to the North-South dialogue) and drawbacks (the disruption of the Bretton Woods system). These developments have been interrupted, and we have instead a fragmentation of conflicting issues, policies and solutions.

Clearly, lasting changes are taking place in our societies: new social and cultural values, new aspirations, new concepts. But the present moment, 1983, offers new opportunities, and new challenges through the conjunction of three events:

- The waning of the energy crisis, which carries with it opportunities to ensure lasting economic recovery, develop a new dialogue with the oil-producing countries, and take measured steps to move the monetary system toward a clearly stated objective of a fixed structure.
- A change of leadership in the U.S.S.R. with its likely effects on the internal evolution of the East European countries and on East-West relations, probably the most important challenge.
- A new strategic balance as exemplified by the decision on the deployment of Euromissiles and recent military technological developments.

We should use these opportunities and challenges to promote a new climate of hope and confidence in the ability of our democratic governments to bring about orderly change internally and to provide the world with a clear vision of a more predictable and desirable future.

## NOTES

1  Martin Feldstein, Chairman of President Reagan's Council of Economic Advisors, "Adjusting the Dollar," The New York Times, June 2, 1983, p. A23.

2  George de Menil and Anthony M. Solomon, Economic Summitry, New York: Council on Foreign Relations, 1983; Helmut Schmidt: "Helmut Schmidt's Prescription: The World Economy at Stake," The Economist, 26 February–4 March 1983; Valéry Giscard d'Estaing: "A Communiqué for Williamsburg: For a useful summit," The Economist, 21–27 May 1983.

3  "Helmut Schmidt's Prescription: The World Economy at Stake," op cit.

# Euro Fantasies: Common Currency as Panacea

*Rudiger Dornbusch*

For nearly 50 years, Europe has been on a course of ever-widening and -deepening integration. For just as long, Germany has been building a reputation as the global champion of hard money to which the deutsche mark stands as its monument. The proposed monetary union to create a common currency in Europe joins these two strands: Europe gets German monetary integrity, and Germany blends into Europe.

The Maastricht Treaty, concluded in December 1991, is the pre nuptial agreement for this marriage. However, on the way to union doubts loom larger than joy. Still in question are the benefits to be derived, the suitability of the partners, and relations with outside parties. These questions are particularly acrimonious because the tight timetable (see p. 112) for converting to a common currency destroys illusions, as does Europe's poor economic performance. Europe has 18 million unemployed, and no one knows what to do with them. German Chancellor Helmut Kohl, German industry, and German banks all agree that the common currency, provided under the European Monetary Union (EMU) is a must. Promoters of "social union" are equally eager; they see integration as a way to ameliorate an economic system that they regard as having too much competition and too little social justice.

RUDI DORNBUSCH is Ford Professor of Economics and International Management at the Massachusetts Institute of Technology.

Those who question the drive toward a common European currency include monetary hawks, that is, most of Germany's population and its central Bundesbank; excluded bystanders, such as Central European countries; and benevolent spectators in the United States. The prospective partners in EMU who financially live from hand to mouth—France, Italy, Spain—are cheering monetary union. They still believe it is a miracle cure for rotten public finance and generations of debased currency, but they are also wincing as they are weighed in for the race to the Maastricht goal. Meanwhile, Britain is searching its soul. The Labour party wisely is favorably inclined toward the monetary union—a safe and pragmatic strategy with which to tear the Conservatives apart.

Achievement of a common currency is being touted as Europe's event of the century even as its real impact is in doubt. EMU could create a powerful and vigorous Europe, politically and economically cohesive and financially strong enough to dwarf the United States and the dollar. Or it might turn out to be a nonevent. Then again, financial markets might blow it away before it even starts, or bureaucratic bean counters might strangle it by rigid application of the Maastricht tests (see p. 112), thus ruling the partners unfit to consummate the union. The most likely scenario is that EMU will occur but will neither end Europe's currency troubles nor solve its prosperity problem. Euro-fantasies envision EMU as a panacea, or at least a pivotal step toward making Europe wonderful—politically, culturally, economically, socially, financially. Do not hold your breath.

## EMU IN PERSPECTIVE

In the past few months, the probability of a European Monetary Union has increased. The turning point was undoubtedly the French government's success in facing down labor opposition and pushing through the bulk of the government's budget cuts. The French also pushed their interest rates below German levels, demonstrating that in the EMU context France could be a hard-currency country. The performance impressed Kohl and gave him confidence that Germany and France could pursue monetary union together.

So EMU has gone from being an improbable and bad idea to a bad idea that is about to come true. High unemployment, low growth, discomfort with a welfare state that is no longer affordable— all these issues have found new hope of resolution in a desperate bid for a common money, as if that could address the real problems of Europe. On the contrary, the hard work of attaining a common currency, meeting the demanding Maastricht criteria for admission to EMU is adding to the burden of an already mismanaged Europe. The struggle to achieve monetary union under the Maastricht formula may be remembered as one of the more useless battles in European history. The costs of getting there are large, the economic benefits minimal, and the prospects for disappointment major.

At the outset, European integration was a historic move to bring Germany and France together and thus avoid the recurrent wars that have plagued this century. Then European integrationists developed bigger ambitions—the creation of a common market with no obstacles to trade in goods and services or the movement of people. Monetary union was seen as the next step on the way to full union. Even as that agenda is being implemented, the circle of candidates for inclusion in the European Union (EU) widens, public disenchantment grows, and the contradictions between enlarging the circle and deepening the integration of members become more apparent. Kohl has recognized that unless he pushes hard for EMU, the concept will fall by the wayside, and he is not alone. The French, too, want EMU. Their reason is surely not to build bridges that avoid future conflict— Germany and France by now are as tight as the United States and Canada. The reason is that no French minister of finance dares go to bed not knowing where the franc will be in the morning. Monetary union will allow them a good night's sleep, the first in a decade. And then there are all the other candidates who are trying to get a bit of credibility for budgetary policies and currency rates that do not quite make it without membership: Ireland, Belgium, Scandinavian countries, Italy, and Spain.

By April 1998 the key membership decisions will be made; by 1999 currencies will be pegged to each other; by 2002 there will be only the new currency, the Euro. But that won't be the end of the story. Frustrating relations between the included and the excluded countries will jeopardize much of the gain from adopting a common money.

## CLEARING THE HURDLES

There is virtually no country, including Germany and France, whose budget today meets the Maastricht criteria. As a result, all Europe is simultaneously plunging into budget-cutting and will likely suffer an economic slowdown. These reductions are appropriate even without emu, but their timing and size will add to its ultimate cost, stunt growth, and raise unemployment. Monetary authorities in these countries have shown no inclination to accommodate these consequences. They have their own agenda of holding tightly to the criteria until the last moment on the timetable, thus shaping the "right" attitude for the new central European bank. The combination of overly tight monetary policy and determined budget-cutting suggests a tough time ahead for Europe.

An even more important issue is what happens to those who cannot or do not want to be part of the monetary union. Britain has shown an aversion to full inclusion. British pragmatism stops at the proposal of inflation-targeting as the common bond. Joining the monetary cult is too much.

Italy, with its undervalued currency, poses another problem. France wants Italy to be in so that further competitive depreciation becomes impossible. But once Italy is in, with an appreciated currency, the country will soon be back on the ropes, just as in 1992, when the currency came under attack. The matter of the "outs" comes down to a simple question: What can be offered to Britain and Italy to induce them to join the emu club? Germany's unlimited, unconditional defense of their currencies is enough of a reward for Italy. Predictably, Germany is utterly unwilling to take that offer, leaving France sulking in the wings. Everybody is waiting and hoping that Italy and Britain, the soft currencies when the Maastricht Treaty was enacted in 1992, will make it a point of pride to show that they are European, they are willing to be hard-currency countries, and they will do the pushups necessary to join. Do not wait for Britain; the Labour government has as much trouble at home with the proposed Social Charter as with the European Central Bank.

Assuming emu is a foregone conclusion, vital questions remain about whether inclusion is the right choice for various parties, the potential for economic benefits, the expected role of the European Central Bank, and the amount of sovereignty emu members will give up.

## MAKING THE CUT

Without Germany and France, of course, there will be no emu. For Germany, emu is a political step reflecting the deeply held belief that domestic stability requires an unbreakable link with France; nothing else matters in this context. Few north European advocates of emu lose sleep over the exclusion of Greece, Portugal, even Italy or Spain. Assuming France and Germany are founders, how will they structure the debate about fulfilling the Maastricht criteria? Where will they draw the line between the "ins" and "outs"?

The present financial condition of most European countries suggests that a narrow reading of the Maastricht criteria sets too-high ratios of debt to GDP and deficit to GDP. Moreover, undue optimism about the strength of a 1997 economic recovery is pervasive. Without a solid recovery, everybody's deficit numbers will look far worse, and prospects will be dim for meeting the Maastricht requirement of a deficit below three percent of GDP. Politicians may not be able to afford to let the market toss around these questions for the next two years. A more likely and practical scenario is that an assumption will be made that France, Germany, and a small group of nations are progressing toward monetary union. They will lay out a demanding three-year program of fiscal adjustment that puts them below the Maastricht targets by 1998.

That will serve as a justification for fudging a bit by these countries on the strict criteria for emu entry.

Which other countries will also be allowed to fudge? Belgium cannot pass even a fudged test unless its debt is written off; it now has twice the maximum indebtedness allowable under the Maastricht Treaty. There is an interesting precedent in the country's 1926 overindebtedness and funding crisis. In a forced consolidation, Belgium gave the national railways to bondholders, an approach that Belgium's plentiful supply of public enterprises would allow today. Belgium is a northern European darling and hard-money partner, which ought to call for some special concessions.

Italy is surely off the list for immediate consideration, even though German and French industry want to put Italian competition on a short leash by excluding competitive currency depreciation. The fact is that they cannot; Italy has such high debt and deficit levels that it could not be cleaned up enough to pass German scrutiny for first-wave entry into emu.

There is an overriding issue in the "ins" versus "outs" debate. Monetary union is like marriage between partners of very unequal assets. Prenuptial arrangements are naturally the rule and must be followed closely. But when the passion is gone, the agreements endure. In forging the agreement, German bondholders, who have the most to lose, rule supreme. While France has oscillated between hard and soft money, Germany has built a strong, consistent coalition of bondholders and the Bundesbank. Kohl would make a big mistake if he threatened the bondholders, who are savers and who fear, if not remember, debased currency. For that reason, Italy will not be a first-wave entrant, since German bondholders view it (rightly or wrongly) as the incarnation of monetary delinquency. A credible case for fudging with the Maastricht timetable can be made for Germany and France, but not for countries with bad fiscal reputations.

If there are "ins" and "outs," which is it better to be? For Italy, out is clearly better initially. Because the French are tied in knots over Italian competitiveness and fear another round of competitive depreciation, they are willing to make deals to help Italy come on board. For Italy, the key to making exchange rate commitments will be an offer from Germany of "unconditional, unlimited intervention" in support of the lira. Hell will freeze over before that comes about. Yet Italy could gain from professing interest in emu membership; doing so would help in the country's inevitable fight over its own budget. More important, a public request for membership is a signal to investors of Italy's economic intentions, which helps bring down interest rates and improve the budget.

If Germany and France do initiate emu as expected, a structured process to incorporate the "outs" would follow. But because Germany will not offer exchange rate guarantees, much of the burden would fall on the "outs" who will have to lay out their convergence programs and do the work. Italy will be urged to consolidate its public finance. London will feel pressured by the prospect of losing large amounts of financial business to Frankfurt. As emu gets under way, the pressure on the "outs" will increase because including them is essential to ultimate emu success. For stragglers like Britain, who are indifferent or picky, the strategy will be to raise the ante. For financially tainted, would-be mem bers like Italy, it will be to push harder.

The emu is a particularly difficult issue for Eastern European countries. They are on a slow course of incorporation into the European Union but remain financially weak. Were emu an integrating mechanism, early inclusion would be critical. But this aspect of emu is overdone. An option for "out" countries like the Czech Republic and Poland would be the adoption of the euro as their national currency, just as Argentina has effectively done with the dollar. Such a move would help with financial stability, but it would come at the cost of losing the exchange rate as an adjustment tool.

## BENEFITS AND PROBLEMS

Whatever persuaded European leaders in 1991 to single out money as the key vehicle of political integration, it is a poor choice. Money at its best is apolitical, and the European central bank will accomplish that. Leaving aside the political benefits, if any, from integrating currencies, can economic gains be reaped? emu is unlike the all-important customs union and the brilliant scheme of completing the internal market. Those dramatic initiatives carried incentives to make the European market, desperately uncompetitive and segmented as it was, into one large unit. The imagination was captured by the vast and highly competitive U.S. market, and the initiative was both bold and worthy. emu has little of that.

Currency integration will bring two benefits in two ways. First, the elimination of cumbersome money-changing will make transactions more convenient and reduce the costs of making payments. Second, exchange-rate volatility will be reduced, to zero in fact, and businesses will be better able to trade and invest across intra-European borders. But by itself a single market does not mean integration of the means of payment. The value of a euro in Barcelona will not necessarily be computed the same in Berlin until and unless a transfer system, akin to the U.S. Federal Reserve's inter-bank wires, is accompanied by a requirement to clear all checks at par. Such a requirement, which would protect against stiff and varying charges by oligopolistic banks, is vitally important to business.

Minor gains in the stability of the deutsche mark-franc rates could be more than offset by the increased volatility of rates to outside markets and investors. Were that so, trade integration would be captured by the "ins" at the expense of Europe's "outs" and the rest of the world, from Eastern Europe to the United States. However, there is little evidence that currency volatility, low as it has been, is an impediment to trade. As a result, reduced volatility between the "ins" will not change the landscape of trade and investment in Europe much. In the meantime, it can be used to pressure countries like Britain to be in or really out.

Will Europe, governed by one money, do fundamentally better? The French view is emphatically positive: if Italy cannot devalue anymore, it cannot steal French jobs. Thus for France, one money is great. But its enthusiasm is based on a fallacy, because what is at issue is the real rate of exchange adjusted for costs. If the nominal exchange rate cannot change, for equilibrium the real rate must change. Expect wages and prices to do the work. The French may be right to believe that it is far more difficult to make adjustments by deflation than by devaluation. But that is small comfort.

In countries with highly flexible wages, the exchange-rate regime makes little difference. In countries with rigid labor markets, like most of those in Europe, flexible exchange rates are all-important. The most serious criticism of emu is that by abandoning exchange rate adjustments it transfers to the labor market the task of adjusting for competitiveness and relative prices. Without wage flexibility, the adjustment process is frustrated; losses in output and employment (and pressure on the European central bank to inflate) will predominate. The overriding cost of an integrated monetary area is that nominal exchange rates disappear as an adjustment mechanism. If a region goes into decline, say, because its exports become obsolete, deflation has to take the place of devaluation. If a region experiences a boom, say, because it has superior research, education, and trade performance, inflation takes the place of ap preci ation.

Exchange rates as an adjustment tool have a good history, Mexico and Latin America notwithstanding. Forcing adjustment into the labor market, the European market with the poorest performance, is bound to fail. In backward regions unemployment will rise, as will social problems and complaints about integration. If exchange rates are abandoned as an economic tool, something else must take their place. Maastricht promoters have carefully avoided spelling out just what that might be. Competitive labor markets is the answer, but that is a dirty word in social-welfare Europe.

## EMU AND SOVEREIGNTY

The creation of a European monetary union is not a natural part of the process of trimming sovereignty in favor of a more integrated Europe. It is not a first step, with foreign policy and defense naturally following soon. On the contrary, depoliticized money is the ambition around the world. Creating an independent central bank in New Zealand or Chile is mostly the same as creating a European central bank. The intent is to transfer the regulation of money from short-sighted and politically vulnerable legislators to conservative managers who have long time horizons and are accountable only for what they achieve.

In a European central bank, money management would be removed from national authorities. Even if money management were already institutionalized in an appropriate way, as in Germany, it would simply be moved up one layer to a Europe-wide level. For many European countries, that would be the only way to liberate their central banks from political influence—literally to move them into a single out-of-town house. For others, it would be merely a lateral move, from an independent body shadowing Germany to one subsuming it. The point is: good central banking is apolitical, and the more apolitical the better. That is what a European Central Bank is all about. And that is why emu is not a transfer of sovereignty over money but a Europe-wide abdication.

Money management by a central bank, of course, is unlike defense and foreign policies, which are intrinsically political. In defense and foreign policies, citizens broadly want peace (most of the time), but that is where agreement ends. The task is reconciling conflicting national objectives, views, traditions, or cultures. In money management, everyone wants the same thing—stable money. So in defense and foreign policies, the transfer of sovereignty means giving up something real and precious. Giving up nationally managed money is just kicking a bad habit! The difference could not be greater.

## CENTRAL BANK ORTHODOXY

Italians dream that the European central bank will make their life easier than the Bundesbank does now. For Germans the prospect is a nightmare. Their fears are unjustified. The new central bank is certain to establish itself at the outset as a direct continuation of the German central bank, the current pillar of European monetary orthodoxy. This result is assured by the narrow rules of the game but even more by other factors. Those selected for the board of a central bank, in the spotlight of public attention, immediately turn conservative, as has routinely happened at the U.S. Federal Reserve. As member nations will also want their representatives to be influential, the European central bank is likely to be composed of prestigious conservatives. Of prime importance will be the board chairman, who will chart the bank's course with no precedents in place. If, as now seems likely, Willem Duisenberg of the Netherlands central bank heads the European central bank, the assurance of hard money is carved in stone. After all, Duisenberg has on occasion expressed the fear that Germany could turn soft!

It is obvious the European central bank will be off to a good start, if that is measured by keeping interest rates high and inflation low. The trouble is that Europe by then may be in deep trouble: accelerated budget-cutting combined with tough central banking led by the Bundesbank spells trouble. Unfortunately, central banking in Europe does not buy into the concept that budget-cutting requires accommodating monetary policy. That means Europe between now and 2000 cannot expect much growth. Europe's new currency, far from creating prosperity, may in the end be blamed for a period of poor performance. If the current national central banks accommodate by easing monetary policy, growth can go on harmoniously and unimpeded. If central banks misread their role, deficit-cutting will wind up as a recessionary debacle, and emu will be blamed for it.

## A BETTER EMU

In setting up the Maastricht criteria, policymakers focused on avoiding pollution of the central bank's objectives by member countries' weak fiscal positions. High debt and deficits, from this perspective, are an invitation to monetization and "inflating away" of fiscal problems. At the extreme, treasury departments go straight to central banks to be accommodated. The separation of the two institutions is entirely appropriate. So is the current emphasis on smaller deficits, if only because of the vast unfunded pension liabilities on the horizon. But it is also true that the reasoning that screens out high-debt and high-deficit countries as threats to the integrity of a European central bank can be used against high-unemployment countries. In these countries, plausibly, policymakers will turn to a central bank to seek help—a bit more money, a few more jobs. The incentive to inflate is just the same as in accommodation of jobs; inflating away debt is just as easy as inflating away unemployment. Neither may work, but the attempt or the expectation of an attempt will be counterproductive.

The implication is that emu should include an outright unemployment ceiling. Countries with more than, say, six percent structural unemployment should not be members. They should be required to undertake the structural and macroeconomic policies (including loosening economic regulations, reducing excessive benefits, etc.) that bring unemployment down to levels that are not a threat to the European central bank. If the Maastricht requirements were structured that way, they would initiate a supply-side revolution. Countries would be falling all over themselves to create jobs by deregulation instead of destroying jobs by taxation. Unfortunately, although the logic is impeccable, Europe's good economics have yet to reach the labor market.

Experimenting with a new money is a bad idea at a time when Europe must face the tough realities of abolishing the welfare state, reintegrating millions of unemployed into a normal working life, deregulating statist-corporatist economies, cultivating the supply side of its economy, and integrating Central Europe. The new money creates insignificant benefits at best while frustrating adjustment and restricting pragmatic cooperation. From outside Europe, a common money and the efforts necessary to get it are viewed as deeply misdirected and ill-timed steps that will make Europe a weak link in the world economy.

Although approving of the evolution of a European common market, the United States is fearful about emu. The first was seen as contributing to prosperity and thus political stability. The second is seen as carrying a high risk of contributing to recession and thus to political trouble, which has always been expensive for the world. Europeans, with their rose-tinted Euro-glasses, do not see that prospect. The U.S. skepticism comes from the belief that tying up currencies forces the adjustment elsewhere, resulting in high interest rates and high unemployment. Having lived through that when the dollar was overvalued in the 1960s, the United States has never been a fan of fixed rates. Watching the recurrent currency crises in Europe in the 1980s has reinforced that opinion. The United States has substantial flexibility in both wages and labor market institutions. With such arrangements it could conceivably enter a regime of fixed exchange rates. Europe has neither flexible wages nor functioning labor markets, but already has mass unemployment. Emu will add to it, both on the way there and once the system is trapped in fixed rates across vastly divergent countries. If there was ever a bad idea, emu is it.

# The Case for EMU: More than Money

## Peter Sutherland

In the intensifying debate over the prospects for European economic and monetary union, there is danger of losing sight of the most fundamental fact about EMU. Like everything else in the push for European integration, it is essentially a political undertaking. To underline that truth is not to deny the compelling economic rationale for EMU but to emphasize that there is more at stake.

The economic rationale is based on the inherent logic of Europe's single-market strategy; EMU may well be essential to the single market's survival. But it has also become a test of both the European Union and the political commitment of its 15 member states, one that goes beyond the technicalities of the project. If Europe fails the test, the consequences for integration will be serious.

Assuming that monetary union will begin as scheduled on January 1, 1999, it is still too soon to know which of the EU's member states will qualify to take part in the first wave; that decision will depend on how each nation's key economic indicators develop. But there is already a growing sense that it could be a substantial minority, perhaps even a significant majority, of the member states.

EMU's critics continue to argue that it is a bad and damaging idea. But the skeptics have changed their tune. They no longer claim that monetary union will be a failure because most member states will be unable to meet the criteria for economic convergence

PETER SUTHERLAND is Chairman and Managing Director of Goldman Sachs International. He was Director General of the World Trade Organization from 1993 until 1996 and European Union Commissioner from 1985 until 1989.

that the 1991–92 Maastricht treaty set for admittance; they instead predict that the member states will realize that EMU is vital to the political enterprise of European integration and cannot be allowed to fail, and will therefore fudge or even disregard the criteria. Either way, in their view, the result is the same: something called EMU will happen, but it will be botched, and will prove to be a grave mistake for the European Union.

The critics maintain that EMU will not work because the member states will fail to reform their rigid labor markets and burdensome welfare systems. Such reforms are exceptionally difficult, to be sure, and will be resisted by vested interests. France's current attempts to solve structural problems relating to social security and public employment and Germany's push to modify pension and sick leave benefits are meeting the resistance one would expect. But predicting that those efforts will not succeed seems unnecessarily pessimistic. Their inevitability is widely recognized, as evidenced by privatization programs under way virtually everywhere in Europe. There is also new realism and a sense of the need for constructive engagement on these issues among many of Europe's trade unionists.

Above all, the competitive liberalization of the global economy will require such reforms even absent EMU. Would the social partners in the German economy, for example, choose to commit collective suicide rather than carry out such reforms? Or would the German body politic be more reluctant to engage reform with European Monetary Union than without it? Anglo-Saxon economists have written off the German economy so many times, and so prematurely, that it seems foolhardy to do so once again. No doubt the liberalization and deregulation of the German economy, like similar efforts in France or Spain, will be less than ideal. But it is unreasonable to assume that they will not occur.

## POLITICAL ECONOMICS

The member governments adopted the EMU project because they were persuaded that it was based on a sound economic and monetary rationale. Specifically, they were convinced that the single market, including the free movement of capital, was not compatible with stable exchange rates and stable monetary policy, except with a single currency. Having tried several schemes to stabilize exchange rates, all of which stopped short of a single currency and all of which failed, they decided to aim for a single currency. It is almost inconceivable that they would have embarked on an undertaking of such ambition and inherent uncertainty had they not been persuaded of the project's political efficacy as a means for furthering integration.

By the same token, however, both governments and central banks have been dogmatic in their pursuit of the Maastricht convergence criteria, and their treaty-driven efforts to control inflation and cut budget deficits may have unnecessarily aggravated the recessionary tendency in the economic cycle. But they have had to tread a narrow path, maintaining the Maastricht process' credibility while dealing with difficult social and economic issues. After all, what is involved is a secular change in economic policy, economic behavior, and, above all, public opinion. Economic and monetary union will not occur at all unless the Bundesbank, the Bundestag, and the German people all believe that the new currency is as good as the deutsche mark. Economic and monetary union will not work well unless the public in each participating country is persuaded that low inflation is inherently desirable and that the new low-inflation policy is serious and permanent. The Bundesbank and the Banque de France may have been conservative in their strict pursuit of the Maastricht criteria, but if they had appeared to have had only a conditional commitment to the policy of low inflation during this critical period of transition to the single currency, they could have jeopardized the credibility of the entire enterprise.

Once the single currency arrives, Europe will be in a different ball game. Government deficits will have been reduced, automatically easing recessionary factors. Moreover, if the practice of low inflation has been established and accepted, central bankers will feel more confident that they can lower interest rates without triggering inflationary reflexes. Once Europe is through the white water of the transition and achieves single currency, the balance of constraints in the system will significantly change: the European Central Bank and the national governments will together have to ensure a constructive tradeoff between fiscal and monetary policy, so as to combine low inflation with reasonable growth. But the nightmare scenario—that Europe's central bankers will bear down ruthlessly hard on inflation while the Maastricht criteria bear down on demand management, driving the entire European economy into permanent recession—is implausible.

European governments are shooting for monetary union not as a mindless act of dogma but as an act of political will. When the member states decide, in the first half of 1998, which of their number qualify for EMU, they will apply the Maastricht criteria in such a way as to give monetary union the best possible chance of survival. After that, the countries taking part in the first wave will be required to do whatever is necessary to ensure that monetary union works properly. I believe this is fully understood and accepted.

## MAGIC NUMBERS?

Two of the key qualifying criteria in the Maastricht treaty are that government budget deficits be less than 3 percent of GDP, and government debt less than 60 percent of GDP. But nobody is under any illusion that there is something magical about those numbers. Some experts believe that a deficit ceiling of 2 percent of GDP would have been better; others hold that 4 percent would have been reasonable enough and more acceptable at the low point of the economic cycle. The German Finance Ministry has argued that eventually the target ceiling should fall lower still—1 percent of GDP or even less. Nevertheless, on judgment day the member states will measure performance against the yardsticks of 3 percent and 60 percent, the figures prescribed in the treaty.

Everybody knows that these yardsticks do not measure some sacred truth; they only suggest which member states can be counted on to deliver economic policies that are stable, disciplined, responsible, and unlikely to spur inflation. Paradoxically, much of the public controversy over the convergence criteria has focused on parameters that may in some cases be of secondary importance, such as the level of public debt, while little attention has been paid to the most important indicator of all: low inflation. The size of its public debt would apparently exclude Belgium from the first wave of monetary union, but in terms of the more important criterion of monetary stability, it should clearly qualify. Economists may differ on whether the lowest possible level of inflation is inherently desirable, or whether—as the evidence seems to suggest—a slightly higher level may be optimal for faster economic growth. But from the business point of view, the prospect of stable and predictable economic policy is EMU's most desirable characteristic. The target figures in the Maastricht treaty are designed as indicators of the ability and willingness of each national political system to conform to that general objective.

Of course, by the time judgment day arrives, the static and slightly backward-looking quality of the Maastricht convergence criteria will have been complemented, or perhaps largely displaced, by a more rhythmic and forward-looking system, the stability pact first discussed at the EU summit in Dublin last December. Judgment day will thus be more about the future than the past, with member states advancing to the single currency only if they are deemed willing and able to enter into a new contractual system of collective economic discipline.

What is ultimately at stake is a political judgment. The final decision as to who will advance in the first wave of EMU will not be made on the basis of the economic numbers chalked up by the end of 1997. It will instead be a group judgment as to which member states can be counted on to meet the future obligations of monetary union—in essence, a political judgment on each others' political systems. This is not usually acknowledged in public, largely because the connotations are uncomfortable, even invidious. But it is unavoidable.

If this is the realpolitik of the Maastricht decision-making process, and if monetary union is to have a reasonable chance of working, the first wave of participating member states should be selected carefully. At one end of the spectrum, the most natural candidates for early membership are member states like the Netherlands that are, in a sense, already in the deutsche mark bloc; they are the countries least vulnerable to questions about their ability to compete inside a monetary union. At the other end are member states that are converging on the Maastricht criteria but have not yet established a stable political or economic record of convergence. EMU will be a high-stakes enterprise, and the European Union cannot afford to include member states that can and should be ready for integration in the near future, but are not ready now.

However, there must be no premature rejection of a candidacy. If a member state meets the criteria in a comparable manner to France or Germany, they cannot reasonably be rejected. Furthermore, it is only legitimate to postpone a membership of EMU if that membership would fail to comply with the criteria in a sustainable manner, thus damaging the system.

## THE FRENCH CONNECTION

France will, of course, be monetary union's most critical test case. French participation will be politically vital for a successful launch of EMU. With a year to go before judgment day, it is too early to know whether France will succeed in bringing its deficit below 3 percent of GDP or its public debt below 60 percent of GDP. But it is important to understand the consequences of failure. If France fails to meet the criteria by a wide and indisputable margin, the European Union will face a triple dilemma of crisis proportions. If other member states were to turn a blind eye to the French failure, they would be jeopardizing the monetary credibility of the entire EMU system; if they were to put the single currency on hold, the temporary delay could become indefinite; if they were to press ahead with the single currency, but without France, the political partnership between France and

Germany, symbol and engine of the European enterprise, would be rocked to its very foundations.

It seems obvious that the other member states will and should be anxious to give France the benefit of the doubt, provided that its budgetary figures are not too far from the Maastricht targets and that it is moving in the right direction. The French policy of low inflation and currency stability, maintained for a dozen years under successive governments of both left and right, lends credibility to the French establishment's political commitment to EMU. In addition, President Jacques Chirac has resisted the populist temptation to revert to the old Gaullist model of French nationalism.

But even if the member states are irreproachably rigorous in determining which of their number qualify for the first wave, the European Union has a vital interest in developing the entry process for those member states left to the second wave. It can do so by building strong institutional links between the "ins" and the "not-yet-ins" on matters both of currency stabilization and macroeconomic policy management. This is the logic of recent negotiations between European finance ministers and central bankers. If successful, those negotiations should help blur the sense (or fear) of political discrimination among the "not-yet-ins" without jeopardizing the credibility or stability of the monetary union itself.

There is, of course, another paradigm among the member states: the United Kingdom. Britain has a strong and stable political system, which ought to promise predictability of policy. In principle, it should also be able to meet the Maastricht criteria, if not quite in time for the January 1999 starting date, at least not long thereafter. In practice, it seems unlikely that a Conservative government would even advocate membership in EMU. And it cannot be taken for granted that a Labour government would be an early candidate.

Under Tony Blair, the Labour Party is adopting a more positive tone, toward the European Union in general and toward economic and monetary union in particular. It is possible that after the general election a Labour government would seek membership in

EMU. But Labour is committed to holding a referendum before joining the single currency, and this would require a powerful campaign of persuasion, since strong support for monetary union does not yet exist. Public opinion could be brought around to the idea; what is in question is whether it could be brought around in the nine months or so between a British election and the moment of decision in Brussels. The real trouble is that Britain has an uninterrupted record of resisting the political implications of closer European integration in general, and of monetary union in particular.

For the majority of the EU member states, the ultimate rationale of monetary union lies in its contribution to the larger political strategy of European integration. Those who wish to be part of economic and monetary union should make clear to their electorates that this is a profoundly political act. It is time to come to terms with the essential nature of the European integration process; it's not about losing one's nationality, but it is about sacrificing some degree of sovereignty. The evidence suggests that an overwhelming majority of the EU's current members are willing to take the next step, and that even the laggards will soon follow suit.'

# EMU and International Conflict

*Martin Feldstein*

## MONNET WAS MISTAKEN

To most Americans, European economic and monetary union seems like an obscure financial undertaking of no relevance to the United States. That perception is far from correct. If EMU does come into existence, as now seems increasingly likely, it will change the political character of Europe in ways that could lead to conflicts in Europe and confrontations with the United States.

The immediate effects of EMU would be to replace the individual national currencies of the participating countries in 2002 with a single currency, the euro, and to shift responsibility for monetary policy from the national central banks to a new European Central Bank (ECB). But the more fundamental long-term effect of adopting a single currency would be the creation of a political union, a European federal state with responsibility for a Europe-wide foreign and security policy as well as for what are now domestic economic and social policies. While the individual governments and key political figures differ in their reasons for wanting a political union, there is no doubt that the real rationale for EMU is political and not economic. Indeed, the adverse economic effects of a single currency on unemployment and inflation would outweigh any gains from facilitating trade and capital flows among the EMU members.

The 1992 Maastricht Treaty that created the EMU calls explicitly for the evolution to a future political union. But even without

MARTIN FELDSTEIN is Professor of Economics at Harvard University and President of the National Bureau of Economic Research.

that specific treaty language, the shift to a single currency would be a dramatic and irreversible step toward that goal. There is no sizable country anywhere in the world that does not have its own currency. A national currency is both a symbol of sovereignty and the key to the pursuit of an independent monetary and budget policy. The tentative decision of the 15 European Union (EU) member states (with the exceptions of Denmark and the United Kingdom), embodied in the Maastricht Treaty, to abandon their national currencies for the euro is therefore a decision of fundamental political significance.

For many Europeans, reaching back to Jean Monnet and his contemporaries immediately after World War II, a political union of European nations is conceived of as a way of reducing the risk of another intra-European war among the individual nation-states. But the attempt to manage a monetary union and the subsequent development of a political union are more likely to have the opposite effect. Instead of increasing intra-European harmony and global peace, the shift to EMU and the political integration that would follow it would be more likely to lead to increased conflicts within Europe and between Europe and the United States.

What are the reasons for such conflicts? In the beginning there would be important disagreements among the EMU member countries about the goals and methods of monetary policy. These would be exacerbated whenever the business cycle raised unemployment in a particular country or group of countries. These economic disagreements could contribute to a more general distrust among the European nations. As the political union developed, new conflicts would reflect incompatible expectations about the sharing of power and substantive disagreements over domestic and international policies. Since not all European nations would be part of the monetary and political union, there would be conflicts between the members and nonmembers within Europe, including the states of Eastern Europe and the former Soviet Union.

Conflicts would also develop between the European political union and non-European nations, including the United States, over issues of foreign policy and international trade. While disagreements among the European countries might weaken any European consensus on foreign affairs, the dominant countries of the EU would be able to determine the foreign and military policies for the European community as a whole. A political union of the scale and affluence of Europe and the ability to project military power would be a formidable force in global politics.

Although 50 years of European peace since the end of World War II may augur well for the future, it must be remembered that there were also more than 50 years of peace between the Congress of Vienna and the Franco-Prussian War. Moreover, contrary to the hopes and assumptions of Monnet and other advocates of European integration, the devastating American Civil War shows that a formal political union is no guarantee against an intra-European war. Although it is impossible to know for certain whether these conflicts would lead to war, it is too real a possibility to ignore in weighing the potential effects of EMU and the European political integration that would follow.

## THE POLITICS AND ECONOMICS OF MONETARY POLICY

The most direct link between EMU and intra-European conflicts would be disagreement about the goals and methods of monetary policy. The Maastricht Treaty established the ECB and transfers all responsibility for monetary policy after the start of EMU from individual national central banks to the ECB. The ECB alone would control the supply of euros and set the short-term euro interest rate.

Maastricht makes price stability the primary objective of European monetary policy, paralleling the charter of Germany's Bundesbank. The treaty also provides that the ECB would be independent of all political control by the member states and by European-level political institutions. (Although the treaty states that the ECB will report to the European Parliament, this was intended to follow the Bundesbank tradition of an information report rather than any political oversight.) These conditions are very much what Germany wants for the ECB and for monetary policy. Because of its historical experience, the German public is hypersensitive on inflation and fears any monetary arrangement that does not give primacy to price stability and insulate monetary policy from political influence.

But German opinion differs sharply from the opinions about monetary policy in France and other European countries. The notion of a politically independent central bank is contrary to European traditions. Until recently, when Maastricht required all prospective EMU countries to give their central banks independence, most of the central banks of Europe reported to their ministries of finance, and the finance ministers were at least partially responsible for setting interest rates.

The French have been particularly vocal in calling for political control over monetary policy. In a televised speech just before the 1992 French referendum on the Maastricht Treaty, then-President Francois Mitterrand assured the French public that, contrary to the explicit language of the treaty, European monetary policy would not be under the direction of European central bankers but would be subject to political oversight that, by implication, would be less concerned with inflation and more concerned with unemployment. Mitterrand's statement was a political forecast; France recognizes that the institutions of the EMU would evolve, and continually presses for some form of political body to exert control over the ECB. It has already made considerable progress toward that end.

The December 1996 meeting of the EU Council of Ministers in Dublin emphasized that growth as well as price stability would be an explicit goal of future EMU monetary policy. It also established a new ministerial-level "stability council" described as a "complement" or a "counterweight" to the ECB. Although this body falls short of one that could exercise political control over the ECB, it marked a first French success in establishing that monetary policy should be subject to some counterweight and that growth (that is, short-run macroeconomic expansion) as well as price stability should be a goal of EMU policy. At the European summit in Amsterdam in June 1997, the newly elected French government of

Lionel Jospin made further progress. The summit added an employment chapter to the Maastricht Treaty, emphasizing that employment is a parallel goal to price stability. More important, statements by politicians at the Amsterdam summit appear to have redefined the role of the political authorities in making exchange rate policy and, therefore, in managing monetary policy.

More specifically, the Maastricht Treaty divided responsibility for exchange rate policy between the ECB and the EU Economics and Finance Council, which consists of cabinet ministers of member governments, in an ambiguous way. The drafters of that part of the treaty (the German participants in particular) intended to limit ECOFIN'S role to fundamental aspects of the exchange rate system and to leave to the ECB policies that cause short-run changes in the value of the euro. For example, a decision to fix the exchange rate between the euro and the Japanese yen permanently would be a decision for ECOFIN. In contrast, raising or lowering euro interest rates to increase or decrease the exchange value of the euro would be left to the ECB. Although this distinction was the German view, the French expected that ECOFIN would eventually get to give orders about short-run variations in the desired level of the euro exchange rate. The formal rules remain ambiguous, but the government leaders at the Amsterdam summit appear to have accepted a shift of responsibility for short-run exchange rate policy to ECOFIN. Since discretionary changes in nominal exchange rates can be achieved only by changes in monetary policy, this shift would establish a much more fundamental role for ECOFIN, a political body, in the making of monetary policy.

One further recent development relating to the independence of the ECB is noteworthy. Members of the key monetary policy committee of the European Parliament have called for a role for the parliament in supervising the ECB, including its interest rate policies. They have specifically pointed to congressional oversight of the U.S. Federal Reserve as a possible model for such supervision. Although this arrangement may strike a reasonable balance between independence and accountability, parliamentary oversight would clearly be a major shift from the complete independence called for in the Maastricht Treaty, and consequently an area for contention.

At present, individual European governments (especially in France and Germany) are suppressing their disagreement about the control of monetary policy to minimize the risk of political disapproval of EMU in their respective countries. But if EMU proceeds, the independence of the ECB and the goals of monetary policy will become a source of serious conflict among member countries.

## INFLATION VERSUS UNEMPLOYMENT

The issue of who controls monetary policy is closely related to the question of the proper goal of monetary policy. In recent years, because of the Maastricht Treaty's requirements for entering EMU, most countries have resisted the temptation to use monetary policy to reduce unemployment and have followed the Bundesbank in keeping inflation rates below three percent. But once the disciplining example of the Bundesbank is eliminated and monetary policy is made by an ECB in which all member countries vote equally, there is a strong risk that the prevailing sentiment will be for higher inflation. Over the past 12 months, international financial markets have anticipated that outcome by depressing the value of the deutsche mark, the French franc, and the other European currencies that move with them by 25 percent relative to the dollar and the yen.

If the German public sees the inflation rate rise under EMU, it will become increasingly antagonistic toward the EMU arrangement and toward the countries that vote for inflationary monetary policy. Moreover, since an inflationary monetary policy would lower unemployment only temporarily (while leaving the inflation rate permanently higher), the persistence of high unemployment would lead to political pressure for recurring rounds of expansionary monetary policy, causing continuing dissatisfaction among the anti-inflationary countries.

Countries that are more concerned about unemployment than inflation might nevertheless be critical of the ECB for not pursuing an even more aggressive expansionary policy. Although countries have been properly reluctant to attempt such policies in recent years, they can regard their decisions not to do so as decisions they made themselves. But with a single currency, such governments would suffer the frustration of not being able to decide for themselves and of being forced to accept the common monetary policy created by the ECB.

This general conflict about the governance and character of monetary policy would be exacerbated whenever a country experienced a decline in exports or other type of decline in aggregate demand that led to a cyclical increase in unemployment. The shift to a single currency would mean that the fall in demand in a country could not be offset, as it could be with an individual national currency, by an automatic decline in the exchange value of the currency (making its exports more competitive) and a decline in its interest rates (increasing domestic interest -sensitive spending by households and businesses) or by using its own monetary policy to shift interest rates and exchange rates. The ECB would have to make monetary policy with a view to the conditions in all of Europe, not just a particular country or region. The result would be a conflict between the country with rising unemployment and the rest of the EU.

## TAXES AND TRANSFERS

Without the automatic countercyclical response of financial markets and the ability to use monetary policy to offset a decline in demand, European governments would want to use tax cuts and increases in government outlays to stimulate demand and reverse cyclical increases in unemployment. But the "stability pact" that was adopted under pressure from Germany tells governments that they cannot run fiscal deficits above three percent of GDP after the start of EMU. This restriction creates an important source of tension between countries with cyclical unemployment increases and the other members of the monetary union. The decision at the 1997 Amsterdam summit to weaken the application of financial penalties for violating this deficit ceiling would undoubtedly encourage more violations and, therefore, more quarrels about "irresponsible" fiscal policies.

Since national monetary and fiscal policies would be precluded, the most likely outcome of the shift to a single monetary policy would be the growth of substantial transfers from the EU to countries that experience cyclical increases in unemployment. Financing those transfers would require a significant increase in tax revenues collected by the EU.

The debates about how large such transfers should be and how the taxes to finance them should be collected would exacerbate the more general disagreement that will inevitably arise as the union seeks to restrict the level and structure of the taxes that individual countries may levy. The European Commission is already trying to get countries to move toward more coordination of their domestic tax policies on the grounds that existing differences in tax rates and rules create competitive advantages for some countries. The shift to a single currency would increase the pressure for tax harmonization. As general responsibility for economic policy shifts from national capitals to the European Commission, the European tradition of focusing taxing authority at a single level would be likely to lead to a shift of the exclusive taxing power from the national to the European level. The EU will therefore be disregarding national preferences about redistribution, the size of government, and the structure of taxes. While the pressures for such coordination might be overwhelming once a single currency has been adopted, the loss of national control over taxes and transfers would be another serious source of irritation within the EU.

## LONG-TERM UNEMPLOYMENT

As the decisions shift away from national governments, it will become harder to reach agreement on policy changes to deal with the high unemployment due to excessive regulation and social welfare payments. The shift of policy decisions from national governments to the European level would eliminate the ability to learn from the experiences of individual countries that try different policies and to benefit from the competitive pressures to adopt national policies that succeed. Moreover, the changes in labor market rules and social benefits that have been proposed by certain national governments are now being opposed not only by labor unions within the individual countries but also by other European governments that fear the resulting gains in competitiveness. Thus we hear of opposition to "social dumping" when an inefficient enterprise is closed and witness the imposition of a Europe-wide limit on the number of hours that employees can work. A politically more unified Europe would make it easier to enforce policies that prevent changes in national labor laws or national transfer payments that would reduce structural unemployment and increase national competitiveness.

If EU legislation succeeds in preventing member countries from competing with each other, they will collectively become less able to compete with the rest of the world. The result would undoubtedly be pressure for increased EU trade barriers, justified by reference to differences in social policy between Europe and other countries. European imposition of such protectionist policies would undermine the entire global trading system and create serious conflicts with the United States and other trading partners.

## INCOMPATIBLE EXPECTATIONS

As the monetary union evolves into a more general political union, conflicts would arise from incompatible expectations about the sharing of power. France sees EMU and the resulting political union as a way of becoming a co-manager of Europe and an equal of Germany, which has nearly 50 percent more people. In the economic sphere, the current domination of European monetary policy by the Bundesbank would be replaced by that of the ECB, in which France and Germany would sit and vote as equals. As the French contemplate the eventual membership of the economic and political union, they may also hope that their natural Mediterranean allies, Italy and Spain, will give France a decisive influence on European policies. And the skillful international French civil servants might come to dominate the administration of the European government.

Germany's expectations and aspirations are more difficult to interpret. Some German leaders no doubt believe, as Chancellor Helmut Kohl frequently says, that joining a political union improves the prospects for peace by "containing a potentially dangerous Germany within Europe." Other Germans are no doubt less self-sacrificing and simply disagree with the French assessment of the consequences of greater economic and political integration. They see Germany as the natural leader within the EU because of its economic weight, military capability, and central location in an EU that will soon include Poland, the Czech Republic, and Hungary. As Kohl has said, not without ambiguity, "Germany is our fatherland, but Europe is our future."

What is clear is that a French aspiration for equality and a German expectation of hegemony are not consistent. Both visions drive their countrymen to support the pursuit of EMU, and both would lead to disagreements and conflicts when they could not be fulfilled.

The aspirations of the smaller countries to have a seat at the table may be frustrated. As the EU expands from 15 current members to include at least 6 more countries of Eastern Europe, the role that smaller countries will be allowed to play will become more and more limited. Current EU voting rules will give way to weighted voting arrangements in which the larger countries have a predominant share of the votes. This change will frustrate countries that recognize that they have sacrificed the ability to control their own domestic policies and their own foreign relations without having received in exchange an effective say in Europe's policies.

This loss of sovereignty would affect not just monetary and tax policies but a wide range of current domestic policies that will gradually come under the jurisdiction of the European Commission or

European Parliament. Rule-making by the European Commission reached a crescendo in 1994 with edicts about such things as the quality of beer and the permissible shape of imported bananas. A fear that complaints about bureaucratic meddling could jeopardize approval of the Maastricht Treaty in national referendums led to a reduction in rule-making by the Brussels bureaucracy and a rhetorical emphasis on Maastricht's principle of "subsidiarity," which asserts that activities will be assigned to whatever level of government is most appropriate—European, national, or local. There is, however, little reason to believe that this vague principle will do much to restrain the substitution of Brussels rules or Strasbourg legislation for what are now domestic policies. Even the Tenth Amendment to the U.S. Constitution, which reserves to the states (or to the people) any powers not delegated to the national government, has not prevented the shift of power to the national government over an enormous range of local issues, such as speed limits on local roads and the age at which individuals may consume alcohol.

## A EUROPEAN MILITARY AND FOREIGN POLICY

The collapse of the Soviet Union has changed the basis for European foreign policy and military collaboration. Although the United States and the countries of Western Europe have had an extremely close alliance since the end of World War II and continue to coordinate military efforts within the NATO structure, many Europeans in positions of responsibility see their economic interests and foreign policy goals differing from those of the United States with respect to many parts of the world, including Eastern Europe, the Middle East, Africa, and even Latin America. The French and German governments also want to develop an independent military capability that can operate without U.S. participation or consent.

Although the European nations could now more readily pursue an independent foreign policy and military strategy, they are clearly hampered in doing so effectively by the decentralized political structure of Europe. Chancellor Konrad Adenauer summarized the situation in stark terms for French Foreign Minister

Christian Pineau on the day in 1956 when England and France gave in to American pressure to abandon their attack on the Suez Canal: "France and England will never be powers comparable to the United States and the Soviet Union. Nor Germany, either. There remains to them only one way of playing a decisive role in the world; that is to unite to make Europe. England is not ripe for it but the affair of Suez will help to prepare her spirits for it. We have no time to waste: Europe will be your revenge." That was a year before the Treaty of Rome launched the Common Market.

The creation of a political union based on the EMU with explicit authority to develop a common foreign and defense policy would accelerate the development of an independent European military structure capable of projecting force outside Western Europe. Steps in that direction are already occurring in anticipation of the stronger political union that will follow the start of EMU. In March 1997, on the 40th anniversary of the Treaty of Rome, France and Germany announced their desire to see a merger of the EU with the existing European military alliance, the Western European Union, so as to strengthen the military coordination of European nations outside the NATO framework. An explicit agreement was reached with the United States that will allow the European members of NATO to use European NATO forces and equipment under European control without U.S. participation.

The attempt to forge a common military and foreign policy for Europe would be an additional source of conflict among the member nations (as well as with those outside the group). European countries differ in their national ambitions and in their attitudes about projecting force and influencing foreign affairs. An attempt to require countries like Portugal and Ireland to participate in an unwanted war in the Middle East or Eastern Europe could create powerful conflicts among the European nations.

## THE RISK OF WAR

There is no doubt that a Europe of nearly 300 million people with an economy approximately equal in size to that of the United States could create a formidable military force. Whether that would be good or bad in the long run for world peace cannot be foretold with any certainty. A politically unified Europe with an independent military and foreign policy would accelerate the reduction of the U.S. military presence in Europe, weaken the role of NATO, and, to that extent, make Europe more vulnerable to attack. The weakening of America's current global hegemony would undoubtedly complicate international military relationships more generally.

Although Russia is now focusing on industrial restructuring, it remains a major nuclear power. Relations between Russia and Western Europe are important but unpredictable. Might a stronger Russia at some time in the future try to regain control over the currently independent Ukraine? Would a stronger, unified EU seek to discourage such action by force? Could that lead to war between Russia and the EU? How would a strong and unified Europe relate to other nations in the vicinity, including those of North Africa and the Middle East, and the Muslim states of the former Soviet Union, which are important or potential sources of energy for Western Europe?

War within Europe itself would be abhorrent but not impossible. The conflicts over economic policies and interference with national sovereignty could reinforce long-standing animosities based on history, nationality, and religion. Germany's assertion that it needs to be contained in a larger European political entity is itself a warning. Would such a structure contain Germany, or tempt it to exercise hegemonic leadership?

A critical feature of the EU in general and EMU in particular is that there is no legitimate way for a member to withdraw. This is a marriage made in heaven that must last forever. But if countries discover that the shift to a single currency is hurting their economies and that the new political arrangements also are not to their liking, some of them will want to leave. The majority may not look kindly on secession, either out of economic self- interest or a more general concern about the stability of the entire union. The

American experience with the secession of the South may contain some lessons about the danger of a treaty or constitution that has no exits.

## IMPLICATIONS FOR THE UNITED STATES

If, as seems most likely, EMU does occur and does lead to a political union with an independent military and foreign policy, the United States must rethink its own foreign policy with respect to Europe. First, the United States would have an opportunity to play a new, useful role within Europe, helping to balance national pressures and prevent the inevitable conflicts from developing into more serious confrontations. The United States should therefore emphasize that it wants its relations with the individual nations of Europe to remain as strong as they are today and should not allow Brussels to intervene between Washington and the national capitals of Europe.

Second, the United States must be aware that an economically and politically unified Europe would seek a different relationship with the United States. French officials in particular have been outspoken in emphasizing that a primary reason for a European monetary and political union is as a counterweight to the influence of the United States, both within European and in international affairs more generally. For the French, American influence is an old issue that frustrated de Gaulle and recurs in attacks on American "cultural imperialism" and U.S. attempts to influence Europe's policies toward countries like Libya, Iraq, and Iran. Such issues would become more widespread in a powerful, independent Europe.

Finally, the United States must recognize that it would no longer be able to count on Europe as an ally in all its relations with third countries. It was safe to assume such support when conflict with the Soviet Union dominated international relations and Europe's interest in containing the Soviet Union coincided with America's. But the global configuration of relations is now more complex. And the Europeans, guided by a combination of economic self- interest, historical traditions, and national pride, may seek alliances and pursue policies that are contrary to the interests of the United States. Although this divergence may tend to happen in any case because of the apparent end of the Soviet threat, the creation of a monetary union that led to a strong political union would accelerate it. If EMU occurs and leads to such a political union in Europe, the world will be a very different and not necessarily safer place.

# The Dollar
# and the Euro

*C. Fred Bergsten*

## THE NEW GLOBAL CURRENCY

The creation of a single European currency will be the most important development in the international monetary system since the adoption of flexible exchange rates in the early 1970s. The dollar will have its first real competitor since it surpassed the pound sterling as the world's dominant currency during the interwar period. As much as $1 trillion of international investment may shift from dollars to euros. Volatility between the world's key currencies will increase substantially, requiring new forms of international cooperation if severe costs for the global economy are to be avoided.

The political impact of the euro will be at least as great. A bipolar currency regime dominated by Europe and the United States, with Japan as a junior partner, will replace the dollar-centered system that has prevailed for most of this century. A quantum leap in transatlantic cooperation will be required to handle both the transition to the new regime and its long-term effects.

The global economic roles of the European Union and the United States are nearly identical. The EU accounts for about 31 percent of world output and 20 percent of world trade. The United States provides about 27 percent of global production and 18 percent of world trade. The dollar's 40 to 60 percent share of world finance far exceeds the economic weight of the United States. This total also exceeds the

C. FRED BERGSTEN is Director of the Institute for International Economics. He was Assistant Secretary of the Treasury for International Affairs from 1977 to 1981 and Assistant to the National Security Council for International Economic Affairs from 1969 to 1971.

share of 10 to 40 percent for the European national currencies combined. The dollar's market share is three to five times that of the deutsche mark, the only European currency now used globally.

Inertia is a powerful force in international finance. For half a century, the pound sterling retained a global role far in excess of Britain's economic strength. The dollar will probably remain the leading currency indefinitely. But the creation of the euro will narrow, and perhaps eventually close, the present monetary gap between the United States and Europe. The dollar and the euro are each likely to wind up with about 40 percent of world finance, with about 20 percent remaining for the yen, the Swiss franc, and minor currencies.

Even an initial Economic and Monetary Union (EMU) comprising only the half-dozen assured core countries would constitute an economy about two-thirds the size of the United States' and almost equal to Japan's. The global trade of this group would exceed that of the United States. If the gap between the current market share of the dollar and that of the European currencies were closed only halfway, that would produce an enormous shift in global financial holdings.

Substantial implications emerge for the functioning and management of the world economy. There will probably be a portfolio diversification of $500 billion to $1 trillion into euros. Most of this shift will come out of the dollar. This in turn will have a significant impact on exchange rates during a long transition period. The euro will move higher than will be comfortable for many Europeans. Europe will probably try to defend itself against this prospect by engineering a further substantial weakening of its national currencies between now and the euro's start-up.

In the long run, the dollar-euro exchange rate is likely to fluctuate considerably more than have the rates between the dollar and individual European currencies. This fluctuation could cause prolonged misalignments that would not only have adverse effects in both Europe and the United States but also provoke protectionist pressures on the global trading system. Creation of the euro will raise many policy issues that will require intensive cooperation, both across the Atlantic and in multilateral settings such as the Group of Seven (G-7) and the International Monetary Fund.

Europe has always accounted for a share of world trade comparable to that of the United States. In addition, Europe has had a common trade policy from the outset of its integration process. Trade policy thus has been bipolar for almost four decades, as evidenced by the necessity of Europe and the United States agreeing on all multilateral trade rounds in the General Agreement on Tariffs and Trade and recent sectoral agreements in the World Trade Organization.

The prospective developments on the monetary side would mirror that evolution, equating Europe's market position and institutional arrangements with those of the United States to produce a similarly bipolar regime. The United States, Europe, and global financial institutions are not prepared for these events. The initial blueprints for EMU ignored the issue, and there has been little subsequent discussion in Europe. The United States and the G-7 have failed to address the rise of the euro seriously, as they failed to address EMU's predecessor, the European Monetary System, even when it spawned currency crises with global effects in 1992–93. It is essential that the United States, Europe, and international financial institutions begin to prepare for the euro's global impact.

## THE EURO START-UP

There is considerable debate in Europe on when, with whom, and even whether the euro will be created. This analysis assumes that the euro will be introduced on or near the scheduled date of January 1999 and that its membership will quickly, if not immediately, encompass virtually the entire membership of the European Union. The euro's systemic evolution will not be affected by whether the currency is launched in 1999 or 2001, or whether the "Club Med" countries—Italy, Portugal, and Spain—are included at the start or join a couple of years later. The same conclusions apply.

The euro will probably be strong from its inception. The Maastricht Treaty gives the European Central Bank (ECB) a mandate to ensure price stability. The bank will place overwhelming emphasis on establishing its credibility as soon as possible. The ECB will be especially chary of any depreciation of the euro's exchange rate, and is likely to view euro appreciation as an early sign of success. The ECB will be the first central bank in history without a government looking over its shoulder. Since it lacks the 50-year credibility of the Bundesbank, the ECB will be tougher than its forerunner in pursuing a responsible monetary policy.

Fiscal policy developments are likely to reinforce this outcome. The fiscal criteria of the Maastricht Treaty will probably be interpreted flexibly to enable EMU to start on time and perhaps, largely for political reasons, to include the Club Med countries. The "growth and stability pact" to govern budget positions after start-up seems likely to have large loopholes. If unemployment remains high at start-up, the national governments will probably deploy their only remaining macroeconomic tool—fiscal policy—in an expansionary direction. That would intensify the pressure on the ECB to pursue a tight monetary policy.

Many Europeans believe that fudging the Maastricht criteria would produce a weak euro. On the contrary, combining such budgetary tolerance with a resolute ECB will further strengthen the new currency. The proper analogy is with the Federal Reserve, which produced a sky-high dollar in the early 1980s in the face of Reagan's huge budget deficits, or the Bundesbank, which produced a strong deutsche mark in the face of large deficits in the early 1990s triggered by German reunification. The ecb is likely to out-Fed and out-Bundesbank its most distinguished role models.

The advent of the euro's global role must be considered across three time periods: the run-up from now until 1999, a transition period of five to ten years during which the euro will attain its new position in international finance, and in the long term, when relatively stable structural conditions will have been established.

## GLOBAL MONEY

Five key factors determine whether a currency will play a global role: the size of its underlying economy and global trade; the economy's independence from external constraints; avoidance of exchange controls; the breadth, depth, and liquidity of the economy's capital markets; and the economy's strength, stability, and external position.

On the first two criteria, a unified Europe is superior to the United States. The European Union's GDP was $8.4 trillion in 1996, compared with $7.2 trillion for the United States. Growth of potential output is similar in the two regions, so their relative position should hold. The European Union also has a larger volume of global trade. EU external trade totaled $1.9 trillion in 1996, compared with $1.7 trillion for the United States.

In terms of openness, the share of exports and imports in total output is now about 23 percent in both the EU and the United States. This ratio has doubled for the United States over the past 25 years while rising only modestly in Europe, but it is also likely to remain broadly similar. Both regions are thus largely independent of external constraints and can manage their policies without being thrown off course by any but the most severe external shocks.

It is almost inconceivable that either the EU or the United States would unilaterally resort to exchange or capital controls. Globalization of capital markets has reached the point where all major financial centers, including many in the developing world, would have to act together to alter international capital flows effectively. Hence the two regions will remain parallel on this key currency criterion as well.

It is less clear when Europe will reach full parity with the United States in terms of the breadth, depth, and liquidity of its capital markets. The American market for domestic securities is about twice as large as the combined European markets. The European financial markets are highly decentralized. There will be no central governmental borrower like the U.S. Treasury to provide a fulcrum for the market. It may take some time to align the relevant standards and practices across the EU, especially if London is included. Germany may oppose wholesale liberalization, as the Bundesbank has traditionally done in Germany, on the grounds that it would weaken the ability of the ECB to conduct an effective monetary policy.

On the other hand, the total value of government bond markets in the EU is 2.1 trillion euros, compared with 1.6 trillion euros in the United States. Moreover, international bonds and equities are much more frequently issued in the European markets than in the United States. Futures trading in German and French government bonds, taken together, exceeded that in U.S. notes and bonds in 1995. Expectations over the launch of EMU have already produced a substantial convergence in the yields of government bonds throughout Europe. An integrated European capital market for private bonds shows clear signs of developing. So European parity on this key criterion is likely to occur eventually.

The final criterion is the strength and stability of the European economy. There is no risk of hyper-inflation or any of the other extreme instabilities that could disqualify the euro from international status. On the contrary, the ECB is likely to run a responsible monetary policy. On the other hand, Europe may not carry out the structural reforms needed to restore dynamic economic growth. But markets prize stability more than growth, as indicated by the continued dominance of the dollar through extended periods of sluggish American economic performance. Hence the euro should qualify on these grounds as well.

In addition, America's external economic position will continue to raise doubts about the future stability and value of the dollar. The United States has run current account deficits for the last 15 years. Its net foreign debt exceeds $1 trillion and is rising annually by 15 to 20 percent. The EU, in contrast, has a roughly balanced international asset position and has run modest surpluses in its international accounts in recent years. On this important criterion, the EU is decidedly superior to the United States.

The relative size of countries' economies and trade flows is of central importance in determining currencies' global roles. A large economy has a naturally large base for its currency and thus enjoys important economies of scale and scope. A high volume of trade gives a country's firms considerable leverage to finance in their own currency. Large economies are less vulnerable to external shocks and thus offer a safe haven for investors. They are more likely to have the large capital markets required for major currency status.

There is a clear historical correlation between size and currency status. Sterling and the dollar became dominant during the periods when the United Kingdom and the United States were the world's main economies and traders. The only global currencies today are those of the world's three largest economies and traders: the United States, Germany, and Japan.

The relevant comparison for present purposes is between the EU and the euro, on the one hand, and Germany and the deutsche mark on the other. It would be improper to compare the euro, which will meet all of the key currency criteria, with the sum of the individual European currencies, most of which do not. The comparison must be with the deutsche mark, the only European currency that is now used on a global basis.

Hence there will be a quantum leap in the size of the economy and trading unit in question. Germany accounts for nine percent of world output and 12 percent of world trade. The euro core group accounts for 18 and 19 percent, respectively. The full EMU accounts for 31 and 20 percent, respectively. The relevant unit will thus increase immediately by at least 50 to 100 percent. Eventually, the rise will be about 65 to 250 percent.

Crude econometric efforts suggest that every rise of 1 percent in a country's share of global output and trade raises its currency share by roughly the same amount. On this premise, the global role of the euro would exceed that of the deutsche mark by 50 to 100 percent if EMU included only the core group and by 65 to 250 percent if all Europe were included. The deutsche mark, by most calculations, accounts for about 15 percent of global financial assets in both private and official markets. The euro's role could thus reach 20 to 30 percent of world finance if EMU included only the core countries and 25 to 50 percent if the entire EU were involved. The midpoints of these ranges, 25 and almost 40 percent, provide rough indicators of the likely future global role of the euro. If these shifts into the euro came largely out of the dollar, they would eliminate half to all of the present gap between the dollar and the deutsche mark.

This evolution could produce a major diversification of portfolios into euros, mainly out of dollars. Official reserve shifts into euros could range between $100 billion and $300 billion. Private portfolio diversification could be much larger. Excluding intra-EU holdings, global holdings of international financial assets, including bank deposits and bonds, are about $3.5 trillion. About 50 percent are in dollars and only about 10 percent in European currencies. A complete balancing of portfolios between dollars and euros would require a shift of about $700 billion. A combination of official and private shifts suggests a potential diversification of between $500 billion and $1 trillion.

Such a shift, even spread over a number of years, could drive the euro up and the dollar down substantially. The extent of the shift will depend on whether the supply of euros rises in tandem with demand. It will also depend on the relationship between the dollar and the European national currencies when the euro is issued. While most Europeans want a strong euro, they also want to avoid an overvalued currency that deepens their economic difficulties. Many believe that their national currencies are already overvalued despite recent substantial declines against the dollar. The only way they can avoid the dilemma is to depreciate the European national currencies further before the launch of the euro. The EMU would then be able to set the initial exchange rate below the fundamental equilibrium exchange rate for the euro. The euro could appreciate modestly without undermining the long-term competitive position of the European economy.

Exchange-market developments from now until the early part of the next century could be a mirror image of the first half of the 1980s. During that period, U.S. budget deficits soared. The elimination of Japanese exchange controls triggered a large portfolio diversification from yen into dollars. Fiscal tightening in Europe and Japan further enhanced the dollar's appreciation. The opposite conditions may apply in the period ahead: further reductions in, or even elimination of, the American budget deficit could coincide with European fiscal expansion and a large diversification out of the dollar triggered by the euro's creation. Substantial euro appreciation and dollar depreciation could thus occur in the transition to EMU.

Many analysts agree that the euro will rival the dollar as the world's leading currency. Most believe, however, that such a shift will take considerable time, since any redistribution of international portfolios occurs incrementally. But there is evidence from the history of major currencies that major shocks can produce rapid changes in portfolio composition. The devaluation of the pound sterling in 1931 permanently reduced the international role of that currency and propelled the dollar into the dominant position. The onset of double-digit inflation in the United States in the late 1970s produced a sharp drop in the dollar's role in just a few years.

These shocks, however, have derived more from poor policy and performance by the lead currency than from the improved position of the new rival. The euro's rise may have to await a serious policy lapse by the United States, as in the late 1970s, or a renewed explosion of America's external debt position, as in the mid-1980s. Even the most successful and best-managed countries undergo occasional setbacks, and the euro's rough parity with the dollar is probably inevitable.

## JAPAN AS JUNIOR PARTNER

The yen will continue to play an important but smaller role, maintaining its 10 to 15 percent market share. But the world is not likely to see a tri-polar monetary system. The Japanese Ministry of International Trade and Industry's latest report on the topic concludes that "the yen is nowhere near achieving the status of a truly international currency." Japan will need to be included in any new EU--U.S. arrangements but will probably remain a junior partner in the management of the international monetary regime.

Japan's economy is about twice the size of Germany's. Its trade is only slightly smaller, and it has an even better record of price stability over the past 15 years. Yet its currency plays a much smaller role than the deutsche mark, suggesting a significant deficiency when it comes to the other key currency criteria—notably the capabilities of its financial markets. Japan's continued failure to deregulate and modernize those markets is likely to remain a barrier for the yen. Indeed, the fragility of Japan's financial sector is more likely to repel than attract international interest.

Many analysts have hypothesized the emergence of three north-south regional blocs centered around Europe, Japan, and the United States. So far, however, major trade groupings have developed around Europe and the United States but not around Japan. With the Asia-Pacific Economic Cooperation forum linking the United States and Japan, bi-polarity may be evolving not only in monetary affairs but in trade as well.

## THE NEW TRANSATLANTIC AGENDA

The euro's rise will convert an international monetary system that has been dominated by the dollar since World War II into a bipolar regime. Hence the structure and politics of international financial cooperation will change dramatically.

The exchange rate between the euro and the dollar will pose a significant policy challenge. The United States and the rest of the world should reject any attempt by Europe to substantially under value the euro's start-up rate. It would represent a blatant effort by Europe to export its high unemployment and to enable the euro to become a strong currency without any significant cost to its competitive position.

France is running sizable trade and current account surpluses, even adjusted for its high level of unemployment. Germany has the world's second-largest trade surplus and is the world's second-largest creditor country. The EU is a surplus region. By contrast, the United States is the world's largest debtor nation. Its trade and current account deficits are headed well above $200 billion in 1997. These facts hardly suggest that the European currencies are too strong or that the dollar is too weak. The G-7 should, at a minimum, actively resist further European depreciation and dollar appreciation.

Portfolio diversification's impact on the exchange rate between the dollar and the euro will also pose a challenge. Unfortunately, there is no way to assess the precise magnitude or timing of that impact, and it is impossible to predict the fundamental equilibrium exchange rate that will emerge for the euro and the dollar. It would, therefore, be a mistake to use target zones or any other predetermined mechanisms to limit dollar-euro fluctuations during the transition period.

However, markets could become extremely unstable. It will be important for the G-7 and the International Monetary Fund to monitor events closely, to form judgments on the likely outcome as the process evolves, and to intervene to limit unnecessary volatility. This monitoring will require much closer cooperation than exists today.

Over the longer run, availability of a more attractive alternative to the dollar could reduce the ability of the United States to finance its large external deficits. With more than $4 trillion in external liabilities and an array of alternative assets available to international investors, however, the United States' policy autonomy already faces considerable limits. Such constraints were felt in Washington in the late 1970s—even though the United States was then the world's largest creditor country—when the dollar's free fall signaled the need to tighten monetary policy and triggered the $30 billion dollar support package of October 1978. They were felt again in early 1987 and early 1995 when the dollar fell sharply against the deutsche mark and the yen.

European countries already pay relatively little attention to fluctuations in their national currencies vis-à-vis the dollar. But external events will play an even smaller role in the larger, unified European economy. Larger and even more frequent changes in the exchange rate of the euro could be accepted with equanimity. The EU might even promote greater currency movements to achieve external adjustment, as the United States has done on occasion.

The euro and the dollar will dominate world finance, but both Europe and the United States will often be tempted to practice benign neglect. If left to market forces, the two currencies will likely experience increased volatility and misalignments. Both outcomes would be destabilizing for other countries and the world economy.

The European Union and the United States must recognize that prolonged misalignments would be costly for their economies too. The United States learned this in the mid-1980s, when dollar overvaluation caused an extended recession in manufacturing and agriculture. Given the pivotal role of the EU and the United States in global trade policy, such lapses would be extremely harmful to the world economy. A structured exchange rate regime should be developed to manage the relationship that will emerge between the dollar and the euro. The EU, Japan, and the United States should negotiate a target zone system with broad currency bands, perhaps 10 percent on both sides of a nominal midpoint, that would avoid large current account imbalances and their attendant problems.

Many Europeans believe that EMU will facilitate such cooperation. Europe will speak with a single voice, enabling it to force the United States to be more cooperative. Some Europeans view this outcome as an important goal of EMU, and one that will offset the continent's enhanced ability to ignore external events.

Trade policy provides support for their logic. The multilateral trading system has been essentially bipolar since the creation of the Common Market in 1958, which has always spoken with a single voice on most trade matters. The united Europe could have chosen to raise barriers against the world, with only modest costs because of its considerable size, but has largely opted to support further global liberalization. Most observers believe that this negotiating structure facilitated the success of the three major rounds of the General Agreement on Tariffs and Trade. It has recently been on display in the forging of the two most important liberalizing measures since the end of the Uruguay Round, the agreement on trade in telecommunications services and the Information Technology Agreement on trade in high-tech goods.

While this pattern may hold, several scenarios can be envisioned. The United States could react defensively to its loss of monetary dominance and seek to create a formalized dollar area, like the United Kingdom's sterling area in the 1930s. The EU could adopt a strategy of benign neglect, arguing that the United States has done so repeatedly and that its turn has now come. Trade protection could result from either course.

When French President Valerie Giscard d'Estaing and German Chancellor Helmut Schmidt decided to create the European Monetary System in 1978, one of their goals was to foster a more stable global monetary regime. The creation of EMU could bring that vision closer to reality. However, in the absence of cooperation between the European Union and the United States, the euro could create greater instability. It is up to the governments of the two regions to achieve a smooth transition from the sterling- and dollar-dominated monetary regimes of the nineteenth and twentieth centuries to a stable dollar and euro system in the early 21st century. The underlying strength and history of the North Atlantic relationship bodes well, but achieving a successful outcome will be a major policy challenge in the years ahead.

# The Degeneration of EMU

*Niall Ferguson and Laurence J. Kotlikoff*

## HERE TODAY, GONE TOMORROW

From conception through gestation and birth, and now in its early infancy, the euro has consistently proved the skeptics wrong. Some Cassandras thought that Brussels-bashing nationalists would reject the single currency in referendums. Others doubted that Italy and other fiscally troubled applicants would fulfill the Maastricht Treaty's strict limits on budget deficits and national debt. Still others predicted that the fierce 1998 dispute over the presidency of the European Central Bank might abort the entire enterprise.

Yet economic and monetary union (EMU) has proceeded more or less according to plan. The French referendum's "petit oui" in 1992 may have required a little gentle massaging; the Maastricht fiscal criteria may have been honored partly in the breach; and of course the currency has, over the past year, depreciated markedly against the dollar. But the fixed exchange rates within the eurozone have held firm, despite warnings about speculative attacks during the transition. And with its depreciation spurring economic growth, the euro is likely to recover somewhat against the dollar this year.

NIALL FERGUSON is Fellow and Tutor in Modern History at Jesus College, Oxford. He is the author of The Pity of War (1999) and has just published the second volume of *The House of Rothschild* (1999).

LAURENCE J. KOTLIKOFF is Professor of Economics at Boston University and Research Associate at the National Bureau of Economic Research. He is the author of Generational Accounting (1993). Both were Houblon-Norman Fellows at the Bank of England in 1998–99.

Nevertheless, the skeptics may have the last laugh. For whether a euro equals a dollar tomorrow or the next day does not really matter. What matters is whether the entire monetary union will hold together in the years ahead. The euro's medium-term future will prove much shakier when Europe is hit by the fiscal crises looming for the majority of the eurozone's member countries.

## THE NEW MATH

The notion that such fiscal problems exist is not new. Nor is the proposition that they could jeopardize monetary cohesion. But fresh evidence, drawn from a recent, comprehensive calculation of "generational accounts," shows the full extent of the fiscal crisis facing the eurozone.

Generational accounting provides answers to the following three questions: How large a fiscal burden does current policy impose on future generations? Is current fiscal policy sustainable without major additional sacrifices on the part of current or future generations? What policies are required to achieve generational balance—i.e., to ensure that future generations will pay to the government the same share of their lifetime incomes in net taxes (taxes paid minus transfer payments received) as do today's generations?

This new method of accounting was developed not to augment the conventional measure of fiscal imbalance—the official government debt—but to replace it. For neither the size of the government debt nor its change over time (the budget deficit) are well-defined economic concepts. Rather, they reflect the arbitrary choice of fiscal vocabulary, specifically in labeling government receipts and payments.

Three things follow from this. First, the debt and deficit criteria laid out in the Maastricht Treaty bear no intrinsic relation to fiscal prudence. Second, one can satisfy the Maastricht criteria simply by using the appropriate accounting terminology—something that observers of Italian entry into EMU may already have guessed. Third, the sustainability of EMU fiscal policies must be measured more objectively.

The bottom line is that generational imbalances across the eurozone gravely threaten the single currency's medium-term viability. The choice for nearly all EMU members is between tax hikes on a scale unprecedented in peacetime or drastic government spending cuts. Given the political weakness of most national governments, it is hard to see either choice being made. But the only other conceivable possibility—a sharp and unanticipated rise in inflation, which "solved" some fiscal crises in the past—also seems improbable, at least within EMU's constraints.

## ADD IT UP

Generational accounts represent the sum of all future net taxes (taxes paid minus transfer payments received) that citizens born in any given year will pay over their lifetimes, given current policy. The sum of the generational accounts of all living generations indicates what those now alive will pay toward the government's bills. The government's bills, in turn, are equal to the sum (in today's prices) of all of the government's future purchases of goods and services plus its official net debt—its financial liabilities minus its financial assets, including public-sector enterprises. Bills not paid by current generations must be paid by future generations. This reflects the zero-sum nature of the government's intertemporal budget constraint: no matter what level of current deficit or debt a government reports, somebody, someday, will have to pay in net taxes what the government spends. Borrowing now to pay for government spending means paying more taxes later.

Generational imbalance results when the generational accounts of current newborns fall short of the growth-adjusted accounts of future newborns. The two accounts are directly comparable because they incorporate net taxes over entire lifetimes, allowing for population and economic growth at current official projections. If future generations face higher generational accounts than do current newborns, current policy is not only generationally unbalanced, it is also unsustainable. The government cannot continue to collect the same net taxes (adjusted for growth) from future generations as it would collect, under current policy, from current newborns without violating the intertemporal budget constraint.

This calculation imposes the entire fiscal adjustment needed to satisfy the government's budget constraint on those born in the future. It also delivers a clear message about the policy changes that governments need to achieve generational balance without foisting all the adjustment on to future generations—either through government spending cuts or tax increases, or a combination thereof. One can then calculate the precise size of the tax hike or spending cut necessary to make the growth-adjusted generational accounts of future generations equal those of newborns.

A critical feature of generational accounting is that the size of the future fiscal burden does not depend on how the government describes its receipts and payments. The same, unfortunately, is not true of the reported size of the government's official debt. Suppose that the Italian government chose to label the roughly 300 trillion lire in social security contributions in 2000 as "loans" instead of "taxes." Also suppose that instead of calling the future benefits it promises to pay current workers in exchange for these contributions "transfer payments," it called them "return of principal plus interest" on these loans minus an "old-age tax." This alternative wording would leave the Italian government reporting a deficit larger by 300 trillion lire, putting the overall deficit far higher than the Maastricht threshold of three percent of GDP. A year from now, the government's total debt would therefore be larger—but so would the generational accounts of currently living generations, since their future "old-age tax" would now be included in their accounts. Since both would be larger by the same amount, the burden on future generations would not change. The economic position of each generation would also be unaffected by this alternative set of labels; each worker would hand the government the same amount of money this year and receive from the government the same amount of money in the future. The only difference would be the words that the government used to describe these flows.

The fact that a government uses a given vocabulary to describe what it is doing does not make those words sacrosanct. Since each set of words results in a different measure of the deficit, which is correct? In economic theory, there is no correct measure. The concept of a deficit has everything to do with semantics and nothing to do with economics. Generational accounting not only dispenses with this arbitrary terminology; it is also forward-looking and comprehensive.

So what does it mean for Europe? The table on page 114 gives results for 14 countries: Austria, Belgium, Finland, France, Germany, Ireland, Italy, the Netherlands, Portugal, and Spain (10 of the 11 members of EMU) as well as Denmark, Sweden, and the United Kingdom (EU members outside the eurozone) and Norway (which belongs to neither). It shows 4 mutually exclusive ways these countries could achieve generational balance: cutting government purchases, cutting government transfer payments, raising all taxes, or raising income taxes (corporate as well as personal). The figures in the table indicate the immediate and permanent percentage adjustment needed, with the magnitudes of these adjustments indirectly measuring a country's generational imbalance. Education is treated as a transfer payment rather than a government purchase, and calculations are for all levels of government—local, regional, state, and central.

According to the table, 9 of the 14 countries need to cut all government spending on goods and services by more than 20 percent if they want to rely solely on such cuts to achieve generational balance. This group includes the three most important EMU members: Germany, France, and Italy. Austria, Finland, and Spain need to cut their noneducation purchases by more than half, as does Sweden; indeed, for Austria and Finland, the cut in spending needed is more than two-thirds.

Not all European countries suffer from generational imbalances. In Ireland, future generations face a smaller fiscal burden than do current ones, thereby allowing for growth. But Ireland is unique: it is the only country considered here whose government could spend more over time without unduly burdening coming generations. Four countries have only moderate generational imbalances in terms of spending adjustment: Belgium, Portugal, Norway, and the United Kingdom. But the last two of these are outside the eurozone.

Generational accounting produces a very different ranking of fiscal vulnerability from the conventional measures used in both the Maastricht Treaty and the 1997 Stability and Growth Pact, which judge fiscal stability by a nation's debt and deficit as ratios of GDP. The first column of the table shows that the EMU countries with the biggest fiscal problems are Austria, Finland, and Spain. But on the basis of Maastricht debt-GDP ratios, the three worst cases are Belgium, Italy, and the Netherlands.

Europe's generational imbalances are far from unique. For the sake of comparison, take the United States. Despite rosy projections of running "surpluses" well into the future, America in fact would have to cut government spending at all levels by 14 percent (or federal spending by 43 percent) to achieve generational balance. The figures for Japan and Brazil are 30 and 26 percent, respectively. Canada and New Zealand, by contrast, are in almost perfect generational balance. And before it recently introduced a pay-as-you-go social security system, Thailand could boast a figure of -48 percent, implying enormous latitude for government spending.

Fiscal policy and demographics explain these differences. For example, the United Kingdom has kept most transfer payments fixed over time in real (that is, inflation-adjusted) terms, thanks to a decision in the 1980s to break the link between state pensions and earnings inflation. Germany is still dealing with the colossal costs of reunification, while Ireland has a more youthful population than the European average.

One alternative to cutting government purchases is to cut transfer payments—e.g., by raising the age of retirement, as is being discussed now in the United States. Here the cuts required are somewhat smaller but nevertheless daunting for the majority of EMU members: over a fifth for Austria, Finland, and Holland; more than ten percent for Germany, Italy, and Spain. Again, only Ireland does not need an immediate cut to achieve generational balance.

These dramatic cuts would be very unpopular—as would tax increases, the third possible policy option. If Germany relied exclusively on across-the-board tax hikes, tax rates at all levels of government (federal, regional, and local) and of all types (value added, payroll, corporate income, personal income, excise, sales, property, estate, and gift) would rise overnight by more than 9 percent. In Austria and Finland, taxes would have to rise more than 18 percent, and in Spain more than 14 percent. If countries relied solely on income tax hikes, then Austria, Finland, and France would have to raise their income tax rates by over 50 percent. The requisite income-tax hikes in Germany and Italy would be just under 30 percent, compared with 10 percent for Britain and 21 percent for the United States. In contrast, Ireland could cut its income tax rates by about 5 percent before it needed to worry about overburdening future generations.

This problem will not go away. On the contrary, the longer countries wait to act, the bigger the adjustments will need to be. Britain, for example, could achieve generational balance with an immediate income-tax hike of just under 10 percent. But if it waits 5 years, that number will rise to 11 percent. After a 15-year delay, it will be 15 percent, and after 25 years, more than 20 percent.

## HEY, BIG SPENDERS

These shocking figures mean that the majority of EMU countries have severe generational imbalances, even if their reported deficits do lie under the Maastricht limit of three percent of annual GDP. Yet none of the four scenarios above is likely to be realized by any government other than that of Ireland, given the immense political opposition to such retrenchment. The tax hikes or spending cuts would be, in most cases, unprecedented in peacetime. But whereas the losers would be today's taxpayers, the winners would be future generations.

Not one of the key European governments has the political strength to effect such fiscal reform. In Germany, Gerhard Schroder's SPD-Green coalition is still struggling to restrain the growth of state pensions and social spending. In France, the left-wing coalition led by Lionel Jospin is even less likely to grasp fiscal nettles now that its talented finance minister, Dominique Strauss-Kahn, has resigned to fight fraud charges. In Italy, Massimo D'Alema's left-of-center coalition limps on in a newly repackaged government, crippled by the chronic divisions of the Italian party system. Total Italian tax revenues have already risen from 39 to 44 percent of GDP since 1990; it is hard to imagine any government surviving if it asked for more.

A significant increase in economic growth could ease the fiscal positions of many European states. But this is unlikely to happen in the core European countries, given their relatively rigid labor markets. True, growth in the 11 EMU countries is generally forecast to be 3 percent in 2000. But with 10-year bond yields around 5.7 percent and inflation below 1.4 percent, real interest rates are very high by historical standards, compounding debt problems and stifling economic recovery.

What course can Europe take in the face of such tight fiscal restraints? Tinkering with the budget limits in the Maastricht Treaty and the Stability and Growth Pact may be possible for some countries, though not necessarily for those states whose generational accounts are most out of kilter. And the possibilities for creative accounting using traditional measures of debts and deficits have not yet been fully exhausted. Because the Maastricht criteria are based on measures of debt that are economically arbitrary, there is every reason to expect enforcement to be lax. Indeed, it already has been. As the German Bundesbank and others have pointed out, as many as 8 of the 11 EMU members had debts above the maximum 60 percent threshold (of debt as a percentage of annual GDP) when they qualified for entry in 1998.

A further possibility is that the countries with the most severe generational imbalances may exert pressure on the ECB to loosen monetary policy. For most of the twentieth century, after all, printing money was often the line of least resistance for governments having fiscal difficulties.

As is well known, issuing money operates as a fiscal tool in three ways. First, it permits a government to swap a depreciated currency for actual goods and services. The private sector pays for this transfer to the government (or seigniorage) while inflation eats away at the money's real value. Second, raising prices by cranking up the printing presses reduces the real value of unadjusted government wage payments, transfer payments, and official debt repayments. Third, rising inflation permits a government to push taxpayers into higher marginal tax brackets if the tax system's degree of progressivity is not inflation-indexed. Historically, this is how many states have coped with severe fiscal imbalances: the defeated powers after World War I, for example, or Russia and Ukraine after the collapse of the Soviet economy.

Here lies the crucial point for Europe's single currency. Those countries under the most severe fiscal pressure will obviously wish to print money sooner and faster than those better situated. Yet the Maastricht Treaty effectively rules out printing money; Article 104 of the treaty (now Article 101 of the treaty establishing the European Community) and Article 21 of the Statute of the European System of Central Banks enshrine a strict "no bail-out" rule. Member states that hope to inflate away their debts will simply be turned away.

Much more likely is a series of collisions between national governments struggling to bring their finances under control and the ECB, which is constitutionally bound to maintain price stability as its primary objective and appears unconcerned by sluggish growth in large parts of the eurozone. The ECB is also likely to ignore the unpleasant monetary arithmetic implied by the budget problems of the member states and instead retort with some unpleasant fiscal arithmetic of its own by keeping its monetary policy strictly anti-inflationary.

If all countries were in the same predicament, they might resolve this conflict politically. But because there is such variation in the eurozone's generational imbalances, and indeed in their rates of growth and inflation, some countries will get into difficulties sooner than others. The political conflicts are easy enough to imagine. If European governments find it hard to agree about the edibility of British beef, it is not easy to imagine them acting in unison over generational imbalances in public finance. Even the recent proposal to introduce an EU-wide withholding tax on the interest from private savings foundered in the face of U.K. opposition. As was depressingly apparent at their Helsinki summit in December 1999, European leaders would rather dream the old Gaullist dream of military independence from America than face hard fiscal facts. If they do not set their generational accounts in order, there will be no European defense budgets in the future, much less a European army.

## DREAMS DEFERRED

History shows that monetary unions can be undone by fiscal imbalances. The difficulty lies in deciding which previous monetary unions most closely resemble EMU, since none does exactly. Some economic historians have sought to draw comparisons with the pre-1914 gold standard. But others see EMU as more like a national monetary union because there is a common central bank and no prescribed right to secede.

In truth, neither of these parallels is very illuminating. The gold standard was an informal system, without a single central bank, that states could always exit—like the European Exchange Rate Mechanism before the euro. On the other hand, comparing EMU with the United States, Italy, or Germany is unconvincing. In each case, political union came before monetary union. Nor is it helpful to compare currency unions between giants and dwarves (such as that among France, Andorra, and Monaco). Rather, the best analogies are with monetary unions among multiple states with only loose confederal ties and negligible fiscal centralization.

The Austro-Hungarian monetary union after 1867 is a useful example. The historian Marc Flandreau has pointed out that post-1867 Austria-Hungary combined the free circulation of goods and capital and a unified central bank on one hand with fiscal autonomy for each constituent state and its multiple nationalities on the other. (Unlike in the EU, however, there was a common army and foreign policy.) Both Austria and Hungary regularly ran quite large deficits until 1914, but these were absorbed with little difficulty by bond markets. Yet the dramatic increase in expenditure and borrowing in World War I caused inflation to accelerate and led ultimately to the breakup of the monetary union in 1917–18.

Another illuminating precedent is the Latin Monetary Union (1865–1927) between France, Belgium, Switzerland, Italy (including the Vatican), and later Greece. True, there was no Latin Central Bank, but the LMU did have a conscious political motivation, as the economist Luca Einaudi has argued. (A driving force was Felix Parieu of France, who dreamt of an eventual "European Union" with a "European Commission" and a "European Parliament.") But the costs to the other members of Italian fiscal laxity were high. The papal government financed its deficits by churning out silver coinage to reap high seigniorage profits. In short, it debased the coinage and allowed private agents to export it to the rest of the union—a flagrant breach of the rules. At the same time, the Italian government introduced largely unconvertible paper currency to finance its growing deficits, breaking the spirit if not the letter of the convention. The war of 1870 removed the political rationale of French continental hegemony; the only reason the LMU survived after 1878 was to avoid the cost of dissolution. Like the Scandinavian Monetary Union founded in 1873 by Sweden and Denmark, the LMU was belatedly pronounced dead in the 1920s.

History therefore suggests that asymmetric fiscal problems—often generated by war—quickly cause monetary unions between fiscally independent states to dissolve. The fiscal problems caused by bloated social security and pension systems could have a similar centrifugal effect on EMU, with welfare substituting for war as the fatal solvent.

## EXIT STRATEGIES

The problem is not simply that European states will continue to run deficits as conventionally measured. Past experience (for example, the German monetary union of Bismarck's day) suggests that monetary unions can coexist with federal fiscal systems where member states issue substantial volumes of bonds. Diverging levels of borrowing in the eurozone today may result in differing bond yields down the road—and the existence of yield spreads is not incompatible with monetary union. Markets cannot be forbidden to attach different default risks to different member states within a monetary union, just as companies issuing euro-denominated corporate bonds offer investors varying returns. Furthermore, high levels of state borrowing do not necessarily lead to inflation. Much depends on the international bond market's demand for high-grade sovereign debt; with more and more people living for two decades or more after retirement, that demand is likely to grow.

But generational imbalance does not simply imply that European states will run deficits. This method already assumes that they will. Rather, it points to an inevitable need to raise taxes, reduce expenditures, or print money to meet a rising burden of debt interest. But what happens when states like Austria, Finland, or Spain reach a political impasse on fiscal reform? Bond markets can absorb only so much debt before demand starts to wane. Legally, withdrawal from EMU is impossible. But history shows there is always an exit. If a country's only viable option is to print money and inflate away some of its liabilities, and if the European Central Bank abides by its "no bail-out" rule, then secession will almost certainly be considered. The question is what the costs would be.

First, higher interest rates would result in the short term, and much would depend on their impact on the government's debt-service bill. In this context, the different term structures of the various national debts are important: a country with a lot of short-term debt would gain much less from inflation. Once again, there are wide disparities among eurozone members. More than half of

Spain's domestic debt is short-term, compared with 0.4 percent of Austria's.

Second, the exchange rate of the seceding currency would almost certainly weaken. This could help boost the economy by making exports cheaper. But legal tangles would also arise as creditors and debtors (foreign and domestic) fought over whether the presecession debts should be valued in euros or in the national currency. This could severely destabilize the seceding country's financial system, as well as those of other countries. Again, the implications would be greater for countries with more debt held abroad.

The political will to implement spending cuts and tax increases may be strengthened by these considerations. Still, history offers few examples of successful adjustments on the scale necessary in certain European countries today. What it does offer are several examples of monetary unions disintegrating when fiscal strains became incompatible with the unpleasant arithmetic of a single currency. In this respect, conventional measures of fiscal balance like debt and deficit ratios to GDP understate the magnitude of the eurozone's problems. Generational accounting suggests that EMU could degenerate—not overnight, but within the next decade.

# The Future of the Euro

## Why the Greek Crisis Will Not Ruin Europe's Monetary Union

*Lorenzo Bini Smaghi*

When the euro was conceived two decades ago, few people expected it to have to weather a storm as great as the recent global economic and financial crisis. And many observers now think the entire European construct—its institutions and currency—has been so damaged by the crisis that it might not survive. A careful analysis of the problems within individual eurozone economies, particularly Greece's, and in the architecture of the monetary union among them reveals what went wrong, how the EU has responded, and what the prospects of the euro really are.

Between 2008 and 2010, several things went wrong in Europe, the biggest of which was Greece's financial crisis. For years, Greek fiscal policy had been unsound. Although private debt had been rising, the country's overall debt-to-GDP ratio had not ballooned, because the Greek economy was growing. But that growth turned out to be unsustainable. When the global economic crisis hit, Greece's deficit more than doubled. The problem was compounded by revelations that the government had grossly falsified and padded its budget in the run up to the 2009 parliamentary elections.

Unlike countries with national currencies, Greece could not address its problems through monetary policy. It can neither print

LORENZO BINI SMAGHI is a Member of the Executive Board of the European Central Bank.

money to inflate its debt away nor depreciate its currency to recover the international competitiveness of Greek goods and grow the economy out of debt. And unlike a subnational federal region in trouble, Greece, as a sovereign unit itself, could not have its falling revenues and rising social expenditures offset through simple fiscal transfers from the rest of Europe. Its labor force, moreover, is not mobile enough for excess to be exported elsewhere in the eurozone.

As far as the euro's architects were concerned, this kind of problem should never have arisen. European financial markets should have put pressure on countries with excessive debt-to-GDP ratios, such as Greece, by charging them higher interest rates for loans. The European Central Bank (ECB) prohibits loaning money to service national debts, and its no-bail-out clause should similarly have discouraged overspending. Additionally, the eurozone's Stability and Growth Pact, which was meant to enforce fiscal discipline in member countries through rules against running high deficits and debts, should have constrained Greek politicians. Finally, the Lisbon process, a 2000 development plan for the eurozone, should have increased Greece's economic competitiveness and spurred real growth.

Unexpectedly, however, European financial markets accommodated Greece's public and private spending with relatively low interest rates. It was only when the global financial crisis gained momentum that the markets reacted and capital flows suddenly stopped. The Stability and Growth Pact was ineffective as well; member states proved unwilling to enforce restrictions against others for fear of being subject to restrictions themselves. Finally, the Lisbon process underestimated the true differences in the member countries' economies and failed to adequately address them.

Once the Greek financial crisis was under way, there were two options for tackling it. The first was for Greece to implement fiscal and structural reform that would bring its debt and deficit under control. Greece, the International Monetary Fund (IMF), the European Commission (EC), and the ECB negotiated just such a plan in June, with the goal of turning Greece's primary deficit of nine percent of GDP into a surplus of six percent by 2015. It rests on fairly standard IMF reforms: substantial expenditure cuts, increases in revenue creation, and improvements in tax collection. It also includes important structural reforms, such as pension reform and privatization, which are aimed at improving long-run debt sustainability and the performance of Greece's labor and manufacturing sectors.

The plan was accompanied by financing from the IMF and loans from the rest of the eurozone worth €110 billion—or 46 percent of Greece's 2010 GDP. Because the Greek crisis spread to other countries—Portugal and Spain, in particular—member states agreed to create a special European Financial Stability Fund to support any eurozone country that decides to undertake economic reform.

Yet there is already widespread skepticism about the IMF plan among some academics, investors, and speculators. Many fear that it is too harsh, imposes too many restrictions, and would ultimately be politically unsustainable. Their alternatives, however, are no better. Some have called for Greece to undertake an "orderly" debt restructuring, including devaluing bonds to alleviate the country's debt burden. In its extreme form, this proposal also calls for the reinstatement of the drachma, because moving to the less valuable currency could restore Greece's economic competitiveness.

In truth, however, these measures would not work and would be much harsher for the people of Greece than the IMF plan. Debt restructuring is never orderly. Undertaken now, it would hammer Greece's domestic financial system and have serious repercussions for the rest of its economy. Greek access to eurozone capital markets would be impaired for years, stalling the public and private sectors. And if Greece did not fully repay the loans from other eurozone countries, it would suffer a major loss of political credibility.

In such an economically integrated area as the eurozone, leaving the currency union would not solve Greece's economic problems either. After Italy left the European Exchange Rate Mechanism (ERM) and devalued its currency in 1992, for example, it suffered from volatile swings in interest rates due to a lack of investor confidence. Inflation rapidly reappeared, and Italy had to tighten its monetary policy further than would have been necessary if it had stayed in the ERM.

The return to a national currency would also involve renegotiating business contracts, both within Greece and between Greeks and others. In the event of legal disputes, EU courts would likely be inclined to rule against Greece, the country that changed its currency. Greek citizens would probably try to maintain the euro as a unit of account and means of exchange, leading to parallel circulation of the drachma and the euro. And, having accepted billions in euro-denominated loans, the Greek debt burden would immediately increase if Greece reinstated the less valuable drachma.

The costs of restructuring debt or abandoning the euro would be too high for Greece to bear. The IMF plan is therefore Greece's best option. That said, it is ultimately quite tough and carries with it two types of risk. The first is if the reforms are not economically sustainable, they might create a debt spiral. The second is that if they are not politically sustainable, the government may adopt the other plan anyway.

A restrictive fiscal policy might well have a negative impact on Greece's growth in the short term, but many of the arguments about its recessionary effects are flawed. They use a baseline model that assumes a given growth rate and an unsustainable fiscal policy. When a restrictive budget is added, growth does indeed decrease at first, due to standard Keynesian principles. But financial markets are completely excluded from this model. It does not account for the fact that unsustainable fiscal policies inevitably provoke financial markets, which tend to react abruptly and generate terrible economic crises. At that point, much harsher measures are required to restore debt sustainability. A well-designed baseline model should include these effects and would show that over the long run uncontrolled fiscal policy is much more recessionary than timely budgetary adjustments.

Greece is a case in point. Due to fears about hindering future economic growth, for many months the Greek government refused to regain control of its budget. Now, even after emergency bailouts last spring, Greece is projected to lose four percent of its GDP in 2010. Had it taken action earlier and avoided the financial crisis, its economy probably would have shrunk more than what was projected before the crisis (in the fall of 2009, the EC projected a 0.3 percent loss for 2010), but it certainly would have fared better than it has now. The fiscal adjustment needed would have been milder, and the loss of political credibility would have been less devastating. Even now, a plan that does not include fiscal retrenchment will be much worse for long-term economic growth.

Beyond economic sustainability, critics cast doubt on the IMF plan's political feasibility, arguing that it is impossible for Greece to retrench if it means that the country must do away with entitlements that the population has come to view as fundamental rights, such as generous unemployment and retirement pensions. Such retrenchment would stir public unrest, they say, and leaders would have no option but to default to devaluation.

It is true that, as is often noted, there is no constituency for budget discipline. And Greece's ruling political class may not have had the ability, or will, to convince Greek citizens of the need for restrictive fiscal measures in advance of the crisis. The current economic situation has shown, however, that politicians can build consensus for unpleasant fiscal action during a crisis. Governments in the euro-zone used the threat that the Greek problem could spread to build support for an expensive rescue package, for example. And the governments of Portugal, Spain, Ireland, and others used the dire state of European financial markets to justify budgetary restraint and major reforms to labor and financial markets.

Citizens do not take fiscal reform lightly, but they are more easily convinced of its necessity if persuaded that something even worse looms as the alternative. This is why public support should coalesce around IMF-style economic reform, not debt restructuring or devaluation. Citizens of countries where those occurred remember their devastating effects. In countries where there is no recent memory of financial crisis, some may harbor the illusion that the current one will pass easily. But in today's world of densely networked economic systems, that is indeed an illusion.

Just as the economic crisis exposed problems in the Greek economy, it also exposed weaknesses in the euro's institutional framework. Restoring confidence will require strengthening that framework. A task force headed by EU President Herman Van Rompuy is scheduled to offer concrete proposals to do so by the end of this year. And in June, the ECB released its own recommendations: stronger independent surveillance of the budgetary policies of the member states with more automatic implementation of sanctions; improved surveillance of country competitiveness to ensure that member states continue to converge economically; and a crisis management structure with strong conditionality to support countries that implement adjustment programs. We acknowledge that it will not be possible to expel member states that fail to comply with EU budgetary guidelines, so such a threat would ultimately not be credible.

The EC and the European Parliament have also called for the creation of three financial supervisory authorities (the European Banking Authority, the European Insurance and Occupational Pensions Authority, and the European Securities and Markets Authority) and a regulatory authority (the European Systemic Risk Board). Because the economies of the eurozone are so interconnected, eurozone-wide supervisory and regulatory authorities are necessary. They would have the discretion to press national governments to remedy problems and would be independent enough to act preemptively, without having to wait for a crisis to galvanize politicians to action. Some may dislike the idea of giving international bodies the power to constrain national economic policy. But financial contagion spreads too quickly, and European taxpayers have had to pay for the failures of other countries too often, for the current system to remain.

Forecasting the euro's demise was premature. The EU and euro-zone countries were able to respond to the financial crisis with appropriate corrective measures: many countries adopted strong fiscal adjustment packages; eurozone countries have announced, and in some cases already implemented, unprecedented structural reforms, not least of which was their joint decision to coordinate and publish the results of their bank stress tests; the new European Financial Stability Fund has been established and can be used to support other eurozone countries in distress, and a task force on reform will offer and approve concrete proposals to strengthen eurozone governance by the end of the year.

One might criticize these measures for having been taken only after a crisis was eminent, but this is ultimately how democracies work in the face of difficulties. Problems in the economies of eurozone countries and in the framework of the monetary union will need to be addressed, but all the constituent countries will emerge stronger if they continue to pursue the right adjustment policies. Europe will need to find the right mix of cooperation, in defending its common interests at the global level, and competition in incentivizing growth. It will need to rely both on the center, which must ensure strong fiscal policy, and on the member states, which control much of the rest of economic policy. But one should take inspiration from the EU's history. Finding these balances has historically been one of Europe's key strengths.

# The Failure of the Euro

## The Little Currency That Couldn't

*Martin Feldstein*

The euro should now be recognized as an experiment that failed. This failure, which has come after just over a dozen years since the euro was introduced, in 1999, was not an accident or the result of bureaucratic mismanagement but rather the inevitable consequence of imposing a single currency on a very heterogeneous group of countries. The adverse economic consequences of the euro include the sovereign debt crises in several European countries, the fragile condition of major European banks, high levels of unemployment across the eurozone, and the large trade deficits that now plague most eurozone countries.

The political goal of creating a harmonious Europe has also failed. France and Germany have dictated painful austerity measures in Greece and Italy as a condition of their financial help, and Paris and Berlin have clashed over the role of the European Central Bank (ECB) and over how the burden of financial assistance will be shared.

The initial impetus that led to the European Monetary Union and the euro was political, not economic. European politicians reasoned that the use of a common currency would instill in their

MARTIN FELDSTEIN is George F. Baker Professor of Economics at Harvard University and President Emeritus of the National Bureau of Economic Research. He was Chair of the Council of Economic Advisers from 1982 to 1984. This article is adapted from an NBER working paper, *"The Euro and European Economic Performance."*

publics a greater sense of belonging to a European community and that the shift of responsibility for monetary policy from national capitals to a single central bank in Frankfurt would signal a shift of political power.

The primary political motive for increased European integration was, and may still be, to enhance Europe's role in world affairs. In 1956, just after the United States forced France and the United Kingdom to withdraw their forces from the Suez Canal, German Chancellor Konrad Adenauer told a French politician that individual European states would never be leading global powers, but "there remains to them only one way of playing a decisive role in the world; that is to unite to make Europe. . . . Europe will be your revenge." One year later, the Treaty of Rome launched the Common Market.

The Common Market expanded in 1967 to form the European Communities, and then, in 1992, the Maastricht Treaty gave rise to the European Union, which created a larger free-trade area, provided for the mobility of labor, and set a timetable for adopting a single currency and an integrated European market for goods and services. The European Commission cast this arrangement as a steppingstone toward greater political unity and made the specious argument that the free-trade area could succeed only if its member countries used a single currency. (There is, of course, nothing in economic logic or experience that implies that free trade requires a single currency. The North American Free Trade Agreement, for example, has stimulated increased trade without anyone thinking that the United States, Canada, and Mexico should have a single currency.)

Germany resisted the decision to create a single currency, reluctant to give up the deutsche mark and the price stability and prosperity it had brought to the country's postwar economy. But Germany eventually gave in, and France and others succeeded in establishing a schedule that would lead to the launching of the euro in 1999. Germany was, however, able to influence some of the characteristics of the ECB: the bank's formal independence, its single policy goal of price stability, the prohibition on purchasing bonds from member governments, a "no bailout" rule for countries that became insolvent, and its location in Frankfurt. Germany also forced the creation of a stability agreement that established financial penalties for any country that had a budget deficit of more than three percent of its GDP or a debt that exceeded 60 percent of its GDP. When France and Germany soon violated these conditions, the Council of Ministers voted not to impose penalties, and the terms of the pact were weakened so that they became meaningless.

## A DEATH FORETOLD

Long before the euro was officially introduced, economists pointed to the adverse effects that a single currency would have on the economies of Europe. (See, for example, my *Economist* article from 1992, "The Case Against the Euro," or my essay from these pages, "EMU and International Conflict," November/December 1997.) Single currencies require all the countries in the monetary union to have the same monetary policy and the same basic interest rate, with interest rates differing among borrowers only due to perceived differences in credit risk. A single currency also means a fixed exchange rate within the monetary union and the same exchange rate relative to all other currencies, even when individual countries in the monetary union would benefit from changes in relative values. Economists explained that the euro would therefore lead to greater fluctuations in output and employment, a much slower adjustment to declines in aggregate demand, and persistent trade imbalances between Europe and the rest of the world. Indeed, all these negative outcomes have occurred in recent years.

Here is why: when a county has its own monetary policy, it can respond to a decline in demand by lowering interest rates to stimulate economic activity. But the ECB must make monetary policy based on the overall condition of all the countries in the monetary union. This creates a situation in which interest rates are too high in those countries with rising unemployment and too low in those countries with rapidly rising wages. And because of the large size of the German economy relative to others in Europe, the ECB's monetary policy must give greater weight to conditions in Germany in its decisions than it gives to conditions in other countries.

The tough anti-inflationary policy of the ECB caused interest rates to fall in countries such as Italy and Spain, where expectations of high inflation had previously kept interest rates high. Households and governments in those countries responded to the low interest rates by increasing their borrowing, with households using the increased debt to finance a surge in home building and housing prices and the governments using it to fund larger social programs.

The result was rapidly rising ratios of public and private debt to GDP in several countries, including Greece, Ireland, Italy, and Spain. Despite the increased risk to lenders that this implied, global capital markets did not respond by raising interest rates on those countries with increasing debt levels. Bond buyers assumed that a bond issued by one government in the European Monetary Union was equally safe as a bond issued by any other government in the union, ignoring the "no bailout" provision of the Maastricht Treaty. As a result, the interest rates on Greek and Italian bonds differed from the rate on German bonds by only a small fraction of a percent.

Before the monetary union was put in place, large fiscal deficits generally led to higher interest rates or declining exchange rates. These market signals acted as an automatic warning for countries to reduce their borrowing. The monetary union eliminated those market signals and precluded the higher cost of funds that would otherwise have limited household borrowing. The result was that countries borrowed too much and banks loaned too much on overpriced housing.

When, in early 2010, the markets recognized the error of regarding all the eurozone countries as equally safe, interest rates began to rise on the sovereign debts of Greece, Italy, and Spain. Market dynamics put in motion a self-reinforcing process in which rising interest rates led countries to the brink of insolvency. In particular, the fear that Greece might have trouble meeting its debt payments caused the interest rate on Greek debt to rise; the expectation of higher future interest payments implied an even larger future debt burden. What started as a concern about a Greek liquidity problem—in other words, about the ability of Greece to have the cash to meet its next interest payments—became a solvency problem, a fear that Greece would never be able to repay its existing and accumulating debt. That pushed interest rates even higher and led eventually to a negotiated partial default, in which some holders of Greek sovereign debt agreed to accept a 50 percent write-down in the value of their bonds. In turn, the Greek experience raised the perceived risk of Italian government debt, causing the interest rate on Italian government bonds to rise from less than four percent in April 2010 to more than seven percent in November 2011—a rate that will cause government debt to rise faster than national income, pushing Italy to the brink of insolvency.

A different market dynamic affected the relationship between European commercial banks and European governments. Since the banks were heavily invested in government bonds, the declining value of those bonds hurt the banks. The banks then turned to their governments to protect their depositors and other creditors, thus magnifying the original problem. In Ireland and Spain, this cycle began with mortgage defaults, harming the banks and leading governments to guarantee the holdings of the banks' depositors and other creditors, thus adding to government debt. The banks' heavy investment in government bonds then meant that the weakness of Irish and Spanish government debt further hurt the banks.

## THE EURO ON LIFE SUPPORT

By the fall of 2011, several European countries had debt-to-GDP ratios that were high enough to make default a serious possibility. Sharp write-downs in the value of their sovereign debts are not a feasible solution because they would do substantial damage to European banks and possibly to banks and other financial institutions in the United States.

European political leaders have proposed three distinct strategies to deal with this situation. First, led by German Chancellor Angela Merkel and French President Nicolas Sarkozy, eurozone officials agreed last October that commercial banks should increase their capital ratios and that the size of the European Financial Stability Facility (EFSF), which had been created in May 2010 to finance government borrowing by Greece and other eurozone countries, should be expanded from 400 billion euros to more than a trillion euros. This latter move was meant to provide insurance guarantees that would allow Italy and potentially Spain to access capital markets at reasonable interest rates.

But the plan to increase the banks' capital has not worked, because banks do not want to dilute the holdings of their current shareholders by seeking either private or public capital, and so instead they have been raising their capital ratios by reducing their lending, particularly to borrowers in other countries, causing a further slowdown in European economic activity. Nor can the EFSF borrow the additional funds, since such a move is opposed by Germany, the largest potential guarantor of that debt. Moreover, even a trillion euros would not give the EFSF enough funds to provide effective guarantees to potential buyers of Italian and Spanish debt if those countries might otherwise appear insolvent.

The second strategy, advocated by France, calls for the ECB to buy the bonds of Italy, Spain, and other countries with high debt to keep their interest rates low. The ECB has already been doing this to a limited extent, but not enough to stop Greek and Italian rates from reaching unsustainable levels. Asking the ECB to expand this policy would directly contradict the "no bailout" terms of the Maastricht Treaty. Germany opposes such a move because of its inflationary potential and the risk of losses on those bonds. (Two German members of the ECB's executive board have resigned over this issue.)

The third strategy is favored by those figures, such as Merkel, who want to use the current crisis to advance the development of a political union. They call for a fiscal union in which those countries with budget surpluses would transfer funds each year to the countries running budget deficits and trade deficits. In exchange for these transfers, the European Commission would have the authority to review national budgets and force countries to adopt policies that would reduce their fiscal deficits, increase their growth, and raise their international competitiveness.

This transfer arrangement has already happened with Greece and Italy. The case of Greece has been the most dramatic. By last October, Greece was unable to borrow in the global capital market and therefore had to depend on credit extended by the ECB and the International Monetary Fund to pay civil servants and maintain its social welfare programs. Merkel and Sarkozy summoned Greek Prime Minister George Papandreou to Brussels and told him that he must abandon the plan he had announced to hold a national referendum on the austerity measures being imposed by the other eurozone members. They told him that instead he must persuade the Greek parliament to accept the tough strategy to reduce the budget deficit created by Merkel and Sarkozy or face expulsion from the eurozone. Papandreou agreed and forced the necessary legislation through parliament. He then resigned, and Lucas Papademos, a former vice president of the ECB, was appointed as a temporary prime minister with the responsibility of implementing the budget cuts designed in Brussels. But the subsequent parliamentary defections and public riots have shown how much the Greek people resent being forced by Germany to change their economic behavior, accept layoffs of government employees who thought they had lifetime jobs, and reduce demand at a time of double-digit unemployment and rapidly falling GDP. At the same time, many voters in Germany resent sending money to the Greeks and seeing the rules of the ECB undergo radical change.

The situation in Italy is different because Italy is not yet dependent on explicit transfers from the ECB or the International Monetary Fund. But Italy does depend on the support of the ECB to limit the rise of the interest rate for its government bonds. France and Germany pressured Italy to adopt new budget policies, leading to the resignation of Prime Minister Silvio Berlusconi in November and the appointment of a technocrat government committed to resolving Italy's fiscal problems. The euro has thus caused tensions and conflicts within Europe that would not otherwise have existed. Further steps toward a permanent fiscal union would only exacerbate these tensions.

## GREECE'S IMPOSSIBLE MATH

Greece's budget deficit of nine percent of GDP is too large to avoid an outright default on its national debt. With Greece's current debt-to-GDP ratio at 150 percent and the current value of Greece's GDP falling in nominal euro terms at an annual rate of four percent, the debt ratio will rise in the next year to 170 percent of GDP. Rolling over the debt as it comes due and paying higher interest rates on it would raise the total debt even more quickly.

Even if a more general write-down of Greek debt were to cut Greece's existing interest payments in half, the deficit would still be six percent of Greece's GDP and the debt-to-GDP ratio would rise to 165 percent of GDP at the end of 12 months. And this does not even take into account the adverse effect the debt write-down would have on Greek banks. The Greek government would be forced to provide payments to Greek depositors, further increasing the national debt.

To achieve a sustainable path, Greece must start reducing the ratio of its national debt to GDP. This will be virtually impossible as long as Greece's real GDP is declining. Basic budget arithmetic implies that even if Greece's real GDP starts growing at two percent (up from the current seven percent real rate of decline) and inflation is at the ECB target of two percent, the deficit must still not exceed six percent of GDP if the debt ratio is to stop increasing. Since the interest alone on the debt is now about six percent of GDP, the rest of the Greek budget must be brought into balance from its current three percent deficit.

Cutting the interest bill in half and simultaneously balancing the rest of the budget would reduce the ratio only very slowly, from

150 percent now to 145 percent after a year, even if no payments to bank depositors and other creditors were required. It is not clear that financial markets will wait while Greece walks along this fiscal tightrope to a sustainable debt ratio well below 100 percent.

The situation in Italy is much better. Italy already has a slightly positive growth rate and a primary budget surplus, with tax revenues exceeding noninterest government outlays by about one percent of GDP. The country's total budget deficit is about four percent of GDP; a reduction of the deficit equivalent to two percent of GDP would be enough to begin reducing the ratio of debt to GDP. That should not be difficult to achieve, since government spending accounts for roughly 50 percent of GDP. The prospect of a declining budget deficit has already reduced the interest rate on new government borrowing from 7.5 percent to 6.5 percent. Eliminating the budget deficit and starting to shrink the debt ratio more rapidly could bring the interest rate back to the four percent level that prevailed in Italy before the crisis began.

## TRADING PLACES

Even if the eurozone countries reduced their large budget deficits and thereby alleviated the threat to the commercial banks that have invested in government bonds, another problem caused by the monetary union would remain: the differences among eurozone members in terms of long-term competitiveness, which leads to sustained differences in trade balances that cannot be financed.

During the past year, Germany had a trade surplus of nearly $200 billion, whereas the other members of the eurozone had trade deficits totaling $200 billion. A more comprehensive measure that factors in net investment income reveals that Germany has a current account surplus of five percent of GDP, whereas Greece has a current account deficit of nearly ten percent of GDP. Put another way, Germany can invest in the rest of the world an amount equal to five percent of its GDP, whereas Greece must borrow an amount equal to nearly ten percent of its GDP to pay for its current level of imports.

If Greece were not part of the eurozone, its exchange rate would adjust over time to prevent this large and growing trade deficit. More specifically, the need to finance that trade deficit would cause the value of the Greek currency to decline, making Greek exports more attractive to foreign buyers and encouraging Greek consumers to substitute Greek goods and services for imports. The rising cost of imports would also reduce real personal incomes in Greece, leading to lower consumer spending and freeing up Greek goods and services to be exported to foreign buyers.

But since Greece is part of the eurozone, this automatic adjustment mechanism is missing. Greece faces the persistent problem of a rising current account deficit, which has now reached ten percent of GDP, because Greece's productivity (output per employee) increases more slowly than Germany's, causing the prices of Greek goods to rise relative to the prices of German and other European goods. More specifically, if output per employee in Germany increases by three percent a year, real wages can also grow by three percent. If the ECB keeps inflation in the eurozone at about two percent, German wages can rise by five percent a year. If Greek wages also rise by five percent a year while productivity in Greece grows by only one percent a year, the prices of Greek goods and services will increase two percent faster than the prices of German products. That increase in the relative prices of goods and services would cause Greek imports to rise and exports to stagnate, creating an increasingly large trade deficit. This problem could be avoided if the annual rise in Greek wages were limited to two percent less than the rise in German wages. This may, of course, be politically difficult in the highly unionized Greek economy.

But limiting the growth of Greek wages would address only further deterioration of Greek competitiveness in the future. Stopping a further decline in Greek competitiveness would not correct the existing annual current account deficit of nearly ten percent of GDP that Greece must continue to finance. Eliminating the existing current account deficit would require making Greek prices much more competitive than they are today, by reducing the cost of producing Greek goods and services by about 40 percent relative to the cost of producing goods and services in the rest of the eurozone. Since that is not likely to be achieved by increased productivity, it must be achieved by lowering real wages relative to the real wages of Germany and other countries in the eurozone. This would be a very painful process, achieved at the cost of years of high unemployment and declining incomes. Greece now has an official unemployment rate of 16 percent, and its real GDP is falling by seven percent per year. Continuing such poor performance for a decade or more is virtually unthinkable in a democracy. Moreover, since such a process would shrink the current account deficit only over a long period of time, Greece would need to continue borrowing to finance its current account imbalance. Even if Germany were willing to formalize such long-term financial assistance by establishing a transfer union to provide those funds, the controls that Berlin would demand to keep wages and incomes declining would create severe political tensions between Germany and Greece.

## THE TEMPTATION OF DEVALUATION

The alternative is for Greece to leave the eurozone and return to its own currency. Although there is no provision in the Maastricht Treaty for such a move, political leaders in Greece and other countries are no doubt considering that possibility. Although Greece is benefiting from its membership in the eurozone by receiving transfers from other eurozone countries, it is paying a very high price in terms of unemployment and social unrest. Abandoning the euro now and creating a new drachma would permit a devaluation and a default that might involve much less economic pain than the current course. This devaluation-and-default strategy has been the standard response of countries in Asia and Latin America with unsustainably large fiscal and trade deficits; they were able to devalue because they were not part of a monetary union.

Germany is now prepared to pay to try to keep Greece from leaving the eurozone because it fears that a Greek defection could lead to a breakup of the entire monetary union, eliminating the fixed exchange rate that now benefits German exporters and the German economy more generally. If Greece leaves and devalues, global capital markets might assume that Italy will consider a similar strategy. The resulting rise in the interest rate on its debt might then drive Italy to in fact do so. And if Italy reverts to a new lira and devalues it relative to other currencies, the competitive pressure might force France to leave the eurozone and devalue a new franc. At that point, the EMU would collapse.

Even though Germany is prepared to subsidize Greece and other countries to sustain the euro, Greece and others might nevertheless decide to leave the monetary union if the conditions imposed by Germany are deemed too painful. Here is how that might work: although Greece cannot create the euros it needs to pay civil servants and make transfer payments, the Greek government could start creating new drachmas and declare that all contracts under Greek law, including salaries and shop prices, are payable in that currency; similarly, all bank deposits and bank loans would be payable in these new drachmas instead of euros.

The value of the new drachma would fall relative to the euro, automatically reducing real wages and increasing Greek competiveness without requiring Greece to go through a long and painful period of high unemployment. Instead, the lower value of the Greek currency would stimulate exports and a shift from imports to domestic goods and services. This would boost Greek GDP growth and employment.

Withdrawing from the eurozone would of course be difficult and potentially painful. The announcement that Greece was leaving the eurozone would have to come as a surprise—otherwise, a bank run would be likely, as Greek depositors would have the time to move their euro-denominated funds to banks outside Greece or to withdraw them and hold euros in cash. Since some flight of deposits from Greek banks is already happening, Athens would have to act before this became a flood of withdrawals.

Another serious problem for Greece in making the transition to the new drachma would be the political risk of being forced out of the EU. Since the Maastricht Treaty provides no way for a member of the eurozone to leave, there is the risk that the other eurozone members would punish Greece by requiring it to leave the EU as well, causing Greece to lose the benefits that the EU offers of free trade and labor mobility. They might do so to discourage Italy and others from pursuing a similar exit strategy. But not all EU members would necessarily seek such a punishment, especially since ten of the 27 EU member countries do not use the euro and Greece's situation is clearly more desperate than that of Italy or Spain.

The primary practical problem with leaving the eurozone would be that some Greek businesses and individuals have borrowed in euros from banks outside Greece. Since those loans are not covered by Greek law, the Greek government cannot change these debt obligations from euros to new drachmas. The decline in the new drachma relative to the euro would make it much more expensive for Greek debtors to repay those loans. Widespread bankruptcies of Greek individuals and businesses could result, with secondary effects on the Greek banks that those individuals and businesses have borrowed from.

But as the experience of Argentina after it ended its link to the dollar in 2002 showed, domestic Greek debtors might end up paying only a fraction of those euro debts. For Greece, the option to leave the monetary union may therefore be very tempting.

Greece's departure need not tempt Italy, Spain, or others to leave. For them, the cost of leaving could exceed that of adjusting their economies while remaining inside the eurozone. Unlike Greece, they can avoid insolvency by adjusting their budget and trade deficits without radical changes in policy.

Looking ahead, the eurozone is likely to continue with almost all its current members. The challenge now will be to change the economic behavior of those countries. Formal constitutionally mandated balanced-budget rules of the type recently adopted by Germany, Italy, and Spain would, if actually implemented, put each country's national debt on a path to a sustainable level. New policies must avoid current account deficits in the future by limiting the volume of national imports to amounts that can be financed with export earnings and direct foreign investment. Such measures should make it possible to sustain the euro without future crises and without the fiscal transfers that are now creating tensions within Europe.

# The Crisis of Europe

## How the Union Came Together and Why It's Falling Apart

*Timothy Garton Ash*

May 10, 1943: German forces are destroying the Warsaw ghetto. Facing armed resistance from Polish Jewish fighters, they set fire to it house by house, burning some inhabitants alive and driving others out from the cellars. "Today, in sum 1,183 Jews were apprehended alive," notes the official report by the SS commander Jürgen Stroop. "187 Jews and bandits were shot. An indeterminable number of Jews and bandits were destroyed in blown-up bunkers. The total number of Jews processed so far has risen to 52,683." An appendix to this document contains the now-famous photograph of a terrified small boy in an outsize cloth cap, his hands held high in surrender. Marek Edelman, one of very few leaders of the Warsaw ghetto uprising to survive, concluded a memoir published immediately after the war with these words: "Those who were killed in action had done their duty to the end, to the last drop of blood that soaked into the pavements. . . . We, who did not perish, leave it up to you to keep the memory of them alive—forever."

Fast-forward exactly 60 years, to May 10, 2003, a month before Poland holds a referendum on whether to join the European Union. At a "yes" campaign rally in Warsaw, a banner in Poland's

TIMOTHY GARTON ASH is Professor of European Studies at Oxford University and a Senior Fellow at the Hoover Institution at Stanford University. © Timothy Garton Ash.

national colors, red and white, proclaims, "We go to Europe under the Polish flag." Outside the rebuilt Royal Castle, a choir of young girls in yellow and blue T-shirts—echoing the European flag's yellow stars on a blue background—breaks into song. To the music of the EU's official anthem, which is drawn from the final movement of Beethoven's Ninth Symphony, they sing, in Polish, the words of the German poet Friedrich Schiller's "Ode to Joy." Soon these young Poles will be able to move at will across most of a continent almost whole and free, to study, work, settle down, marry, and enjoy all the benefits of a generous European welfare state, in Dublin, Madrid, London, or Rome. "Be embraced, ye millions! This kiss to the entire world! Brothers, a loving father must live above that canopy of stars!"

To understand how a predicted crisis of European monetary union became an existential crisis of the whole post-1945 project of European unification, you have to see Europe's unique trajectory from one May 10 to the other. Both the memories of World War II and the exigencies of the Cold War drove three generations of Europeans to heights of peaceful unification that were unprecedented in European history and unmatched on any other continent. Yet that project began to go wrong soon after the fall of the Berlin Wall, as western European leaders hastily set course for a structurally flawed monetary union.

While many governments, companies, and households piled up unsustainable levels of debt, young Europeans from Portugal to Estonia and from Finland to Greece came to take peace, freedom, prosperity, and social security for granted. When the bubble burst, it left many feeling bitterly disappointed and led to excruciating divergences between the experiences of different nations. Now, with the current crisis still unresolved, Europe lacks most of the motivating forces that once propelled it toward unity. Even if a shared fear of the consequences of the eurozone's collapse saves it from the worst, Europe needs something more than fear to make it again the magnetic project it was for a half century. But what can that something be?

## WAR ON THE MIND

Historians have identified many factors that contributed to the process of European integration, including the vital economic interests of European nations. Yet the single most important driving force across the continent was the memory of war. Among those parading down the streets of Warsaw in May 2003 was the bearded professor Bronislaw Geremek, who, as a ten-year-old Polish Jewish boy, had seen the Warsaw ghetto burning before his eyes. It was no accident that he became one of Poland's most ardent advocates of European integration, as a leader of the Solidarity movement, the Polish foreign minister, and then a member of the European Parliament.

To be sure, the Warsaw ghetto survivor, the Nazi soldier, the British officer, the French collaborator, the Swedish businessman, and the Slovak farmer had very different wars. Yet from all their throats rose the same passionate cry: "Never again!" For all the differences in national and subnational experiences across a hugely diverse continent, the historian Tony Judt could still title a history of Europe that covers the 60 years up to 2005 with a single word: *Postwar*. In this respect, if in no other, the European Union's favorite catch phrase, "Unity in diversity," was strictly accurate.

Those memories played an important role for those British Conservatives, most of them World War II veterans, who took the United Kingdom into the European Economic Community, the precursor to the European Union, in 1973. But above all, personal experience motivated those continental Europeans, up to and including French President François Mitterrand and German Chancellor Helmut Kohl, who created the EU of today. In a conversation I had with him after German reunification, Kohl delivered a line I will never forget. "Do you realize," he asked, "that you are sitting opposite the direct successor to Adolf Hitler?" As the first chancellor of a united Germany since Hitler, he explained, he was profoundly conscious of his historical duty to do things differently.

European integration has rightly been described as a project of the elites, but Europe's peoples shared these memories. When the project faltered, as it did many times, the elites' reaction was to seek some way forward, however complicated. Until the 1990s, when the custom of holding national referendums on European treaties began to spread, Europeans were seldom asked directly if they agreed with the solutions found, although they could periodically vote in or out of office the politicians responsible for finding them. Nonetheless, it is fair to say that for about 40 years, the project of European unification could rely on at least a passive consensus among most of Europe's national publics.

These 40 years were those of the Cold War, the other conflict that shaped the EU. From the 1940s through the 1970s, a central argument for Western European integration was to counter the Soviet threat, visible for all to see in the presence of the Red Army in East Germany and divided Berlin. Beside the memories of Europe's own self-inflicted barbarism, there were, so to speak, the barbarians at the gate. Soviet leaders from Joseph Stalin to Leonid Brezhnev should be awarded posthumous medals for their service to European integration.

Cold War competition also goes a long way to explaining why the United States lent such strong support to European unification, from the Marshall Plan of the 1940s to the diplomacy surrounding the reunification of Germany and the dissolution of the Soviet Union in 1989–91.

For the half of Europe stuck behind the Iron Curtain—what the Czech writer Milan Kundera called "the kidnapped West"—the will to "return to Europe" went hand in hand with the struggle for national and individual freedom. The growing prosperity of Western Europe had a magnetic effect on those who saw it, whether at first hand or on Western television.

It is the most elementary historical fallacy to suggest that an event was caused by one that occurred after it, yet something that was only to happen in 1992 was a contributing cause of the velvet revolutions of 1989. The target year 1992, the widely trumpeted deadline that the European Economic Community had given itself for completing its single market, conveyed an urgent sense of being left ever-further behind, not just to the peoples of Eastern Europe but also to reform-minded Soviet-bloc leaders, including Mikhail Gorbachev.

This brings us to the last great motor of European integration until the 1990s: West Germany. The West Germans, both the elites and a large part of the populace, demonstrated an exceptional commitment to European integration. They did this for two very good reasons: because they wanted to, and because they had to. They wanted to show that Germany had learned from its terrible pre-1945 history and wished to rehabilitate itself fully in a European community of values, even to the point of surrendering much of its own sovereignty and national identity. Having been the worst Europeans, the Germans would now be the best. (As a joke at the time went, if someone introduced himself just as "a European," you knew immediately that he was German.) But they also had a hard national interest in demonstrating that European commitment, for only by regaining the trust of their neighbors and international partners (including the United States and the Soviet Union) could they achieve their long-term goal of German reunification. As Hans-Dietrich Genscher, the former West German foreign minister, once observed, "The more European our foreign policy is, the more national it is." West German Europeanism was not simply instrumental—it reflected a real moral and emotional engagement—but nor was it purely idealistic.

After the two German states were reunited in 1990, many observers wondered whether what was essentially an expanded West Germany would continue this extraordinary commitment to European integration. Well before the crisis of the eurozone broke, the answer was already apparent. Reunited Germany had become what some participants in the post-Wall debate called a "normal" nation-state—a "second France," in the commentator Dominique Moïsi's striking phrase. Like France, the new Germany would pursue its national interests through Europe whenever possible, but on its own when it deemed it necessary—as it did, for example, when securing its energy needs bilaterally with Russia, notably in the Nord

Stream gas pipeline deal of 2005. Its leaders, in Berlin now, not Bonn, would still try to be good Europeans, but they would no longer open the checkbook so readily if Europe called.

## THE BIRTH OF A MALFORMED UNION

The immediate origins of the malformed currency union that is at the epicenter of today's European crisis also lie in the tempestuous moment of German reunification and its aftermath. Following the fall of the Berlin Wall on November 9, 1989, Mitterrand, alarmed by the prospect of German reunification, pushed hard to pin Kohl down to a timetable for what was then called economic and monetary union. That proposal had already been elaborated to help the European Economic Community complete its single market and address the difficulty of managing exchange rates within it. Mitterrand's general purpose was to bind a united Germany, if united those two Germanies really must be, into a more united Europe; his specific purpose was to enable France to regain more control over its own currency, and even win some leverage over Germany's.

In a remarkable conversation with Genscher, the West German foreign minister, on November 30, 1989, Mitterrand went so far as to say that if Germany did not commit itself to the European monetary union, "We will return to the world of 1913." Meanwhile, Mitterrand was stirring up British Prime Minister Margaret Thatcher to sound the alarm as if it were 1938. According to a British record of their private meeting at the crucial Strasbourg summit of European leaders in December 1989, Mitterrand said that "he was fearful that he and the Prime Minister would find themselves in the situation of their predecessors in the 1930s who had failed to react in the face of constant pressing forward by the Germans."

David Marsh, the best chronicler of the euro's history, concludes that the "essential deal" to proceed with monetary union was done at Strasbourg. Tough negotiations followed, and exactly two years later a treaty was agreed on in the small Dutch city of Maastricht, setting the basic terms of what would become today's eurozone. It is too simplistic to characterize this as a straight tradeoff: "the whole of Deutschland for Kohl, half the deutsche mark for Mitterrand," as one wit quipped at the time. But Germany's need for its closest European allies—above all, France—to support its national reunification had a decisive influence on both the timetable and the design of Europe's monetary union.

To be sure, Kohl was a deeply committed European. He never tired of repeating that German and European unification were "two sides of the same coin." So now, he told U.S. Secretary of State James Baker three days after the Strasbourg summit, he had even agreed to a European monetary union. What stronger proof could he offer of Germany's European credentials? Kohl "took this decision against German interests," the German minutes of that meeting record him telling Baker. "For example, the president of the Bundesbank was against the present development. But the step was politically important, since Germany needed friends." As one does, when one is trying to unite Germany without blood and iron.

The design of the resulting monetary union can also be understood, like so much else in the history of European integration, as a Franco-German compromise. At the insistence of Germany, and especially of the Bundesbank, the European Central Bank would be a Bundesbank writ large, fiercely independent of governments (unlike in the French tradition) and devoted with Protestant fervor to the one true god of price stability (lest the Weimar nightmare of hyperinflation return). To his credit, Kohl wanted the monetary union to be complemented by a fiscal and political union, so there could be control of public spending and coordination of economic policy among the states, and more direct political legitimation of the whole enterprise. "Political union is the essential counterpart to economic and monetary union," he told the Bundestag in November 1991. "Recent history, not only in Germany, teaches us that it is absurd to expect in the long run that you can maintain economic and monetary union without political union."

But France was having none of that. The point was for it to gain some control over Germany's currency, not for Germany to gain control over France's budget. So the discussion of a fiscal union withered away into a set of "convergence criteria," which required would-be members of the monetary union to keep public debt under 60 percent of GDP and deficits under three percent.

Thus, in the Sturm und Drang of the largest geopolitical change in Europe since 1945, a sickly child was conceived. Most Germans opposed giving up their treasured deutsche mark. But they would not be asked; the West German constitution did not envisage referendums. Kohl had no intention of changing that. Alexandre Lamfalussy, the head of the European Monetary Institute, the precursor to the European Central Bank, later recalled telling him, "I don't know how you will get the German people to give up the D-Mark." Kohl's reply: "It will happen. The Germans accept strong leadership."

In France, meanwhile, the Maastricht Treaty scraped through in a September 1992 referendum with a yes vote of just over 50 percent. The passive consensus for further steps of European integration, advancing ever closer to the heart of national sovereignty, was beginning to break down even in heartlands of the postwar project.

## A CRISIS FORETOLD

With a hat tip to Gabriel García Márquez, a history of Europe's monetary union could be called *Chronicle of a Crisis Foretold*. By the time the eurozone's 11 founding member states were preparing to introduce a common currency on January 1, 1999, most of the problems that would beset the euro a decade later had been predicted.

Critics at the time questioned how a common currency could work without a common treasury, how a one-size-fits-all interest rate could be right for such a diverse group of economies, and how the eurozone could cope with economic shocks that varied from region to region—what economists call "asymmetric shocks." For

Europe had neither the labor mobility nor the level of fiscal transfers between states that characterized the United States.

"Since 1989, we have seen how reluctant West German taxpayers have been to pay even for their own compatriots in the east," noted one article in these pages in 1998. "Do we really expect that they would be willing to pay for the French unemployed as well?" Reporting a widespread view that the monetary union would face a crisis sooner rather than later, and that this would catalyze the necessary political unification, the author cautioned, "It is a truly dialectical leap of faith to suggest that a crisis that exacerbates differences between European countries is the best way to unite them."

Since I was that author, I should add that I did not anticipate three important things. First, I did not expect that the monetary union would flourish for so long. For nearly a decade, the euro appeared to be strong, edging up toward the dollar as a global trading and reserve currency. For businesses, it removed the risk of exchange-rate fluctuations inside the eurozone. For the rest of us, it was a delight to be able to travel from one end of the continent to the other without having to change currencies. To visit Dublin, Madrid, or Athens was to see cities booming as never before. Small wonder that in 2003 those young Poles sang Schiller's "Ode to Joy" at the prospect of joining the happy Irish, Spaniards, and Greeks. And I, like others sympathetic to the project, was lulled into a false sense of security.

Because the crash came later than originally expected, it was worse when it came. Over time, enormous imbalances had built up between the core, mainly northern European countries (above all, Germany), and the peripheral, mainly southern European countries (especially Portugal, Ireland, Italy, Greece, and Spain, which have sometimes been unkindly labeled "the PIGSs").

To be sure, the initial shocks that started the earthquake came from outside Europe, in the U.S. subprime mortgage market. In this sense, the travails of the eurozone are part of a broader crisis of Western financial capitalism.

Yet the second thing we did not fully anticipate in the 1990s was the extent to which the eurozone would generate its own asymmetric shocks. Whereas Germany, still staggering under the financial burden of German reunification, impressively massaged down its labor costs, trimmed its welfare spending, and became competitive again, many of the peripheral countries allowed their unit labor costs to soar.

While Germany and some other northern European countries maintained fiscal discipline and moderate levels of debt, many of the peripheral countries went on the mother of all binges. In some places, such as Greece, it was public spending that skyrocketed; in others, such as Ireland and Spain, it was private spending. The open sesame to both kinds of excess was the same: governments, companies, and individuals could borrow at unprecedentedly low interest rates thanks to the credibility that eurozone membership lent their countries. In effect, Greece, which had snuck into the eurozone in 2001 with the aid of falsified statistics, could borrow almost as if it were Germany.

When, therefore, Germany was asked to help bail out those countries, German voters were understandably indignant. Why should we work even harder and retire even later, they asked, so these feckless Greeks, Portuguese, and Italians can retire earlier than we do and go sun themselves on the beach? "Sell your islands, you bankrupt Greeks," snorted *Bild*, Germany's largest tabloid, in October 2010.

The Germans had a good point: they had demonstrated remarkable prudence; the peripheral countries had not. But there was another side to the story. The moment the Stability and Growth Pact (the formalized successor to the convergence criteria) was revealed to be toothless was when Germany itself, along with France, violated the deficit limit of three percent of GDP in 2003–4. The penalties envisaged in the pact were not even enforced.

Moreover, Germany had fared so well partly because the peripheral countries had fared so badly. The peripheral eurozone countries could no longer compete with Germany on price by devaluing their own national currencies, and part of their binge spending went to buying more BMWs and Bosch washing machines. The euro also enabled German exporters to price their goods more competitively in markets such as China. (One study, by Nathan Sheets and Robert Sockin of Citigroup, estimated that Germany's lower real exchange rate, courtesy of the euro, has lifted its real trade surplus by about three percent of GDP annually.) As the economist Martin Feldstein noted in these pages, in 2011 Germany's $200 billion trade surplus roughly equaled the rest of the eurozone's combined trade deficit. Germany was to Europe what China is to the world: the exporter that requires others to consume.

In addition, Germany and other northern European countries with current account surpluses recycled those surpluses partly by lending to Greeks, Irish, Portuguese, and Spaniards. So when Germany bailed out the peripheral eurozone countries, it was also bailing out its own banks.

The third element few foresaw in the 1990s was the spiraling scale, speed, and folly of global financial markets. Most egregious, bond markets contributed to the burgeoning imbalances by mispricing sovereign risk in general and the differential risk between various eurozone government bonds in particular. Despite the presence of a "no bailout" clause in the Maastricht Treaty, bond traders acted as if the risk associated with lending to the Greek or Portuguese governments was only fractionally higher than that of lending to Germany or the Netherlands.

When belief in the solidity of the eurozone began to collapse, soon after its tenth birthday, the markets plunged to the other extreme. Again and again, they punished eurozone leaders' belated half measures with soaring bond yield spreads, so that country after country found its borrowing costs whizzing upward. At interest rates of five to eight percent, it becomes very difficult for a government to sustain its debt burden, even with the most exemplary German-style fiscal discipline and structural reform. There was only so much that even the wisest and most economically responsible leaders, such as Italian Prime Minister Mario Monti, could ask of their own people.

## EUROPE'S DYSFUNCTIONAL TRIANGLE

Structurally, Europe now finds itself caught in a dysfunctional triangle, between national politics, European policies, and global markets. Ever since the European Coal and Steel Community was founded, in 1951, integration has proceeded through the development of common European policies: from those on agriculture, fisheries, and trade, all the way to monetary policy. The democratic politics of the EU have, however, remained stubbornly national.

While the volcanic magma was heating up under the outwardly calm crust of the eurozone, European leaders spent much of this century's first decade engaged in an ambitious attempt to write what some called a constitution for Europe. To cope with both the deepening of the EU, through monetary union, and its widening, through the historic enlargement to eastern Europe, they proposed a new set of institutional arrangements for the EU's 27 states (since 2007) and 500 million people. But in referendums, voters in France and the Netherlands rejected even a watered-down version of these lofty plans. "The nations don't want it," commented Geremek, that passionate but also realistic European, shortly before he died in 2008.

So the mountain labored again, and brought forth a mouse. The Treaty of Lisbon, which came into force in 2009, did give more powers to the directly elected European Parliament. But decision-making in today's EU still consists mainly of national politicians cutting deals behind closed doors in Brussels. And the politics and media they worry about are national, not European. There are Europe-wide political groupings, based on those in the European Parliament, but there are no truly European politics. The average turnout for elections to the European Parliament has declined with every vote since direct elections began in 1979. Although there are some good Europe-wide media outlets, watched and read by a happy few, there is no broader European public sphere.

The French historian Ernest Renan said that a nation is "an everyday plebiscite." Well, today's EU has an election almost every day, but these are national elections, conducted in different languages and in national media. Increasingly, the election campaigns feature parties that blame the country's current travails on other European nations, or on the EU itself, or on both. Visiting Maastricht earlier this year—a city now a little worried about its place in the history books—I was told how the anti-immigrant and anti-Islamic Dutch populist Geert Wilders has redirected his political fire against "Europe." That's where he thinks the votes are now.

At the same time, panicky global markets instantly impinge on both European policies and national politics. As country after country finds its credit rating cut and its borrowing costs going through the roof, governments tremble and call yet another emergency summit in Brussels. As the clock ticks into the early hours, exhausted national leaders are torn between their terror of what the markets will do to them when trading opens the next morning and their terror of what their national media, coalition partners, parliaments, and voters will do to them when they get back home.

As soon as the meeting ends, each leader will dash out from the conference room to brief his or her own national media, so that every time, there is not just one version of a European summit but 27 different ones—plus a 28th, the implausibly irenic conclave described by the EU's own clutch of institutional heads. This is Europe's political *Rashomon*, with 28 conflicting versions of the same event delivered in 23 languages. It is an odd way to run a continent

## THE MISSING INGREDIENTS

Europe's monetary union was a bridge too far—meaning not a bridge that should never have been crossed but a bridge that was crossed too soon, before Europe was strategically prepared to defend it. To be sure, carrying on for another decade or two with a system of fixing the margins within which exchange rates could fluctuate—the so-called Exchange Rate Mechanism—would have been demanding. But it is hard to disagree with this retrospective judgment by the economic commentator Martin Wolf: "Consider how much better off Europe would have been if the exchange rate mechanism had continued, instead, with wide bands."

We also have to consider other roads not taken. What if, instead of introducing the euro, Europe had deepened its still-far-from-complete single market? What if the whole EU had concentrated on improving its competitiveness, as Germany did so impressively, and not merely paid lip service to that goal in a catalog of good intentions called "the Lisbon agenda"? What if it had used this time to develop a more effective foreign policy? But regret is futile. An old and now politically incorrect English joke has an American couple arriving at a crossroads, deep in the Irish countryside, and asking a tweed-clad farmer the way to Tipperary. "If I were you," says the Irishman, "I wouldn't start from here." Yet here is where we are.

At the end of June this year, the EU held yet another "save the euro" summit—by a rough count, the 19th of the crisis. Germany said it would allow special European funds to be used to help imperiled Spanish banks, and the eurozone states resolved to create a single banking supervisory structure run by the European Central Bank. Although nobody noticed, the summit communiqué was a reminder of useful things the EU continues to do. For example, European leaders reached agreement on a unitary European patent system, which is expected to lower patenting costs for European companies by as much as 80 percent. They also decided to open accession negotiations with Montenegro, a newly independent state that just 13 years ago was still embroiled in the wars of former Yugoslavia.

As of this writing, no one knows how the euro saga will end. The possibilities include a total, disorderly collapse of the eurozone, a continued muddling through, and, most optimistically, systemic consolidation into a genuine fiscal and political union. Yet even if the eurozone crab-marches toward a political union, it will still have to generate the solidarity among its citizens necessary to underpin it, a degree of European compatriotism that does not yet exist. Another open question is how a more united eurozone core, which would itself contain creditor and debtor nations with very different perspectives, would relate institutionally and politically to EU member states not in the zone, such as the United Kingdom, Sweden, and Poland.

According to one projection by analysts at ING, a total collapse of the eurozone could cause GDP to fall by more than ten percent over two years in all the leading European economies, including Germany. Coming on top of the hardships already endured, that could lead to dangerous political radicalization. (Unlike in the 1930s, such radicalization, to the far right and the far left, has been remarkably limited so far, even in Greece—a tribute to the resilience of contemporary European democracies.) But even if the eurozone falls apart, there will still be a place called Europe and probably a set of institutions called the European Union. And there will be a new yet also familiar historic challenge for Europeans: to pick themselves up from the ruins and rebuild.

Today's crisis is the greatest test yet of what has been called "the Monnet method" of unification, after Jean Monnet, a founding father of European integration. Monnet proposed moving forward, step by step, with technocratic measures of economic integration, hoping that these would catalyze political unification—not least through moments of crisis. "Crises are the great unifier!" he once explained. Yet even in the first 40 years of European integration, crises sometimes pulled Europe together and sometimes did not. If they tended more often to promote unity than division, that was in large part thanks to wartime memories and Cold War imperatives. So where are the drivers of integration now? Go back down the list.

A single market of 500 million consumers remains a powerful economic attraction for most European countries. However, it no longer seems as evident as it once did that Europe brings steadily growing prosperity and welfare to all its citizens. Exporting nations, especially Germany, and global service providers, such as the United Kingdom, are increasingly looking to emerging markets, where the growth is.

Unlike during the Cold War, there is no obvious external threat in Europe's front yard. Try as he might, Vladimir Putin just does not match up to Stalin, or even Brezhnev. Could China step into that role? Without stigmatizing China as an enemy, the most compelling new rationale for European unification is indeed the rise of non-Western great powers: China, mainly, but also India, Brazil, and South Africa.

One cannot simply extrapolate from current economic and demographic trends, but in any likely world of 2030, even Germany will be a small to medium-sized power. Then, the only effective way to defend the freedoms and advance the shared interests of all Europeans will be to act together and speak with one voice. Intellectually, this argument is persuasive. But emotionally, to sway a wider public, it does not compare with the visible presence of the Red Army at the heart of Europe.

If Russia no longer fits the bill for an external threat, the United States no longer plays the part of active external supporter. Already in 2001, President George W. Bush could ask, in a private meeting, "Do we want the European Union to succeed?" Part of his administration, at least in his first term, was inclined to answer no. President Barack Obama would definitely answer yes, but until the eurozone crisis threatened the U.S. economy, and hence his reelection prospects, it was hardly a priority. His administration has taken Europe as it has found it and dealt pragmatically with Brussels or with individual countries—whatever worked. Its geopolitical focus has been on China and Asia more generally, not Russia and Europe.

Conceivably, the United States' attitude could change if China really came to be seen as the new Soviet Union, a global geopolitical threat to the West. Then one option would be for Washington to seek a closer strategic partnership with a more united Europe, including, for example, a transatlantic free-trade area. Old Europe and its cousins across the water would work toward what Édouard Balladur, the former French prime minister, has imagined as a "Western Union." But there is scant evidence of such thinking at the moment. Rather, both the United States and Europe are making their own tense accommodations with China.

Another past driver of integration, eastern European yearnings, still has some traction today. Eastern Europeans have more recent memories than other Europeans do of dictatorship, hardship, and war. Many appreciate the new freedoms they enjoy in the EU; for some, belonging to the same club as western Europeans is the realization of a centuries-old dream. One Polish economist explains why Poland still aspires to join the eurozone thus: "We want to be on board the ship, even if it is sinking!" Of course, they would rather the ship stays afloat. Last fall, in a speech in Berlin, Radoslaw Sikorski, the Polish foreign minister, memorably observed, "I will probably be the first Polish foreign minister in history to say so, but here it is: I fear German power less than I am beginning to fear German inactivity."

## EUROPEAN GERMANY, GERMAN EUROPE

Germany is the key to Europe's future, as it has been, one way or another, for at least a century. The irony of unintended consequences is especially acute here. If Kohl was the first chancellor of a united Germany since Hitler, François Hollande is the first Socialist president of France since Mitterrand, and it is Mitterrand's legacy he has to wrestle with. Monetary union, the method through which Mitterrand intended to keep united Germany in its proper place—co-driver with France, but still deferential to it—has ended up putting Germany at the wheel, with France as an irate husband flapping around in the passenger seat ("Turn left, Angela, turn left!").

At the time of German reunification, German politicians never tired of characterizing their goal in the finely turned words of the writer Thomas Mann: "Not a German Europe but a European Germany." What we see today, however, is a European Germany in a German Europe. This Germany is an exemplary European country: civilized, democratic, humane, law-abiding, and (although Mann might not have rated this one) very good at soccer. But the

"Berlin Republic" is also at the center of a German Europe. At least when it comes to political economy, Germany calls the shots. (The same is not true in foreign and defense policy, where France and the United Kingdom are more important.) This is not a role Germany sought; leadership has been thrust upon it.

Moreover, if the need to win support for German reunification drove Kohl to accept European monetary union on a tight timetable, and without the political union he thought essential to sustain it, German reunification has changed the German attitude to the European project. The very same set of closely linked historical developments that has now produced, 20 years on, the need for a special German contribution to Europe has in the meantime reduced both the country's idealistic desire and its instrumental need to offer that contribution.

Were he still chancellor, Kohl would surely insist that the euro must be saved by moving decisively toward a political union. Merkel and her compatriots have reacted very differently, reluctantly doing the minimum needed to prevent collapse. The modest and plain-speaking Merkel is in many ways the personification of the civic, modern European virtues of this new Germany. She is also a brilliant and ruthless domestic political tactician. Whatever her personal convictions, she knows she faces what may be called the four Bs: the Bundestag (the lower house of the national parliament, from which Germany's most pro-European politicians have largely migrated to the European Parliament, another unintended consequence of that well-intended institution), the Bundesverfassungsgericht (the country's constitutional court, deliberately established after 1945 to be a U.S.-style check on a leader's power), the Bundesbank (still very influential in the German debate), and, last but by no means least, the populist tabloid *Bild*.

Many Germans resent the idea of bailing out Greeks and Spaniards and recall that they were given no say on Kohl's decision to give up the deutsche mark. In a German opinion poll conducted in May 2012, no less than 49 percent of respondents said it had been a mistake to introduce the euro. So far, the benefits they have derived from the euro have not been adequately explained. Yet this European Germany is a free country, open to argument, and some are now making the attempt.

## MEMORY, FEAR, AND HOPE

The greatest single driving force of the European project since 1945, personal memories of war, has disappeared. Where individual memory fades, collective memory should step in. Remember Edelman's appeal: "We, who did not perish, leave it up to you to keep the memory of them alive—forever." Yet most young Europeans' consciousness of their continent's tortured history is shallow. Their formative experiences have been in a Europe of peace, freedom, and prosperity. Even younger eastern Europeans from states such as Estonia, which did not exist on most maps just 22 years ago, have come to take these hard-won achievements for granted. In this sense, the deepest problem of the European project is the problem of success.

Over the last decade, European peoples with historical complexes about being consigned to the periphery of Europe felt themselves to be at last entering the core. Eastern Europeans joined the EU. Southern Europeans thought they were flourishing in the eurozone. In Athens, Lisbon, and Madrid, there was a sense of a leveling up of European societies, of a new, not merely formal equality among nations.

Now that illusion has been shattered. In Greece, the homeless line up at soup kitchens, pensioners commit suicide, the sick cannot get prescription medicines, shops are shuttered, and scavengers pick through dustbins—conditions almost reminiscent of the 1940s. In Spain, every second person under the age of 25 is unemployed; across the eurozone, the average is nearly one in four. But the pain is unevenly spread. In Germany, youth unemployment is comfortably under ten percent. There is a new dividing line across Europe, not between east and west but between north and south. Now, and probably for years to come, it will be a very different experience to be a young German or a young Spaniard, a young Pole or a young Greek.

Think back to those two May 10 moments in Warsaw. Someone whose formative teenage experience was of the terrors of 1943 would find today's crisis shocking, but still not half as bad as what he remembered—and he would insist that Europe must never fall back to that. The teenager of 2003 has a different mental lens: this is terrible, she thinks, and not what she was led to expect.

Europeans such as Geremek and Kohl witnessed Europe tear itself apart, and then dedicated themselves to building a better one. The generation of Spain's *indignados*, young protesters who have rallied across the country since May 2011, grew up in that better Europe, and have now been thrown backward. The trajectory of those who were, say, 15 years old in 1945 went from war to peace, poverty to prosperity, fear to hope. The trajectory of those who were 15 in 2003, especially in the parts of the continent now suffering the most, has arched in the opposite direction: from prosperity to unemployment, convergence of national experiences to divergence, hope to fear.

Could this very discontent provide the psychological basis for a popular campaign to save Europe? The signs are not promising. Popular movements have arisen during the crisis, but they have pointed in other directions. One of the largest was against the Anti-Counterfeiting Trade Agreement, which many young Europeans saw as a threat to their online freedom. The *indignados* of all countries, Europe's counterparts to the Occupy Wall Street movement, rail against bankers, politicians, and baby boomers, whom they see as having stolen their future. An interview-based survey of activists in these diverse campaigns, coordinated by Mary Kaldor and Sabine Selchow of the London School of Economics, found that the EU is either invisible among them or viewed somewhat negatively.

Fear should not be underestimated as a motivating force in politics. When, in a repeat election this June, the Greeks narrowly voted for parties that were serious about keeping the country in the eurozone, the Swiss cartoonist Patrick Chappatte drew a weary-looking man standing next to a ballot box in the shadow of the

Acropolis and exclaiming, "Good news! Fear triumphed over despair." Adapting a famous phrase of U.S. President Franklin Roosevelt, one might almost say that today Europe has nothing to put its hope in but fear itself.

The fear of collapse, the Monnet-like logic of necessity, the power of inertia: these may just keep the show on the road, but they will not create a dynamic, outward-looking European Union that enjoys the active support of its citizens. Without some new driving forces, without a positive mobilization among its elites and peoples, the EU, while probably surviving as an origami palace of treaties and institutions, will gradually decline in efficacy and real significance, like the Holy Roman Empire of yore. Future historians may then identify some time around 2005 as the apogee of the most far-reaching, constructive, and peaceful attempt to unite the continent that history has ever seen.

# Can Europe's Divided House Stand?

## Separating Fiscal and Monetary Union

*Hugo Dixon*

C onventional wisdom has it that the eurozone cannot have a monetary union without also having a fiscal union. Euro-enthusiasts see the single currency as the first steppingstone toward a broader economic union, which is their dream. Euroskeptics do, too, but they see that endgame as hell—and would prefer the single currency to be dismantled. The euro crisis has, for many observers, validated these notions. Both camps argue that the eurozone countries' lopsided efforts to construct a monetary union without a fiscal counterpart explain why the union has become such a mess. Many of the enthusiasts say that the way forward is for the 17 eurozone countries to issue euro bonds, which they would all guarantee (one of several variations on the fiscal-union theme). Even the German government, which is reluctant to bail out economies weaker than its own, thinks that some sort of pooling of budgets may be needed once the current debt problems have been solved.

A fiscal union would not come anytime soon, and certainly not soon enough to solve the current crisis. It would require a new treaty, and that would require unanimous approval. It is difficult to imagine how such an agreement could be reached quickly given the fierce opposition from politicians and the public in the eurozone's

HUGO DIXON is Founder and Editor of Reuters Breakingviews.

relatively healthy economies (led by Finland, Germany, and the Netherlands) to repeated bailouts of their weaker brethren (Greece, Ireland, Italy, Portugal, and Spain). Moreover, once the crisis is solved, the enthusiasm for a fiscal union may wane. Even if Germany is still prepared to pool some budgetary functions, it will insist on imposing strict discipline on what other countries can spend and borrow. The weaker countries, meanwhile, may not wish to submit to a Teutonic straitjacket once the immediate fear of going bust has passed.

But there are more than just two ways forward: fiscal union or a breakup of the euro. There is a third and preferable option: a kind of market discipline combined with tough love. Under this approach, individual states would take as much responsibility as possible for their own finances, but they would also embrace the free market more vigorously. Governments that borrowed too much money would have to be free to default. Limited bailouts for governments and banks in lesser trouble would also be required, albeit in return for economic reforms and belt-tightening. The result would be fitter economies and a Europe that has the strength to play a bigger role on the world stage.

As this article went to press, the eurozone crisis was in a particularly acute phase. Markets were in a high state of anxiety, Greece's latest rescue package was in difficulty, and much of the region was teetering on the brink of recession. Spain was in the midst of a general election campaign, and Silvio Berlusconi's government in Italy was losing authority. Nevertheless, amid the turmoil, there were signs that the eurozone might be clumsily muddling along toward something like the market-discipline-plus-tough-love option for dealing with the immediate crisis. It should also adopt it as a long-term model.

## DISUNION

In theory, a common currency has many advantages for the European Union's single market, which also includes countries, such as the United Kingdom, that decided to stay out of the eurozone. When people do not have to worry about fluctuating currencies, they can more easily do business across borders, make long-term investments anywhere in the market, and build transnational enterprises. The ability to harness economies of scale and the opportunity to compete across an entire continent are worthwhile prizes.

But there is also a big disadvantage: individual countries lose the ability to tailor their monetary policies to their particular needs by setting their own interest rates. Instead, interest rates are set by the European Central Bank, which is a problem because different economies move at different speeds. For example, low rates throughout the whole eurozone in the years running up to 2007 amplified Spain's subsequent housing bubble.

Whether the benefits of having a common currency outweigh the costs depends largely on three factors: the similarity among the economies covered by the single monetary policy, their flexibility, and the existence of a large central budget that can be used to transfer money from flourishing regions to struggling ones. Economies with similar structures and cycles find it easier to live with a one-size-fits-all monetary policy. Even economies that are different can cope with a single currency so long as they are adaptable—in particular, so long as their businesses can easily hire and fire employees and people are willing to cross borders in search of work.

The eurozone does not come out well by any of these measures, especially in comparison with the United States. Europe's economies are diverse, its labor markets are hemmed in by elaborate restrictions, and it has only a small central budget with which to help troubled regions. This is why Euro-enthusiasts and Euroskeptics alike—from Jacques Delors, a former president of the European Commission and one of the principal architects of the single currency, to Boris Johnson, the mayor of London—argue that a fiscal union is needed to oil the wheels of monetary union.

## RACKING UP DEBT

But there is another way of living within the constraints of a one-size-fits-all monetary policy: strengthen Europe's weaker members, particularly by making their economies more flexible. Before the single currency was launched in 1999, governments did not have an incentive to undertake the hard reforms needed to make that happen. Whenever the likes of Greece or Italy found themselves becoming uncompetitive, their governments devalued their currencies. After the monetary union came about, the eurozone's unfit economies found another escape route: they borrowed money. This allowed those governments to finance high expenditures without raising taxes. But as these economies became weaker, their competitiveness suffered.

Many states also accumulated mountains of debt, sowing the seeds of the current crisis. Under the Maastricht Treaty, which began the process of forming the monetary union, governments are not supposed to run up debts that equal more than 60 percent of GDP, but every major economy of the eurozone exceeded that level significantly. After the world economy slowed down early in the century, supposedly virtuous states, such as France and Germany, started flouting rules meant to limit budget deficits. There was then no chance of disciplining the others. Last year, the debt-to-GDP ratios of France and Germany exceeded 80 percent; Italy's hit 119 percent, and Greece's 143 percent.

Debt grew not only because governments were breaking the rules; it also grew because governments managed to persuade investors, in particular banks and insurance companies, to lend them money. Beginning in early 2010, investors finally stopped funding Greece; then they stopped funding Ireland and Portugal. But this bond strike took an awfully long time to emerge. The market's failure to discipline governments any sooner was largely the result of the governments themselves. They took advantage of the widespread view that European nations could not default. This was reinforced by the way that banks were (and still are) regulated. The so-called Basel rules, recommendations on banking regulations devised by central bankers of the G-20 countries and others, say that government bonds are risk-free assets and so banks do not have to hold any capital when they invest in them. Not surprisingly, banks piled in, with the consequence that sovereign debt problems in-fected them, too. Both before and after Lehman Brothers went bust in September 2008, moreover, central banks on both sides of the Atlantic flooded the world with cheap money, distorting money markets and making it easy for governments to rack up debt. It was deliberate rule breaking by governments and their rigging of the market in favor of government bonds, not the lack of a fiscal union, that led to the current crisis.

## EURO BONDAGE

This, however, has not stopped Europe's weak economies from calling for a fiscal union. Quite the opposite: they are looking for yet another way to continue living beyond their means. George Papandreou, the Greek prime minister, and Giulio Tremonti, the Italian finance minister, want their countries to be able to issue euro bonds. One can see the appeal: euro bonds would insulate weak states from the discipline of the market by signaling to inves-tors that Germany and other fit countries would ultimately pay the bill if Greece or Italy defaulted. But from the strong countries' perspective, allowing the issuance of euro bonds would give weak economies the license to be profligate, unless it was done in an extremely controlled manner. Moreover, the need to carry the en-tire eurozone's debt could ultimately break the strong countries' backs, too.

Some supposedly more palatable versions of this idea have been proposed. A paper published last year by Bruegel, a Brussels-based think tank, suggests limiting euro bonds to 60 percent of each na-tion's GDP. The snag is that the troubled countries already carry debt well above that level, which raises the question of how they would fund themselves. This is the reason that George Soros and other market gurus have argued for a much higher figure.

Germany, the eurozone's main paymaster, has been willing to countenance the idea of a fiscal union, but only after a long process of integration once the crisis has been resolved. It is also insisting on strong new rules limiting the amount of money that individual countries can borrow and inflicting penalties on those that break those rules. Meanwhile, Mark Rutte, the Dutch prime minister, has suggested creating the position of European Commission budget czar to police the rules. If countries continued to flout the rules, the czar would have the right to tell them how to run their economies, for example, by telling them to raise taxes. If they did not do what they were told, they would have to quit the single currency.

But all of this lies far in the future—if at all. So far, managing the current crisis has consisted of case-by-case bailouts. In return for low-interest loans from various different European war chests and the International Monetary Fund, troubled countries have had to reform their economies and cut back on their borrowing. These bailouts do involve aid from fiscally strong countries to weaker ones, but not as much as would occur in a full fiscal union.

As market conditions have deteriorated and more countries have been sucked into the vortex of economic collapse, there have been several different versions of these bailouts. The 17 eurozone countries have found it hard to agree on what to do, leading to zig-zagging policymaking, which has undermined investor confidence and created unnecessary economic hardship.

For all its warts, however, the policy has had some successes. The weaker European governments have been forced to embrace reforms that they had shirked for decades. They are liberalizing their labor markets, rooting out tax evasion, pushing up excessively low retirement ages, slashing bureaucracies, privatizing industries, and opening up cartel-like industries, such as pharmacies and taxi services. This is happening not only in Greece, Ireland, and Portugal, the three countries that have taken bailouts. Italy and Spain have also adopted their own fitness regimes, albeit falteringly. Had these states just been able to issue euro bonds, they would not have had the incentive to shape up.

## THE FREEDOM TO FAIL

Still, the current crisis management has been deficient in one important respect. At least by the time this article went to press, no insolvent country had been allowed to go bust. Greece's debts were spiraling out of control at the time, but the bailout plan that was devised for the country at a European summit in July encouraged banks that had lent it money to roll over their debts or extend their repayment terms. That is a long way from a proper debt restructuring, which would leave Athens with a lower level of debt, one it could realistically support.

Companies and individuals all around the world restructure their debts. Governments outside Europe default. Why should the eurozone countries be exempt from bankruptcy? Defaulting is not nice, of course. Lenders lose money; borrowers can be boycotted for years or have to pay higher interest rates. But this is how things ought to be. Like investors who make unwise loans, governments that borrow too much should not get off scot-free. If they do not feel any pain, they will repeat the same mistakes. Indeed, the fear of being forced into bankruptcy might prevent governments from running up excess debts in the first place. The option of defaulting in a controlled manner ought to be part of the current crisis-management approach for those governments that really cannot support their debts: certainly Greece and possibly Ireland and Portugal, too.

Yet most European policymakers have so far viewed default as anathema because they have been scared of contagion. If Greece defaulted, the banks that lent it money might also go bust. The market might conclude that other weak governments will default, too, making it hard for them to raise money. Some policymakers are frightened that the mayhem unleashed would be like, or even worse than, the chaos that followed Lehman Brothers' bankruptcy. As this article went to press, there were indeed signs that the crisis was spreading to Italy: its government was finding it increasingly expensive to borrow money on the bond market.

But the lesson of Lehman's collapse is not that banks or governments should never be allowed to go bust. It is that defaults should be controlled and that those that are exposed to possible contamination should prepare for it. But the eurozone seems not to have learned this yet. Banks stuffed with government bonds have merely been nudged to shore up their balance sheets. Whereas the United States and the United Kingdom conducted rigorous stress tests on their banks in early 2009, Europe has done three fairly limp reviews in the past two years. Even the most recent one, in July, failed to model for a possible Greek default. Meanwhile, governments that are exposed to contagion have been slow to reduce their budget debts and liberalize their economies. Berlusconi, for example, has acted like a latter-day Nero, fiddling while Rome burns. Even French President Nicolas Sarkozy behaved until recently as if France lived in a charmed world where borrowing was its privilege.

But it is not too late to put the controlled-default option back on the table. Given the policy errors for which France and Germany are responsible—from flouting the original deficit rules to standing in the way of a sensible restructuring of Greece's debt—they should pay some penance. And they will, in the form of low interest rates on the money they have already lent struggling economies and in the form of the extra capital they may need to pump into their own banks to cover the cost of their bad loans to Greece and possibly others. This will cost a lot, but less than throwing more good money after bad to avoid defaults. And it will certainly be cheaper than a full-fledged fiscal union.

## LENDERS OF LAST RESORT

Part of the art of managing a financial crisis is distinguishing insolvent institutions from merely illiquid ones. The debts of insolvent institutions should be restructured, whereas illiquid institutions should get funding. Like a country with its own currency, the eurozone needs a lender of last resort. The key, however, will be to ensure that it does not become a lender of first resort, as that would remove the incentive for states and banks to manage their own affairs responsibly.

Having entered the 2007 credit crunch without a properly thought-out plan for how a lender of last resort would operate, the eurozone has had to make up policy on the fly. The European

Central Bank has been showering banks with liquidity since the crisis hit, but this really should have been done hand in glove with integrated banking supervision across the eurozone. Instead, regulation was fragmented and, to some extent, continues to be. The European Central Bank has also helped fund troubled governments—first, Greece, Ireland, and Portugal; then, Italy and Spain—by buying their bonds. It hoped that this would push up the value of the bonds and make it easier for the governments to issue new ones. (As bonds are bought on the market, this is not quite the same as giving the governments cash.)

The European Central Bank was uncomfortable with this role, however, because it does not believe that governments should print money to reduce their deficits. So the eurozone countries decided at a summit in July that this task should be transferred to the European Financial Stability Facility (EFSF), a new slush fund set up to help manage the crisis. At the same time, they agreed to expand the size of the facility, give it the authority to provide money to cash-strapped banks, and grant it the power to provide emergency credit lines to governments that are not in full bailout programs.

But this has not ended the debate over which policy is best. Willem Buiter, Citigroup's chief economist, among others, has argued that despite its expanded 440 billion euros, the EFSF is still too small to handle full bailouts of Italy and Spain. Although this is true, a lender of last resort should not be used as a permanent prop anyway. Italy and Spain could solve their own problems if they had the political will to tighten their belts. Full bailouts will become necessary only if they shirk that responsibility.

The EFSF will be replaced in mid-2013 by a new bailout fund called the European Stability Mechanism, a permanent facility. In one important respect, the ESM will be better than the EFSF: it will be required to distinguish insolvent from illiquid governments when it makes loans. In the case of insolvent governments, the debt held by private-sector creditors will have to be restructured so as to make the governments' debts sustainable. Too bad this mechanism will not kick in for almost two more years.

## THE THIRD WAY

Given these complexities, many Euroskeptics think it would be better to abandon the euro project altogether. But this is a bad idea. The monetary union may have developed prematurely, but nobody has come up with a way of putting the toothpaste back in the tube. If Athens ever decided to reintroduce the drachma, for example, people would promptly pull their euros out of Greek banks, causing the country's financial system to collapse even before the new currency was minted. Depositors in other weak countries would then pull their money from those countries' banks, triggering a chain of collapses and a deep depression. There is another option: market discipline plus tough love. This medicine will be difficult to swallow, but in the end, it will lead to a healthier Europe.

# Saving the Euro Will Mean Worse Trouble for Europe

## Charting the Disastrous Ahead

*Vivein A. Schmidt*

The EU has tried repeatedly, and failed repeatedly, to calm the markets. That is not for a lack of solutions at hand. Consider three: make the European Central Bank (ECB) a lender of last resort, spread exposure by pooling eurozone debt via eurobonds, or massively increase the European Financial Stability Facility (EFSF) and start bailing out weak economies in earnest.

Any of those solutions would reinstate confidence and lead to stability, but each is easier said than done. The first and arguably best solution—in which the ECB simply buys debt without limits from Italy or any other member state in trouble—is legally questionable under the EU treaty; what's more, Berlin rejects the idea, citing the bank's limited mandate, and says it could spark inflation. The creation of eurobonds is a political nonstarter for northern European states distrustful of their profligate, crisis-prone counterparts in the south. And eurozone leaders have already tried—unsuccessfully—to create a bigger EFSF on the cheap by asking the BRIC countries to buy in.

VIVIEN A. SCHMIDT is Jean Monnet Professor of European Integration and Director of the Center for the Study of Europe at Boston University. She is the author of Democracy in Europe.

Simply put, markets are reeling because eurozone countries have failed to go beyond half-measures to resolve the crisis. The longer they delay taking any one of the three possible solutions, the closer the markets push them to the brink of disaster. But here's the rub: if the eurozone survives, the consequences may be just as ruinous. Austerity will be a drag on growth in the center and the north of Europe, and on competitiveness in the south. Add to this increasing unemployment, inequality, and poverty, and the continent has prepared a recipe for rising social unrest and polarization on the political extremes. Not until European leaders realize the fundamental flaw in their current approach—a lack of real political and economic integration—will there be an end to the crisis in sight.

First, consider the euro going bust. Europe would undergo a vast and painful transformation. How exactly it would happen remains uncertain, but there is little doubt that it would be ugly. Just think of spreads on Italian or Spanish debt zooming past ten percent; one would default, then possibly the other. France would surely follow, given the exposure of its banks to Italian debt, then, even, Germany. The EU as such would nonetheless survive, along with the single market. But that is where the certainty ends.

One of two post-euro scenarios could emerge. In the first, a small group of northern European countries rally around Germany to create a new currency outside the eurozone and, arguably, the EU. The problem is that the new currency would skyrocket in value overnight because, without the dilution from the less competitive south, it would become much too strong to sustain powerful export-oriented economies.

In the second, the southern Europeans leave the eurozone in exchange for a modern-day Marshall Plan funded by, say, the richer eurozone members through the EFSF. The upside is that they would regain competitiveness through the depreciation of their currencies, rather than through the reduction of workers' wages and entitlements. The downside is they would have to go back to national currencies, near-zero liquidity, inflation spurred by the higher price of imports, and, most likely, a ruined banking system.

Accordingly, no country is seriously contemplating an exit from the EU, however unpopular staying in has become. By the best estimate, at the very last minute and at great cost, the euro will most likely be saved. The ECB will finally decide that because the eurozone's financial stability and, indeed, the single currency's very existence is at risk, it can buy member-state debt without limit and still remain under the terms of the treaty. At the same time, the member-states will greatly increase the financial firepower of the EFSF, with further support from the IMF, reinforced by money from the BRIC countries.

But even if Europe saves its common currency, it will not solve the continent's biggest problems. Hiding behind Europe's debt crisis is both a growth crisis and a competitiveness crisis. The former is a result of the austerity policies that EU leaders signed onto last May in exchange for Germany's agreement to bail out Greece and establish the EFSF. Radical deficit reductions and fiscal consolidation was the answer. Rather than calming markets and restarting growth, however, it has produced an economic slowdown across Europe, which is now likely heading toward a double-dip recession, and less rather than more market confidence.

Austerity has already taken a toll. Across Europe, there has been a rapid increase of poverty, inequality, and unemployment. Very little has been done at the EU level to ease the pain. One has to wonder where Social Europe is. The structural funds designed to promote economic development in regions in need have gone mostly unused by the poorest of the southern European regions, largely because they lack the administrative capacity to jump through the bureaucratic hoops required to access the funds. Likewise, the European globalization adjustment fund (EGF), set up in 2007 with great fanfare to address unemployment problems resulting from globalization, turns out to have disbursed almost no money in 2010, even as unemployment continues to rise.

Then there is the competitiveness crisis. As the across-the-board cuts mandated by EU authorities for southern Europe spare nothing—including investment in areas required for future growth, like training and education, support for job and business creation, and economic modernization—these countries will not be able to get out from under their debts, let alone prosper. Austerity measures designed on the so-called German model may work for Germany's export-fueled economy. But it spells nothing short of decline for Europeans on the Mediterranean.

The EU's crises are not just economic and social. They are also political. Politics in Europe are already becoming more national. Euroskepticism is on the rise both in southern Europe, where citizens see the EU as imposing unnecessarily harsh austerity to placate northern Europe, and in the north, where citizens see the EU as imposing unnecessarily high costs in bailing out the south. European leaders have done little to counter these perceptions.

In Germany, for example, Chancellor Angela Merkel's discourse in the months before agreeing to the first Greek bailout and creation of the EFSF did nothing to prepare the public for it, and instead seemed to agree with the tabloid press bent on castigating the lazy Greeks. As such, "saving" the euro proved a much harder sell. The same problem holds for today. Although she now proclaims the need for deeper political and economic integration, Merkel remains the primary holdout to the ECB's becoming a lender of last resort.

Accordingly, political extremes are surging in capitals across Europe. Populist parties have become increasingly vocal in opposition to bailouts, from France's extreme right National Front to Germany's extreme left Die Linke (the Left Party). In the Netherlands, Gert Wilders has succeeded in making his Freedom Party the second most popular in the Netherlands by shifting his emphasis from anti-Muslim to anti-European politics, while the far-left Socialists, equally opposed to the eurozone rescue packages, have also moved up in the polls. Anti-European sentiment has even increased outside the eurozone, most noticeable recently in Britain, with the backbenchers' revolt in the Conservative party.

Those really pulling the political levers now are the so-called technocrats. For national democracies, the resignations of elected prime ministers, whether Silvio Berlusconi in Italy or George Papandreou in Greece, and their replacement by presidentially appointed economists, have raised direct questions about the democratic legitimacy of unelected officials taking the place of elected governments.

But whereas Italy's shift to a technocratic government could very well be a chance to make democracy work anew—with a replay of the country's mid-1990s success in reforming to join the euro, now to stay in—this is much less clear in the case of Greece, which, under the harsh orders of the troika technocrats (IMF, ECB, and European Commission), imposed increasing pain on a disenfranchised public. In this light, Papandreou's call for a referendum could be seen as a genuine desire to bring participatory democracy back in, by allowing the electorate to vote on whether to accept the bailout package and, by extension, to stay in or to leave the eurozone.

The catch, however, is that in re-enfranchising the Greek public Papandreou was single-handedly disenfranchising the greater public of eurozone countries, who all knew that the fate of the euro suddenly hinged on the referendum vote.

Given the delays and hesitant solutions that have repeatedly failed to calm the markets, the real European power centers—and Germany in particular—have not, to put it bluntly, led. The European Parliament, the only directly elected body in the EU, has barely been involved, so there has been no political debate to change the conversation over the efficacy of austerity. EU leaders do not seem to see a problem with the rise of technocracy, or the recourse to automatic rules, agreed without parliamentary debate, whether in the EU or national government. But they are likely to be in for a rude awakening, in particular if markets decide that Italian, Spanish, or French debt is too much to handle.

The EU needs more than deeper economic integration. It also needs deeper political integration. Talk has surfaced about a new fiscal pact that would impose restrictions on national budgets. Although this is the right move to convince the ECB that becoming lender of last resort will not open the door to moral hazard, since the pact is to bind all countries to fiscal probity, the austerity policies embedded in it are likely only to reinforce the growth crisis. Moreover, by undermining one of the main tenets of parliamentary democracy—budgetary responsibility—it will only increase the Eurozone's democratic deficit.

Blinkered by their increasingly euro-critical electorates and, dare it be said, by their neoliberal and ordoliberal (read: German) economic ideas, EU leaders have so far ruled out the appropriate economic initiatives that could solve the debt crisis. Equally problematic, they have cut off the political debates that might provide better policies with greater public legitimacy. As a result, EU leaders, rather than saving the euro and, with it, Europe, may kill off both.

# Can the Eurozone Be Saved?

## Yes, but the EU Summit Was Too Little, Too Late

*Kathleen R. McNamara*

T he European Council summit, held in Brussels on March 24–25, presented an all-too-familiar tableau: European leaders in Brussels squabbling over questions of economic governance and how to stabilize the eurozone in the midst of roiling financial markets and mounting political crises. As investors questioned the European Union's willingness to address ongoing financial turmoil in Greece, Ireland, and Portugal, Portuguese bond spreads skyrocketed and Prime Minister José Sócrates' minority government collapsed.

By the end of the summit, EU countries had agreed to build and fund the European Stability Mechanism (ESM), a permanent bailout facility for the eurozone that extends the temporary European Financial Stability Facility enacted last year. They also agreed to strengthen macroeconomic policy rules to encourage good fiscal housekeeping. But these achievements seem tepid in the face of the European Union's instability after the financial crisis and may prove to be too little, too late.

Observers could be forgiven for viewing the summit as the last chapter in the failed experiment of European governance. But in

KATHLEEN R. MCNAMARA is Associate Professor and Director of Georgetown's Mortara Center for International Studies.

fact, if one looks beyond the *son et lumière*, the European Union remains a remarkably solid and vital political structure nowhere near the brink of collapse. The dramatic headlines mask the ongoing evolution of an extraordinary constitutional order that is more robust than any other interstate relationship. It has profoundly Europeanized national policies, laws, and practices, and its institutions touch almost everything, from citizens and politicians to private firms and government bureaucracies. Despite the operatic drama surrounding the Brussels summit, the real action of the European Union happens daily at a lower level, from the generation of trucking laws through the enforcement of gender equity. No longer rooted only in treaty law, the European Union is enmeshed in the domestic laws of each member state. As such, it would be extremely difficult to disentangle.

Of course, that does not mean that high-level political bargaining and institutional reform are not needed. At this point, the European Union can only move forward if European leaders, particularly German Chancellor Angela Merkel, finally seize the ongoing financial crisis as an opportunity for deepening the European Union's economic governance system. If they do not, harder economic times and increasing political tensions will be difficult to avoid.

The only long-term solution to the European Union's currency problems is for eurozone states to commit to enhanced fiscal institutional capacity at the EU level. This way, the entire union's economic health would not depend solely on a set of unrealistic macroeconomic rules based on the 1997 Growth and Stability Pact, which caps national deficits and debts, and on ad hoc bailouts whenever a country's economy collapsed. Such a reform would require further political integration, which, in the long run, would calm national markets. Like all other currencies, the euro would finally become a part of a broader confederal government, rather than a political tool masquerading as a technocratic solution to a putative economic problem (the costs of transacting in different currencies across a single European market), as it was originally promoted by euro supporters.

The creation of the ESM at this year's summit is a step in the right direction. If the eurozone is to hold together economically, it needs financing at the EU level to deal with the insolvency crises of member states. But the ESM is most certainly too little, too late, because the amount of money on the table—700 billion euros—will most likely be inadequate to deal with another major financial crash. Moreover, amassing enough funding after a crisis has already begun is always a Sisyphean task.

A more effective way to ensure eurozone stability would be to create a new EU bond. At the moment, there is no EU-wide official debt-financing instrument. National bonds are denominated in euros but are backed solely by the issuing government. This means that eurozone bond markets are fragmented, with each pooling a relatively small amount of financing. Much as U.S. Treasury bonds are stable and attractive investments because of the broad strength of the U.S. economy, a Eurobond would overcome individual European countries' economic weaknesses by reflecting the total economic heft of the European Union.

Jean-Claude Juncker, Luxembourg's prime minister and the chairman of the Eurogroup of eurozone finance ministers, recently endorsed a proposal to gradually create a Eurobond market equal to 40 percent of EU GDP. But Merkel quickly squashed the proposal, fearing that Germany's less fiscally stringent neighbors would push up the interest rates on the bonds—and make all of the European Union collectively responsible for maintaining the eurozone's stability. It seems unlikely, however, that the small, troubled states (for example, Portugal, which accounts for about two percent of EU GDP) would have such a large impact on its worth, and the overall benefits of financial stability are greater than the potential risks. After all, the wealthier countries, such as Germany, have a huge stake in eurozone-wide financial stability. Their banks are heavily invested in the same countries that are facing crises. And although the German public may resent putting money into European financing schemes, Irish citizens are equally angry at the notion that they must pursue draconian austerity regimes to pay back private German banks as the European Union sits idly by. These types of disputes would likely be lessened with an EU-wide bond.

Nonetheless, the creation of the Eurobond would represent a politically difficult transformation: it would move the European Union ever closer toward a traditional nation-state model and require a clear-eyed assessment of the politics involved in creating a workable economic and monetary union—something that, if the recent summit is any indication, EU leaders do not currently have the will to do.

The summit's second key decision, now being called the "Euro Pact Plus," builds on the eurozone's old macroeconomic code of conduct, the Stability and Growth Pact. It extends the original pact's rules into new areas, such as wage negotiation procedures, and gives the European Union a stronger legal framework to increase compliance. The new pact also tightens budget planning, reporting, and surveillance to prevent states from running excessive deficits. Finally, it coordinates EU macroeconomic policy to promote convergence and competitiveness.

Yet this initiative is more a dead end than a step forward. The Stability and Growth Pact has never worked, because it is too rigid and thus often ignored, a problem that the new compliance measures are insufficient to overcome. Even Germany, a major supporter of the goals of the Stability and Growth Pact, found itself in noncompliance when, earlier last decade, it ran higher budget deficits for several years. And instead of creating a set of EU-level institutions similar to a national treasury or department of finance, the Euro Pact Plus only reinforces the old nationally enforced Stability and Growth Pact rules. Moreover, its German supporters have suggested relying on the markets to act as a disciplining force. But the subprime crisis and global financial meltdown should have made politicians wary of relying on markets to assess government positions appropriately.

Of course, the creation of a Eurobond and a European federalist fiscal system are not small steps. They certainly would not be possible without a new political grand bargain, which can only happen with constructive and enthusiastic commitments from Germany and France. The single-market program of 1986, which dramatically deregulated product markets, and the 1992 Maastricht Treaty, which created the monetary union, were revolutionary, moving the European Union from national governance to a true supranational entity. But they came amid some degree of consensus among Europeans about how to best manage markets. Today, there is a palpable lack of convergence on policies for government spending, taxing, and borrowing.

The process of fiscal confederation is politically different than monetary union, too. The Single European Act's changes and the Maastricht Treaty's rules for monetary instruments were relatively opaque and sheltered from partisan politics. Fiscal policies' winners and losers are clear, and the effects of fiscal choices can be socially wrenching—yet so, too, are the consequences of the intensive budget cuts that the eurozone may have to implement to crawl out of the current financial pit. But it would be far better to make hard decisions and put the eurozone on a path to financial stability, growth, and employment by developing a eurozone debt and fiscal capacity now, rather than trying to avoid these wrenching decisions and wait until another financial meltdown raises the stakes even higher.

In the eyes of markets and skeptical observers, the European Union is more than an intergovernmental organization but not yet a state. When the European Union bickers and dithers, the markets have no idea what may happen. The euro is the only single currency in history that has not been tightly linked to broader state- and nation-building efforts (often following wars, during which military action required budgeting and taxation). Although the euro is an extraordinary peacetime achievement, it suffers from a lack of supporting political institutions that can make broader macroeconomic policy. The European Union needs to change that and move beyond the structure of its current economic and monetary union—which were seemingly designed for a world in which private and public actors never over-borrow and financial markets never question their ability to repay—to real political and economic cohesion, something international markets would recognize as parallel to a nation state.

Such a grand bargain would be incredibly difficult to achieve and would require a real change in the recent German intransigence over further integration. That, of course, is what makes the whole proposal so difficult to pursue, but it may be the only way to make Europe financially, and politically, viable in the long run.

# How to Save the Euro—and the EU

## Reading Keynes in Brussels

*Henry Farrell and John Quiggin*

T he European Union is in danger of compounding its ongoing economic crisis with a political crisis of its own making. Over the last year, crises of confidence have hit the 17 EU members that in the years since 1998 have given up their own currencies to adopt the euro. For the first decade of this century, markets behaved as though the debt of peripheral EU countries, such as Greece and Ireland, was as safe as that of core EU countries, such as Germany. But when bond investors realized that Greece had been cooking its books and that Ireland's fiscal posture was unsustainable, they ran for the door. The EU has stopped the contagion from spreading—for now—by creating the European Financial Stability Facility, which can issue bonds and raise money to help eurozone states. Together with the International Monetary Fund, the European Financial Stability Facility has already lent Greece and Ireland enough money to cover their short-term needs.

But such bailouts are only stop-gap measures. Portugal and Spain, and to a lesser extent Belgium and Italy, remain vulnerable to pressure from bondholders. Portugal is likely to receive 50–100 billion

HENRY FARRELL is Associate Professor of Political Science and International Affairs at George Washington University and a Fellow at the Woodrow Wilson International Center for Scholars.

JOHN QUIGGIN is Australian Research Council Federation Fellow at the University of Queensland and the author of Zombie Economics.

euros over the next few months. But should Spain also need a bailout—which could cost as much as 600 billion euros—the 750 billion euro European Financial Stability Facility would soon be exhausted. In that event, the main euro creditors, primarily British, French, and German banks, might have to accept so-called haircuts, substantial cuts in the principals of their loans. (The banks' tax-avoidance strategies might inflate this total, but the Bank for International Settlements has estimated that the exposure of British, French, and German banks to the group of vulnerable debtor states referred to as the PIGS—Portugal, Ireland, Greece, and Spain— amounted to more than $1 trillion in mid-2010.) Encouraged by Germany, some of the states in difficulty have sought to placate bond markets by making ruthless cuts in government spending. But as many economists have pointed out, these measures are hindering growth without satisfying bondholders that their money is safe; bondholders worry that these measures are not politically sustainable. In fact, they are likely to undermine Europe's political union.

Nevertheless, Germany has been pressing European countries to institutionalize more stringent cuts in spending. In February, it, along with France, proposed that members of the eurozone introduce "debt brakes," inflexible limits on deficit spending. Germany had already incorporated such a cap into its own constitution, one that severely restricts any government deficit spending, including the kind that might benefit the country's long-term growth. In early March, the other 16 eurozone states agreed to introduce such debt brakes or some equivalent into their domestic laws and to make them as durable and binding as possible, for example, by incorporating them into their national constitutions.

But institutionalizing austerity will badly damage European economies in the short term—and the long-term consequences will be even worse. European politicians worry about the economic consequences if their attempts at fiscal stabilization fail. They should be far more worried about the political consequences. Even if these strict spending limits do calm bond markets somehow, they will destroy what little is left of the EU's political legitimacy.

## BAD AS GOLD

The EU is now drifting toward a thinly disguised version of the gold standard, which wreaked economic havoc in the 1920s and led to a toxic political fallout. Under that system, European states had fixed exchange rates. During economic crises, they refused to increase government spending because of a failure to either understand or care that monetary disturbances and shocks to demand could lead to joblessness. The result was generalized misery. Governments responded to economic crises by allowing unemployment to go up and cutting back wages, leaving workers to bear the pain of adjustment. As *Golden Fetters*, Barry Eichengreen's classic history of the period, shows, the gold standard began to collapse when workers in Europe gained the power to vote out of office the parties that supported austerity.

The measures that the eurozone states have recently decided to adopt will be even harsher, if they make the mistake of following Germany's example. Germany's debt brake, which at first Berlin implicitly proposed as a model for other European countries, turns austerity into a constitutional obligation. In theory, it provides some flexibility during hard economic times, but in practice it makes deficit spending as difficult as possible: only the vote of a supermajority of German legislators can relax it. And it rules out debt-financed investment, such as in infrastructure, even though that can spur long-term growth.

As they begin to adopt Germany's model, or something along those lines, the other eurozone states will find it nearly impossible to use fiscal stimulus in times of crisis. And with monetary policy already in the hands of the dogmatically anti-inflationary European Central Bank, their only means of adjusting to crises will be to stand by as wages fall and unemployment soars. Ireland—with its collapsed tax revenues, massive cuts in government spending, shrinking wages, and skyrocketing unemployment—is the unhappy exemplar of rigid austerity measures in the new Europe.

This approach cannot be sustained for long. The EU has never had much popular legitimacy: many voters have gone along with it so far only out of the belief that their politicians knew best. Today, they are more suspicious. And if they come to think that further European integration is causing more economic hardship, their suspicion could harden into bitterness and perhaps even xenophobia. Ireland's new finance minister, Michael Noonan, has told voters that the EU is a game rigged in Germany's favor; editorials in major Irish newspapers warn of Germany's return to racist imperialism. As economic shocks hit other EU countries, politicians in those states will also look for someone to blame.

If the EU is to survive, it will have to craft a solution to the eurozone crisis that is politically as well as economically sustainable. It will need to create long-term institutions that both minimize the risk of future economic crises and refrain from adopting politically unsustainable forms of austerity when crises do hit. They must offer the EU countries that are the worst hit a viable path to economic stability while reassuring Germany, the state currently driving economic debates within the union, that it will not be asked to bail out weaker states indefinitely.

The short-term solution is clear—even if the European Central Bank, which is still fighting the war against the inflation of the 1980s and 1990s, refuses to recognize it. The solution is a one-off combination of market purchases of bonds and other financial assets, temporarily higher inflation, and fiscal support with the issuance of a common European bond. Quantitative easing and higher inflation would help ease the pain of adjustment, and a European bond would allow the weaker eurozone states to raise money on international markets. All of this would shore up the euro long enough to allow for further-reaching reforms down the road. The major euro bondholders would have to bear some of the costs—as they should, since they lent excessively during the first years of this century—through either explicit haircuts (in effect a discount of their bonds' value) or inflation. Germany might not enjoy experiencing temporarily higher inflation, but if this were a one-time cost, it could probably live with the results—as long as it was also reassured that the long-term gain would be stability in the eurozone.

## IN THE BEST OF TIMES, FOR THE WORST OF TIMES

Instituting effective long-term reforms will be a harder sell. Germany adopted its own large-scale fiscal stimulus in 2009, but it returned to its traditional anti-Keynesian stance as soon as the danger of total systemic collapse had passed. Yet Keynesianism, at least properly understood, is the only way forward.

Contrary to the beliefs of nearly all anti-Keynesians—and, regrettably, some Keynesians, too—Keynesianism demands more, not less, fiscal rectitude in normal times than does the orthodox theory of balanced budgets that underpins the EU. John Maynard Keynes argued that surpluses should be accumulated during good years so that they could be spent to stimulate demand during bad ones. This lesson was well understood during the golden age of Keynesian social democracy, after World War II, when, aided by moderate inflation, the governments of the countries in the Organization for Economic Cooperation and Development greatly reduced their ratios of public debt to GDP. This approach should not be confused with the opportunistic support for large budget deficits evident, for example, among advocates of supply-side economics. If anything, "hard" Keynesianism suggests that the problem with the macroeconomic rules governing the euro is not that they are too tough and too detailed but that they are not tough or detailed enough. States in the eurozone should not be allowed to run moderate budget deficits in boom years, the Keynesian argument goes; instead, they should be compelled to run budget surpluses. The surpluses could then be saved in rainy-day funds or used to pay down government debt or, if the country had reached a satisfactory debt-to-GDP ratio, spent as a fiscal stimulus in the event of a crisis. Unlike the kind of budget management advocated by the German government, this approach does not seek to eliminate or minimize governments' leeway to conduct fiscal policy. It gives governments up-front the means to manage demand whenever they might need to.

Resorting to hard Keynesianism to deal with the euro crisis would require making far-reaching changes to the rules and practices of the EU's economic and monetary union. It would mean both toughening the requirements of the Stability and Growth Pact, which governs the euro, and strengthening the enforcement of these rules. As they stand, the Stability and Growth Pact's by-laws require the eurozone states to maintain budget deficits under three percent of GDP and debt-to-GDP ratios under 60 percent. The system does not provide enough flexibility during downturns: even German politicians ignored these requirements a few years ago, when Germany was suffering from a recession—much as they prefer not to remember this today.

To be more effective, the system needs to be stricter. The Stability and Growth Pact should be strengthened so that it requires countries to put aside surpluses during auspicious years. Since governments are persistently tempted to squander surpluses, a new supervisory institution should be introduced at the EU level. It should be granted access to detailed budget-planning and other economic information from the eurozone states and should be empowered to sanction misbehaving states. Such a reform could be integrated into other proposals under consideration today, such as the "European semester system," which would give the European Council the responsibility to assess member states' budgetary policies. A new European college of budgetary supervisors, with one supervisor from each member state, could assess the budget-planning processes of the member states and provide short-term flexibility in times of real crisis. Its staff would come from the ministries of finance of the eurozone states. When states faced hard economic times, the college could decide, with a simple majority, to relax fiscal strictures on a six-month basis.

The Stability and Growth Pact, a semi-formal protocol of dubious legal standing, should also be properly incorporated into the EU's basic treaties. That would allow the European Court of Justice to adjudicate disputes between EU bodies and member states and help with the pact's enforcement. These arrangements would prevent national governments from unjustified deficit spending while giving them flexibility in times of real need.

Such an active use of fiscal policy requires the coordination of fiscal and monetary policies. This, in turn, means that the European Central Bank can no longer be totally independent, as it has been since the implementation of the euro. As it stands, the European Central Bank is possessive about its powers. For example, it has resisted oversight by the European Parliament even though it has begun to take on an increasingly important political role through its support for the European banking system. It has assiduously avoided mingling monetary policy and fiscal policy, focusing instead on targeting inflation. But it nonetheless failed to prevent asset price booms, and these could only have been prevented with much more direct institutional control over unsound financial innovations. As the interaction between governments and central banks is unavoidable and the role of the European Central Bank is increasingly political, it would be better to properly define the relations of authority among these bodies. The European Central Bank must be more willing to adjust its policies so that they do not undercut those of elected national governments. Even if this were not necessary economically, it would be necessary politically. Handing the power to destroy national economies to unelected technocrats is simply not politically sustainable.

Creating an active fiscal policy regime of this kind would reduce the volatility of interest rates, the result of an excessive reliance on monetary policy. Manipulating interest rates helped stabilize inflation during "the great moderation," the era of relative economic calm between the late 1980s and the late years of the first decade of this century. But in the long term, it contributed to the growth of the asset price bubbles that almost destroyed the entire system in the global financial crisis. To be most effective, these reforms would have to go together with the creation of a limited fiscal union that would balance out the asymmetric effects of economic shocks by allowing limited fiscal transfers between member states. Managing surpluses as hard Keynesianism recommends would go some way toward providing the eurozone states with an important buffer against crises. But in hard times, imperfect monetary unions, such as the eurozone, require temporary transfers to the countries most hurt from the countries that are less affected. This is not to argue that the EU should become a "transfer union," with the extensive fiscal transfers of a full-fledged federal system, as the German government fears. But the eurozone should allow for more short-term fiscal transfers to deal with asymmetric shocks. A common bond mechanism, for example, would help states in difficulty raise money on international markets or allow resources that are, say, earmarked for agriculture to be redirected to an emergency fund.

## ROOM WITH A VIEW

Hard Keynesianism would not solve all of the EU's economic and political problems. But it would steer the union away from the disaster toward which it is now sleepwalking. A new set of rules based on this approach could form the basis of a solution that is politically viable for both Germany and its European partners most suffering from the crisis. With only limited fiscal transfers allowed, Germany could be further assured that it would not have to continually bail out its profligate partners. Such an approach would maximize the fiscal room that states in distress need in order to deal with economic shocks while ensuring the eurozone's long-term fiscal sustainability. In the short term, hard Keynesianism, like enforced austerity, would impose real adjustment costs on the eurozone's weaker economies; there is no cost-free path to fiscal balance. But if the costs were shared with bondholders and were alleviated by a one-off loosening of monetary policy, they could be politically acceptable.

By concentrating on its economic problems but ignoring their political consequences, the EU is setting itself up for failure. The case for austerity does not make sense. And if the EU fails to deal with the political fallout of its own institutional weaknesses, it is going to collapse. No political body can force voters to repeatedly shoulder the costs of adjustment on their own and expect to remain legitimate. During the gold standard, nation-states tried this and failed—and they had considerably more authority than the EU has today. Hard Keynesianism offers a means to combine fiscal discipline with flexibility in order to cushion the political costs of adjustment in times of economic stress. EU leaders must institute it in a hurry.

# Why Only Germany Can Fix the Euro

## Reading Kindleberger in Berlin

*Matthias Matthijs and Mark Blyth*

"Never did a ship founder with a captain and a crew more ignorant of the reasons for its misfortune or more impotent to do anything about it." This was Eric Hobsbawm's damning judgment of the policy elite's response to the Great Depression. As these leaders reached for the old truisms of balancing budgets, lowering tariffs, and restoring the gold standard, they merely worsened the crisis. The same judgment may soon be passed on Germany for its role in the ongoing European sovereign debt saga.

After watching the economies of Greece, Ireland, and Portugal founder, the world has now turned its attention to Italy, home to the world's eighth-largest national economy and third-largest sovereign bond market. The diagnosis is sadly redolent: Europe should deflate its way to growth by sticking with a gold standard of sorts: the hard-money German-dominated euro. Meanwhile, under enormous international pressure, the Greeks replaced socialist Prime Minister George Papandreou with Lucas Papademos, a former official of the European Central Bank, and the Italians placed

MATTHIAS MATTHIJS is Assistant Professor at the School of International Service of American University and a Lecturer at the Johns Hopkins School of Advanced International Studies.

MARK BLYTH is Professor of International Political Economy at Brown University.

economist and former European Commissioner Mario Monti, hailed "super Mario," in the stead of Silvio Berlusconi. Yet despite the EU's coup d'état, the yield on ten year Italian debt went back above seven percent within twenty-four hours of Monti showing up for work.

It is more than ironic that those two foundational Western civilizations—the Greeks and the Romans—who were among the very first to experiment with democracy, now have to let unelected Eurocrats run their economic affairs. There is even a whiff of the 1930s here, too, as weak democrats are pushed aside in favor of strong leaders at the behest of international creditors. As Hobsbawm noted, this did not end well last time.

What, we must ask, has driven Europe to this point? Since the beginning of the current economic crisis, analysts have offered multiple explanations. American economists call it a "crisis of de- sign," arguing that Europe had it coming. Fiscal hawks the world over prefer the budgetary explanation, focusing on Greece's under- reported public spending, bloated state, and generous pension sys- tem. They then generalize these problems to all of Europe (never mind that Italian private debt is relatively low, as is its public spending in comparison to most other developed countries). For their part, elites in Germany blame lagging competitiveness and "too-high" real wages in the Mediterranean countries. Still others point to intra-European macroeconomic imbalances. There is probably something to all of these explanations. But the depth and duration of this crisis call for a more complex, systemic, and his- torical account. After all, when explaining the collapse of a bridge, there is little point in blaming the last vehicle that crossed it.

This complex of causes does however have a common root: Ger- many's failure to act as a responsible hegemon in Europe. It is not that Germany should be unseating democracies and enforcing de- flation, as it has attempted to do by installing Papademos in Greece and Monti in Italy. Rather, it should be stabilizing the eurozone by providing a set of public goods that the institutions and policies of the region have singularly failed to supply. To solve the European crisis and avoid repeating the mistakes of the late 1920s and the 1930s, those sitting in Berlin and Brussels should put down their Andrew Mellon and read Charles Kindleberger.

In *The World in Depression: 1929–1939*, Kindleberger argued that "the 1929 depression was so wide, so deep, and so long because the international economic system was rendered unstable by British inability and U.S. unwillingness to assume responsibility for stabilizing it." Indeed, Kindleberger's critique of the United States' role in that era's crisis summitry might well have been written about Germany today: "The World Economic conference of 1933 did not lack ideas . . . [but] the one country capable of leadership was bemused by domestic concerns and stood aside."

In order to guarantee the strength of any international economic system, Kindleberger explained, a stabilizer—only one stabilizer—needs to provide five public goods: a market for distress goods (goods that cannot find a buyer), countercyclical long-term lending, stable exchange rates, macroeconomic policy coordination, and real lending of last resort during financial crises. The United States did not supply these things in the 1930s. Germany fails the test on all five items today.

First, rather than providing peripheral countries with a market for their distress goods, the Germans have been enthusiastically selling their manufactured goods to the periphery. According to Eurostat, Germany's trade surplus with the rest of the EU grew from 46.4 billion euro in 2000 to 126.5 billion in 2007. The evolution of Germany's bilateral trade surpluses with the Mediterranean countries is especially revealing. Between 2000 and 2007, Greece's annual trade deficit with Germany grew from 3 billion euro to 5.5 billion, Italy's doubled, from 9.6 billion to 19.6 billion, Spain's almost tripled, from 11 billion to 27.2 billion, and Portugal's quadrupled, from 1 billion to 4.2 billion. Between 2001 and 2009, moreover, Germany saw its final total consumption fall from 78.5 percent of GDP to 74.5 percent. Its gross savings rate increased from less than 19 percent of GDP to almost 26 percent over the same period.

Second, instead of countercyclical lending, German lending to the eurozone has been pro-cyclical. Indirectly (through buying bonds) and directly (by spreading its exchange rate through the euro), the country has basically given the periphery the money to buy its goods. During the economic boom of 2003–2008, Germany extended credit on a massive scale to the eurozone's Mediterranean countries. Frankfurt did quite well for itself. "European Financial Linkages," a recent IMF working paper, reveals that in 2008, Germany was one of the two biggest net creditors within the eurozone (after France). Its positive positions were exact mirrors of Portugal, Greece, Italy, and Spain's negative ones. Of course, as the financial crisis began to escalate in 2009, Germany abruptly closed its wallet. Now Europe's periphery needs long-term loans more than ever, but Germany's enthusiasm for extending credit seems to have collapsed.

And what about the third public good, stable exchange rates? By definition, the euro gives the countries that choose to join it a common external float, the credibility that comes with banking in a potential global reserve asset, and the credit rating of its strongest member. This is both true and where the problems begin. At the core of the eurozone lies a belief that, if countries adhere to a set of rules about how much debt, deficit, and inflation they can have, their economies will converge, and the same exchange rate will work for all members. This is true in theory, but only so long as countries obey the rules. And, despite being the author of many of those rules, Germany showed a singular lack of leadership and responsibility when it came to following them. When it broke the Stability and Growth Pact (SGP) in 2003, it sent the signal to the smaller countries that fiscal profligacy would go unpunished. The result was heightened public sector borrowing and increased public spending. Germany's enthusiastic lending to the periphery only exacerbated the problem.

Fourth, economic health requires the stabilizer to coordinate macroeconomic policy within the system. In this domain, Germany failed spectacularly, by insisting that the rest of the world follow its peculiar ordoliberal economic philosophy of export-oriented growth. By ignoring long-established ideas such as the Keynesian "paradox of thrift" or the "fallacy of composition," Germany is advocating a serious dose of austerity in the European periphery without even a hint of offsetting those negative economic effects with stimulus or inflationary policies at home. German growth, after all, was partially fueled by demand in Southern Europe (made possible by excess German savings). By the iron logic of the balance of payments, one country's exports are another country's imports and one country's capital inflows are another's capital outflows. So, the eurozone as a whole cannot become more like Germany. Germany could only be like Germany because the others countries were not. Insisting on ordoliberal convergence is guaranteed to produce economic instability, not stability.

Finally, Kindleberger would want Germany—or, rather, the ECB, which is dominated by Germany—to act as a lender of last resort by providing liquidity during the current crisis. Germany instead insisted on IMF conditionality for the bailout countries and on severe fiscal austerity measures in exchange for limited liquidity, thus failing Kindleberger's final test. The most obvious example is German obstinacy against letting the ECB play the role that the Federal Reserve played in the United States in 2008 and 2009. By lending heavily, the Fed was able to arrest the United States' slide into despair. Only a couple of days ago, Jens Weidmann, the president of Germany's powerful Bundesbank, flat-out rejected the idea of using the ECB as "lender of last resort" for governments, warning that such steps "would add to instability by violating European law." It is hard to see how yet one more violation of European code will add significantly to the already horrendous levels of instability, when brushing democracy aside is considered good for the euro.

Throughout much of the twentieth century, the "German Problem"—the fact that Germany was too strong, too powerful, and too economically dynamic for the rest of Europe—bedeviled European elites. "Keeping Germany down" through NATO and

European integration was seen as the solution. The problem today is not German strength but German weakness—a reluctance to take up its hegemonic role. It is not too late for Germany to change course. Even though they have profited handsomely so far from the current arrangement, they must realize by now that its model was always based on shaky foundations, cannot be generalized to all states, and has reached the limits of its sustainability. If the euro ends up collapsing—and the European Union with it—Germany will clearly be much worse of. Many of its markets will disappear while the new deutschmark soars to unknown heights. In such a world, the 'old' German problem would be back at the heart of the 'new' Europe.

Former U.S. Secretary of State Dean Acheson once observed that the United Kingdom had lost an empire but had yet to find a role. In a way, by signing the Maastricht Treaty in the early 1990s, Germany has accidentally grown an economic empire. It has a role—a leader, not a rule maker—but is clearly not yet conscious of it.

# The Myth of German Hegemony

## Why Berlin Can't Save Europe Alone

### Daniela Schwarzer and Kai-Olaf Lang

I n 2010 and 2011, the first two years of Europe's sovereign debt crisis, Germany seemed to emerge as the continent's dominant power, possessing an unrivaled ability to shape its neighbors' destinies. Enjoying unabated economic strength, Germany agreed to bear the largest burden in the eurozone's financial rescue, and so it was able to determine the pace and methods of managing the crisis. It also influenced the economic and budgetary policies of Europe's debt-ridden countries, such as Greece and Spain, and it used that authority to impose an agenda of reform and austerity across the eurozone. Witnessing these developments, some observers went so far as to proclaim the onset of German hegemony and argued that only Berlin could solve the continent's woes.

Although Germany is, to be sure, the most important European country for overcoming today's problems, its abilities to project its power at the EU level are substantially restricted—and they will diminish further in the months ahead. Germany's position as the chief backer of the eurozone's stabilization arrangements does not

DANIELA SCHWARZER is Head of the EU Integration Research Division at the German Institute for International and Security Affairs (on leave) and currently Fritz-Thyssen Visiting Scholar at the Weatherhead Center for International Affairs at Harvard University.

KAI-OLAF LANG is Acting Head of the EU Integration Research Division at the German Institute for International and Security Affairs.

necessarily translate into political supremacy. And as the euro crisis has escalated and Germany has lost political allies, it will now have to accept that the common currency area will only partly conform to its vision.

The first reason Berlin will struggle to implement its plans for Europe is that political developments of the last six months have left Germany a rather isolated giant. In 2010–11, it was largely because of cooperation between Berlin and Paris—and the close partnership between their two leaders that came to be known as Merkozy—that Germany was able to set European policy and disregard the attitudes of other eurozone members, generally the southern countries with large deficits. Now, France's new president, François Hollande, has advocated a European pro-growth agenda that clashes with German Chancellor Angela Merkel's preference for austerity and, in the view of many Germans, would not encourage national governments to implement necessary reforms. Meanwhile, Austria, Finland, and the Netherlands— smaller eurozone members that traditionally side with Germany on economic matters—have ceased to be reliable partners for Berlin, as populist forces have pressured their governments to withdraw from rescue mechanisms or demand stricter regulation of the recipient countries' budgets in exchange for financial help. Berlin's other usual allies in balancing against Mediterranean-style policy approaches, the United Kingdom and Poland, lack importance in the present crisis. Neither country uses the euro, and the eurozone is where the main political decisions on the future of Europe will be made.

In this new context, Germany risks losing out in several regards. For starters, it can no longer demand substantial debt reductions and budget cuts in return for financial backing, nor can it threaten to veto any rescue package that does not include its preferred policies. This was not the case last year, when Germany was able to impose a budget-balancing fiscal compact on eurozone member states. Then, Germany's threat to withhold financial support was credible. Now, however, the crisis has escalated to such a degree that a German veto of a rescue package would trigger a systemic crisis—one that could unravel not only the common currency but also other, larger achievements of European integration such as the single market. Because Germany is liable for approximately 27 percent of the European rescue mechanisms and enjoys a singular position as the largest economy in Europe, it cannot refuse to back the euro without causing continent-wide damage.

On the flip side, because they are less important to the overall functioning of the eurozone, the smaller, fiscally healthy states that help finance the rescue mechanisms now have more leeway to adopt harsh policies toward the deficit countries. They can ask for guarantees, as the Finns did of the Greeks. They can call for throwing noncompliant member states out of the eurozone, as the Austrian foreign minister did in August. They might even threaten to withdraw from the eurozone themselves—something that would be unthinkable for Germany or France. If the crisis deteriorates and the euro's breakup seems likely, these small member states with comparatively low public debt levels may seek an early exit. By preemptively leaving the euozone, they would avoid getting stuck with the mess resulting from southern European countries' abandoning the common currency.

Germany, however, cannot make such threats—mainly because no one would believe them. A German exit would spell the imminent death of the single currency, which would not only be an economic disaster but also carry a historical legacy that even Germany's euro skeptics would not want to assume. If a disorderly German exit pushed southern European states into political, social, and economic chaos, German voters would no longer remember that the move was supposed to serve their best interests and would punish their government for letting the European idea fail. Moreover, the economic and financial losses for Germany would be incalculable. If Germany introduced a new currency, its value would skyrocket, destroying the country's export competitiveness. Germany's nearly two trillion euros of claims in Target 2, an interbank payment system for processing cross-border transfers throughout the EU, would make its withdrawal from the eurozone extremely costly, as much of that money would be lost.

As the continent's crisis worsens, Germany will find it increasingly difficult to influence other European countries' domestic policies according to its own norms. Berlin may want sanctions and controls to go into effect automatically when eurozone members run up large deficits, but in practice the decision to implement such measures will remain a political choice in each individual country. And as European publics grow more disillusioned with Germany's agenda of structural reforms and austerity, they will demand a loose interpretation of the recently redesigned fiscal rules of the eurozone. What is more, the EU's past experiences with big reform projects suggest that any attempt to establish a fiscal or full-fledged political union would involve complicated negotiations that would result in a compromise, not a German-made solution. So although Germany knows that market pressure is on its side, it will not simply be able to rearrange the euro area and the EU in its own image.

Berlin must also consider the possible political fallout from its intransigent fiscal conservatism: Germany's reputation in Greece, Italy, and Spain has already deteriorated, and it is beginning to erode elsewhere, too. If Berlin continues to demand balanced budgets, it could damage its bilateral relations with not only the eurozone's debt-ridden countries but also European governments that normally favor German self-restraint. In the struggle to stabilize the euro, Germany does not enjoy sufficient ideological power to forge a consensus behind fiscal consolidation. Throughout Europe, the Merkel government's call for austerity is perceived as a self-interested plea that would only stifle growth, not stimulate it. Pushing relentlessly for a Europe that abides by its vision, Germany risks losing many of its partners and turning its friends into skeptics.

Furthermore, the Merkel government's preferred solutions for the future of the eurozone would carry underestimated financial and political costs for Germany itself, making voters less likely to go along with its plans. A political bargain enabling the great leap forward toward a European political union could involve countries' sharing debt responsibilities, forming a banking union, and transferring money across political borders—all of which would impose great costs and risks on German taxpayers.

Moving forward, eurozone countries will most likely establish what is known as a liability union, sharing responsibility for one another's debts, either private (in the banking sector) or public. Neither of these outcomes would match Germany's preference for minimizing collective risks. Even pushing Greece out of the eurozone, so that Germany would not have to back it up, would probably lead to some sort of joint liability. If Greece leaves the eurozone, bank runs and bond market contagion would threaten the rest of the common currency area and require immense financial firewalls, a mutualization of debt, and some sort of union in the banking sector. If it pushes Greece to the brink, Germany may end up having to accept substantial responsibility for the rest of Europe's fiscal and financial woes. And it would have to do so in an uncontrolled way, without being able to guarantee any further economic coordination or regulation of member states' budgets.

Berlin needs to be aware that stabilizing the euro and reforming the EU will not lead to a Germanized Europe. And indeed, Germany's leaders are already coming to realize the limits of their particular vision. They know that the measures taken under strong German influence in 2010–11 were not sufficient to contain the crisis, which can be achieved only through further integration and reforms following a long negotiation process. Germany alone will not be able to push reluctant member states into surrendering more of their national sovereignty, nor will it be able to determine the outcome of the process. If it is to exert a strong influence, Berlin must reestablish close ties with Paris and buttress that partnership by bringing various other countries on board to advocate for deeper integration. This new openness will have to include both eurozone countries—to consolidate the common currency—as well as outsiders such as the United Kingdom and Poland, whose inclusion will be necessary to reshape the institutions of the EU. Germany must take the lead in building bridges between south and north, between givers and takers, and between the pro-austerity and pro-growth caucuses.

In short, it is unlikely that Germany will be able to dictate how Europe resolves its sovereign debt crisis or reforms its institutions. Going it alone is not possible, because even the biggest payer and member state cannot unilaterally shape the rules. The coalitions necessary to rebuild the economic and political architecture of Europe will dilute German plans. Market pressure on crisis countries may have allowed Berlin, for some time, to implement its supply-side policy approach in the eurozone. But the crisis will not enable Germany to push through, without restriction, its own vision of European integration.

# Europe's Optional Catastrophe

## The Fate of the Monetary Union Lies in Germany's Hands

*Sebastian Mallaby*

Two decades ago, when the European currency system was last on the brink of collapse, the ultimate question was how much Germany, the continent's economic powerhouse, would do to save it. The peripheral economies were hurting, weighed down by a monetary policy that was appropriate for Germany but too austere for weaker European countries. Germany's central bank, the Bundesbank, had to make a choice. It could continue to set high interest rates, thus upholding its commitment to stable prices. Or it could cut rates and accept modest inflation—and so save the rest of Europe from a prolonged recession.

We know which option Germany chose then. The Bundesbank brushed off suggestions that it should risk inflation for the sake of European solidarity; speculators correctly concluded that this made a common monetary policy intolerable for the weaker economies of Europe; and in September 1992, the continent's Exchange Rate Mechanism, a precursor of today's euro, shattered under the pressure of attacks from hedge funds. Almost 20 years later, the

SEBASTIAN MALLABY is Paul A. Volcker Senior Fellow for International Economics at the Council on Foreign Relations and the author, most recently, of *More Money Than God: Hedge Funds and the Making of a New Elite.*

world is waiting for a new answer to the same question. How far will Germany go to keep Europe together?

The economist Rudiger Dornbusch observed that in economics, crises take longer to come to a head than you think they will, and then they happen faster than you thought they could. By the time you read this, the eurozone may have splintered. But whether or not that has happened, or soon will, one thing is certain. Since the beginning of the crisis, Germany has had the power to save the monetary union if it wanted to. The union's disintegration would be an optional catastrophe.

## SUPERMAN CENTRAL BANKERS

To see why the euro's failure could be averted, one must first grasp the awesome power of today's central banks. Until World War I, the advanced economies were tethered to the gold standard, meaning that central banks could not print money in unlimited quantities. Likewise, for almost all the years since World War II, the power of the printing press has been checked, first by a diluted version of the gold standard and then by the fear of inflation. But the combination of fiat currencies and economies that are in a slump changes the game. Money, no longer tied to gold or any other firm anchor, can be created instantly, in infinite quantities, on the technocrats' say so. And so long as factories have spare capacity and unemployment keeps wages in check, there is unlikely to be any significant penalty from inflation.

Of course, central banks had this same power in the 1930s, when the world was in a depression and the gold standard had been abandoned. But they hesitated to use it, a decision documented and lamented by monetary historians from Milton Friedman to Ben Bernanke (the current chair of the U.S. Federal Reserve). Since 2008, by contrast, central bankers have been determined to prove that they understand history's lessons. Appearing on Capitol Hill shortly after the investment bank Lehman Brothers filed for bankruptcy in 2008, Bernanke himself informed Barney Frank, then chair of the House Financial Services Committee, that the Federal

Reserve would stabilize the insurer AIG at a cost of more than $80 billion. "Do you have $80 billion?" Frank asked. "We have $800 billion," Bernanke responded. In fact, by December 2008, the Fed had extended fully $1.5 trillion in emergency financing to markets, dwarfing the $700 billion bailout fund authorized by Congress through the Troubled Asset Relief Program (TARP).

Central banks on the other side of the Atlantic have acted with equal resolve. For much of 2011, Europe's political leadership bickered about the details of the European Financial Stability Facility (EFSF), a TARP-like bailout fund with an intended firepower of 440 billion euros. Then, one day last December, the European Central Bank provided 489 billion euros to the continent's ailing banks, and in February 2012, it repeated this stunt, effectively conjuring the equivalent of two EFSFs out of thin air through the magic of the printing press. Since the start of 2007, the ECB has purchased financial assets totaling 1.7 trillion euros, expanding its portfolio from 13 percent to over 30 percent of the eurozone's GDP. That means that the ECB has printed enough money to increase its paper wealth by an amount exceeding the value of eight years of Greek output.

This superman act has, at least as of this writing, saved the euro system from breaking up. Without the central bank's extraordinary support, private banks across the eurozone would have struggled to raise money and would have collapsed. Private firms, unable to take out bank loans, would also have gone under. The debtor countries would not have been able to rely on banks to purchase their government bonds and thus would have defaulted, in turn devastating the private banks that already held their bonds. The ECB's printing of money duly improved sentiment in the market. The interest rate on Italy's ten-year bonds, for example, tumbled, from around seven percent to about 5.5 percent, although it has since risen.

The ECB will eventually use up its room for maneuver. Some observers fear that the sheer volume of freshly minted euros is bound to lead to serious inflation, either when money begins to circulate faster or when the mere prospect of that event creates self-fulfilling inflationary expectations. But the best bet is that, with growth flat and unemployment over ten percent, the threat of inflation spiking across the continent is remote: with plenty of spare capacity on hand, any rise in demand will be met with increases in supply rather than with higher prices. For the foreseeable future, therefore, the ECB can keep on printing money to prop up banks. It can expand its modest direct purchases of government securities to ensure that finance ministries can raise money at less than punitive interest rates. It could even extend its support to nonfinancial firms, for example, by announcing that it stands ready to hold loans to small businesses on its own balance sheet. Most obviously, the ECB can help manage the crisis by keeping short-term interest rates low.

Increasing the money supply is sometimes dismissed as a mere palliative. But in addition to propping up banks, businesses, and governments, easy money can facilitate structural adjustment. If the ECB prints enough money to hit its target of two percent inflation across the continent, this is likely to mean zero inflation in the crisis countries, where unemployment is high, and three to four percent inflation in Europe's strong economies, where workers are confident enough to demand wage increases. By delivering on its inflation target, in other words, the ECB can help Italy and Spain compete against Germany and the Netherlands, gradually eroding the gap in labor costs that lies at the heart of Europe's troubles. At the same time, a determined and sustained period of monetary easing would probably weaken the euro. That would boost the competitiveness of the crisis economies against the rest of the world, further increasing the odds of an export-led recovery.

In short, the ECB has real power. It can avert a market meltdown and at the same time gradually make the periphery more competitive. But for the ECB to deliver on its potential, Germany must resolve not to get in the way. It must allow for an expansion of the ECB's innovative rescue measures and accept German inflation of three to four percent. Over the past year, unfortunately,

German financial leaders have sent mixed signals. The big question of 1992—how far would Germany go for the sake of European solidarity?—has not been clearly answered. And so Europe's future remains cloudy.

## THE PATH OUT

Germany's leaders are correct that the countries in crisis must earn their own recoveries; the ECB cannot save them on its own. In particular, they must improve the administration of public finances, cracking down on tax evasion and wasteful spending, and remove product and labor-market regulations that undermine competitiveness. But these reforms tend to pay off in the long term. In the short term, slashing budgets will shrink demand and quell growth, while some labor-market reforms that make it easier to fire workers may initially drive up unemployment, undermine consumer confidence, and reduce growth further. The most urgent complements to the ECB's response therefore lie elsewhere—and they demand initiative from Germany.

Germany first needs to recalibrate its attitude toward public finances in the periphery. Thus far, the German strategy has emphasized deficit reduction, on the theory that countries that borrow less will accumulate less debt in the long run. But because deficit reduction keeps an economy from growing, it may defeat its own purpose. Over the past year, the eurozone has indeed cut deficits sharply, but the debt-to-GDP ratio has worsened. Germany needs to accept that aggressive austerity programs are neither politically sustainable nor economically wise. To get its debt under control, a country must attack its debt stock directly.

If Europe's leaders had mounted a forceful response earlier in the crisis, they could have imposed a meaningful debt reduction on private creditors across the continent. But by now, most private creditors have sold out, transferring their debt to the International Monetary Fund, the ECB, and other official creditors. (To be sure, private European banks hold large portfolios of European government bonds. But since the public sector stands ready to bail out these banks, they are not true private creditors.) Last year's restructuring of Greece's debt illustrated the problem. Almost two years into the Greek crisis, the country's private creditors were forced to accept a reduction of about 65 percent in the value of their claims. But at that point, most private creditors had already shed their government debt, so the resulting debt relief for Greece was far short of what the country needed to fix its finances.

Given that governments in the surplus countries and multilateral lenders have become significant creditors to the crisis countries, debt relief has to involve leniency on their part. This is unlikely to take the form of an explicit reduction in debt claims: the credibility of the International Monetary Fund and the ECB would suffer too much from an admission that their loans can be defaulted on. Nor is it likely to involve taxpayers in Europe's core explicitly paying off debts owed by the periphery: that would be politically explosive. The most plausible route to debt reduction is to create a eurozone bond, so that part of the debt of the crisis countries can be replaced by debt issued by the whole region. The German government's economic advisers have put forward a plan that would achieve this goal; now, the government needs to embrace it.

In addition to tackling governments' debt overhangs, Europe's leaders need to shore up the continent's banking system, which has been plagued by a surfeit of bad loans and, until recently at least, a deficit of honesty about them. Until the banks confess that loans to unemployed homeowners or ailing businesses won't be repaid on time, and until they set aside capital to cover their losses, their unacknowledged frailty will inhibit their lending: too few individuals and businesses will be able to borrow money, and growth will remain anemic. Moreover, the banks' return to health is a precondition for restoring confidence in the market, since the possibility of costly bank failures casts a shadow over the crisis countries. For the moment, the ECB's generous financing has guaranteed the banks' liquidity, inoculating them against the lending strike they have suffered in the private bond markets. But if millions of depositors begin to desert the banks at once, the ECB's liquidity may not be enough, and no amount of liquidity can address the banks' solvency. Unless banks keep more capital on hand, they risk collapse. Private investors are unlikely to provide these funds, and the governments of the crisis countries are too stretched to do the job alone. Some of the money will therefore have to come from stronger European governments.

## GERMANY'S CHOICE

In 1992, Germany prioritized managing its own economy over supporting European integration. It then seemed to show remorse and came around to supporting the creation of a common European currency. Despite the clear risks in binding disparate economies to a single monetary policy, the political drive to unite Europe won out. "The history of the European monetary unification is characterized by slow, but steady, progress in the face of constant skepticism and predictions of catastrophes," Otmar Issing, a German member of the ECB's executive board, proclaimed in 2001. "The launch of the single monetary policy was a resounding success."

Yet despite Issing's triumphalism, Germany today seems confused about which way it wants to go. The weight of blood and history argues in favor of keeping Europe together, and Germany's industrial captains understand that their success as exporters would be choked off by a return to a strong national currency. At the same time, however, Germany's leaders resist even modest inflation and are understandably wary of backing up other countries' debt or rescuing their banking systems. Germany is of course free to choose whichever path it wants. But if it replays 1992, the "resounding success" of the euro will go down in history as a resounding failure.

resolve each successive stage of the crisis by cooperating and sharing decision-making powers. They have created a host of new continent-wide institutions, built a substantial financial firewall to prevent debt problems from spreading, and are now well on their way to creating a banking union and a partial fiscal union. When the dust settles, the common currency, and indeed the entire project of European integration, is likely not only to survive but to emerge even stronger.

## WATCH WHAT THEY DO, NOT WHAT THEY SAY

The European crisis is rooted in a failure of institutional design. The Economic and Monetary Union (EMU) that Europe adopted in the 1990s comprised an extensive, if incomplete, monetary union, anchored by the euro and the European Central Bank (ECB). But it included virtually no economic union: no fiscal union, no banking union, no shared economic governance institutions, and no meaningful coordination of structural economic policies.

The EMU's architects assumed that economic union would inexorably follow monetary union. But European countries faced no pressure to create one during the years of expansion prior to the Great Recession. When the crisis hit, the absence of crucial policy tools constrained Europe's ability to reach a solution quickly, triggering severe market reactions that continue to this day. Europe now has only two options. It can jettison the monetary union, or it can adopt a complementary economic union. Given how much is at stake, Europe will almost certainly complete the original concept of a comprehensive economic and monetary union.

From its creation in the 1990s, the common currency has lacked the institutions necessary to ensure that financial stability can be restored during times of acute uncertainty and market volatility. The task before the eurozone's leaders today therefore consists of much more than putting together a financial bailout sufficient to restore market confidence. They must rewrite the eurozone's rule book and complete the half-built euro house. This will require both creative financial engineering to resolve the immediate crisis and the establishment of a wave of new institutions to strengthen the real economy and restore growth.

To divine the likely trajectory of the euro, one should look at what the Europeans have done rather than what they have said. They have resolved the many crises that have threatened the integration project throughout its more than six-decade history in ways that ultimately resulted in a more unified Europe. At each key stage of the current crisis, they have done whatever was necessary to avoid the euro's collapse. In the crunch, both Germany and the ECB—the continent's financial powerhouses—have demonstrated that they will pay whatever is necessary to avert disaster.

The problem for the markets is that for two reasons these central players cannot say outright that they will always come to the euro's rescue. First, an explicit commitment to unlimited bailouts would represent the ultimate moral hazard. It would relieve the debtor countries of the pressure their leaders need to sell tough political decisions to their parliaments and publics in order to effectively adjust their economies.

Indeed, it is the intention of neither Germany nor the ECB to end the crisis quickly. Rather, their goal is to use the crisis to further the economic reforms needed to create a strong European economy over the long run. This helps explain why the eurozone authorities have not built as large a financial firewall as the markets have craved.

Second, each of the four main classes of creditors—Germany and the other strong northern European governments, the ECB, private-sector lenders, and the International Monetary Fund (acting as a conduit for funding from non-EU governments, such as Beijing)—will naturally try to transfer as much as possible of the cost of a financial rescue to the other three.

Europe's financial turmoil, then, is not only a crisis of faulty institutions; it is also one of presentation. The markets will not receive the sweeping declarations that they want and so will periodically revert to states of high anxiety. But every policymaker in Europe and even the European publics know that the collapse of the euro would be a political and economic disaster. And fortunately, since Europe is an affluent region, solving the crisis is a matter of mobilizing the political will to pay, rather than the economic ability.

Each of Europe's key political actors will exhaust all options in trying to secure the best possible deal for itself before at the last minute coming to an agreement. The result is a messy process, exacerbated by the cacophony of voices within each country, which understandably unsettles markets. The possibility of miscalculation will continue to loom over Europe. But pressure from the financial markets will ultimately prod the eurozone to find the way forward. And Europe's overriding political imperative to preserve the project of integration will drive its leaders to secure the euro and restore the economic health of the continent.

## AN IMPERFECT UNION

More than anything else, the project of European integration was driven by the geopolitical goal of halting the carnage that had ravaged the continent for centuries and reached its murderous zenith in the first half of the twentieth century. This overriding imperative has driven successive generations of political leaders to subordinate their states' national sovereignty to the greater goal of maintaining and extending the European project.

The region's vision of that project always included the concept of a common currency. In early plans for monetary integration, such as the 1970 Werner report and the 1989 Delors report, monetary union was supposed to go hand in hand with an economic union that would place binding constraints on member states. But when the common currency finally came to be, it was not because of a carefully considered and detailed economic analysis. It was instead a result of geopolitics. The unforeseen shock of German reunification in October 1990—and the fear this produced in Paris of a newly dominant Germany—provided the impetus for the Maastricht Treaty of 1992, which paved the way for the creation of the euro.

The imperative of quickly launching the euro meant that politically necessary compromises, rather than unambiguous rules, would determine the currency's framework. For example, since the founding members of the eurozone came from very different economic starting points, it was politically infeasible to impose firm fiscal criteria for membership. As a result, by 2005, the eurozone was a common currency area that was composed of very dissimilar countries, lacked a central fiscal authority or any way to enforce budget discipline, and had made virtually no progress toward bringing its countries' macroeconomic policies into line.

Initially, none of these design flaws mattered. But as borrowing costs in private financial markets across the eurozone fell toward the traditionally low interest rates of Germany, many new members suddenly had access to unprecedented amounts of credit regardless of their economic fundamentals. The financial markets failed to assess the riskiness of different countries, and European leaders continued to deny any problems in the common currency's design. As a result, in the run-up to the global financial crisis, governments and private sectors built up unsustainable amounts of debt. So when the eurozone was finally struck by its first serious financial crisis in 2009, it had to contend not only with huge debt overhangs but also with a faulty institutional design that prevented an expeditious solution.

## PLAYING CHICKEN

The eurozone was woefully unprepared for the Great Recession. It entered the crisis as a common currency zone flying on just one engine—the ECB—without the kind of unified fiscal entity that traditionally helps countries combat large financial crises. The eurozone's leaders have had to build from scratch their crisis-fighting capacities and bailout institutions: the European Financial Stability Facility (EFSF) and, subsequently, the European Stability Mechanism. And in the midst of stemming an immediate crisis, they have had to reform the flawed foundational institutions of the area.

The ECB, as the only eurozone institution capable of affecting financial markets in real time, wields tremendous power. Its institutional independence is enshrined in the EU treaty, and it does not answer to any government. Unlike normal central banks, which always have to worry about losing their independence, the ECB in this crisis has been able to issue direct political demands to national leaders, as in August 2011, when it conveyed an ultimatum for reform to then Italian Prime Minister Silvio Berlusconi and engineered his ouster when he failed to comply.

On the other hand, unlike the Federal Reserve in the United States, the ECB has not had the luxury of responding to the crisis within a fixed set of national institutions. When the financial crisis hit the United States, the Federal Reserve could immediately create trillions of dollars to steady market confidence with the knowledge that it had a federal government that could formulate a longer-term response (although it has not yet fully done so). The ECB cannot act similarly because there is no eurozone fiscal entity to which it can hand off responsibility. Moreover, to commit to a major monetary rescue would undermine the chances of a permanent political resolution to the eurozone's underlying problem: a lack of effective institutions. Were the ECB to cap governments' financing costs at no more than five percent, for instance, national politicians would probably never adopt the adjustment policies and structural reforms they need to sustain economic growth in the long run.

Saddled with administering a common currency and endowed with governing institutions flawed by early political compromises, the ECB is, not suprisingly, focused on forcing the eurozone's leaders to prioritize reforms. It is not the primary purpose of the ECB to end market anxieties and thus resolve the eurozone crisis as soon as possible. It instead aims to induce national leaders to fundamentally reform the eurozone's institutions and structurally overhaul their economies. The central bank cannot directly compel democratically elected leaders to comply with its wishes, but it can refuse to bail their countries out and thereby permit the crisis to pressure them to act.

So far, the ECB has been quite effective in its strategic bargaining with national authorities. The initial Greek crisis in May 2010 led to a deal whereby the ECB agreed to set up the Securities Markets Program to buy European sovereign bonds in exchange for a commitment from the eurozone governments of 440 billion euros for the newly created EFSF, which proved to be an effective way of channeling resources to Greece, Ireland, and Portugal.

The EFSF, however, would simply not be large enough to rescue Italy and Spain. So in August 2011, the ECB itself bought Italian and Spanish bonds to drive down their interest costs. In return, Rome and Madrid committed to making specific reforms, such as substantial budget tightening, detailed by the ECB in secret letters to their leaders. Then, in December 2011, the ECB provided the continent's banks with huge amounts of fresh liquidity in the form of three-year loans as a quid pro quo for the eurozone's governments to agree to the new European fiscal compact, which seeks to assure budget discipline. Most recently, in June 2012, after the eurozone governments agreed to accept common banking supervision, the ECB signaled a willingness to provide targeted support for Spanish banks and subsequently reduced its benchmark interest rate.

And yet at each stage of the crisis, many pundits and even serious economists have proclaimed the end of the euro. This outlook utterly fails to recognize just how effective the type of bargaining described above has been. All the key political decision-makers in Europe—the ECB, Germany, France, Italy, Spain, and even Greece—harbor no illusions about the catastrophic costs of the common currency's collapse. Most Greek politicians and voters, as evidenced by the latest elections, know that without the euro, their country would become a vulnerable economic wasteland. German Chancellor Angela Merkel knows that were the eurozone to disintegrate, Germany's banks would also fall under the weight of their losses on loans to the periphery; the new deutsche mark would skyrocket, undermining the entire German export economy; and

Germany would once again be blamed for destroying Europe. The ECB, of course, would not want to put itself out of business.

These actors are playing a game of political chicken, but in the end, they will all compromise. Once Germany and the ECB feel they have gotten the best possible deal, they will pay whatever it takes to hold the eurozone together. Neither can afford the alternative. But neither can say so in advance.

It is still possible that Greece will abandon the common currency. But this would leave the eurozone stronger, not weaker, because it would be rid of its weakest economy. The eurozone would address a Greek exit by bolstering its financial firewall and speeding the pace of integration, particularly by creating a banking union, in order to counter the resulting risks of contagion. Most important, the total chaos that would descend on Greece would prompt the other debtor countries to do whatever was necessary to avoid suffering the same fate. Europe's leaders should try to prevent a Greek exit if at all possible, and they will probably do so, but its occurrence would certainly not doom the euro.

## LIVE LONG AND PROSPER

The eurozone has already taken some decisive steps to complete its economic and monetary union. It decided at the EU summit in June to implement a banking union, jointly supervised and regulated, with the authority to shut failed banks and to provide regionwide deposit insurance to prevent bank runs. The eurozone countries have begun to develop a partial fiscal union by sharing responsibility for modest amounts of debt and by adopting firm common rules for budget discipline. And more and more European leaders have talked about moving toward some sort of political union that would address the questions of democratic legitimacy that surround these economic reforms.

It is thus highly likely that the eurozone will emerge from the crisis having done more than just fix the flawed institutions that produced much of the current difficulties. As in the continent's past crises, national governments will move to preserve the project of integration by enlarging Europe's mandate even further.

Even the most successful financial and institutional engineering will ultimately fail, however, if the debtor countries cannot get their economies to grow again. This is a difficult task in almost all high-income countries, including the United States, due to the prolonged slowdown that inevitably follows financial crises and the subsequent need to reduce debt levels. But there must be light at the end of the tunnel if the eurozone's strategy is to succeed.

Restoring growth will require at least three major steps. First, in addition to controlling their deficits, the borrowing countries must adopt convincing structural reforms. In particular, they must increase the flexibility of their labor markets by easing firing procedures and thus encouraging hiring, by raising retirement ages as part of pension reforms, and by allowing for collective bargaining within industries or even firms instead of only on the national level. They need to open up restricted professions, especially in their service sectors. And they should boost productivity by intensifying competition, especially by helping small firms and start-ups grow rapidly. Recent studies by the Organization for Economic Cooperation and Development have demonstrated that although some structural reforms pay off only in the long term, others can bring faster growth and increased competitiveness in as little as three years. Meanwhile, the fiscal tightening that comes with budgetary austerity will lead to lower interest rates and more investment in the debtor countries, also spurring economic growth.

Second, the strong economies in the northern core of Europe, especially Germany, must stop focusing on deficit reduction for a while and generate more spending and inflation. They should buy more of Greece's and Italy's goods and services and less of their debt. For years, Germany kept its wages and domestic spending too low, creating competitiveness problems for the rest of Europe, and it now needs to help offset those results.

Finally, the eurozone needs to continue working on a continent-wide stimulus program. At the June 2012 EU summit, the EU member states agreed to boost spending by roughly one percent of the region's GDP. The pending relaxation of deficit-reduction targets in some of the debtor countries will also help them grow, as will the ECB's recent decision to cut interest rates by 0.25 percent. But the eurozone can do considerably more on all these fronts. The ECB can stimulate the economy through quantitative easing, and European countries can jointly issue so-called project bonds aimed at boosting spending on infrastructure. These bonds would simultaneously accelerate the continent's progress toward fiscal union.

As it stumbles forward, the eurozone must combine the financial engineering that is necessary to overcome the immediate crisis with a growth strategy to restore the area to economic vitality. Fortunately, the way the eurozone's leaders have responded to the current turmoil suggests that the economic self-interests of all the key countries, creditor as well as debtor, will coalesce. The markets, too, might come to understand this reality and start betting on the euro rather than against it.

After Europe adopted a common currency, it took almost ten years for the first serious economic and political crisis to hit. Now that it has arrived, Europe must use the opportunity it presents to get the continent's basic economic institutions right and complete the euro's half-built house. This process will require more treaty revisions and fixes to the eurozone's institutions. If the history of the continent's integration is any guide, however, Europe will emerge from its current turmoil not only with the euro intact but also with stronger institutions and far better economic prospects for the future.

# Avoiding the Next Eurozone Crisis

## How to Build an EU that Works

*Lorenzo Bini Smaghi*

T he Greek debt crisis has shaken the euro just in time for its 10th birthday. This latest challenge should have come as no surprise; it would have been a miracle had the currency been immune to such problems. If anything, the past few years have shown that although the euro is a remarkable construct, it is incomplete: the eurozone is financially unified but not yet politically unified enough. This deficiency underlies the euro's current problems and makes them more difficult to address.

Monetary unity entails a much greater degree of political unity than many European commentators, politicians, academics, and publics assumed it would. In a monetary union, political decisions taken in one country affect the economies of other countries in very direct and sometimes dramatic ways. This means that many national problems can only be dealt with jointly, across the whole currency area. The Greek economy accounts for only two percent of eurozone GDP, but its current sovereign debt crisis is causing economic instability throughout the whole region. It needs to be resolved through tough political decisions in both Athens and Brussels; it will be up to the Greek government to implement any economic adjustment program, but the financing for that plan is in the European Council's hands.

LORENZO BINI SMAGHI is a member of the Executive Board of the European Central Bank.

The EU's current institutional framework does not allow for smooth European decisionmaking. Political life in Europe is still essentially domestic. Economic policies are created individually, and largely with national interests in mind. There are very few bodies that hold a eurozone-wide perspective, the European Central Bank being one of them. Unlike other institutions that coordinate policy among eurozone nations, the ECB is tasked with implementing a single monetary policy—one interest rate—for all of them. This forces it to look at the overall macroeconomic and financial picture.

It has proved difficult for countries that have already started recovering from the 2008 economic recession—Germany being the main one—to grasp the global ramifications of the Greek debt problem, the potential for contagion, and the risks to taxpayers. In May 2010, the German parliament had called on Jean-Claude Trichet, the president of the ECB, and Dominique Strauss-Kahn, the head of the International Monetary Fund, to explain the eurozone-wide risks associated with the brewing Greek crisis. Berlin saw no evident danger, but Trichet and Strauss-Kahn reminded that all eurozone countries, including Germany, would eventually feel the effects of a weakened euro.

For its part, Germany, along with the Netherlands and others, has even suggested that private creditors bear part of the burden to finance Greece's fiscal restructuring. This seems a good idea in theory—why should taxpayers in the rest of the EU bail out irresponsible Greek banks? Yet, in the midst of this crisis, forcing the private sector to take on losses could end up costing taxpayers even more. The reason has to do with the structure of Greek debt. In other emerging economies, debt is spread among many foreign and national lenders, who can each absorb small losses. But most of Greece's debt is held within the country by a few private banks. They could never shoulder a debt writedown and would collapse. In the end, the EU would have to bail out both the banks and the Greek economy—a much more expensive proposition. In spite of these higher costs, policymakers in several countries believe that the only way they can get domestic support for the Greek bailout is if banks are seen as paying part of the bill.

Nation-level decisionmaking is problematic in another way. Many of the European Council's decisions during the crisis, particularly those related to bailouts and financial assistance, required unanimity among the representatives of member states. Yet each of those representatives answers to a national government, which, in turn, answers to a parliament. Each of those parliaments has a slightly different set of goals, procedures, and concerns. While Germany demands that Greek banks accept losses, for example, Finland has requested collateral in exchange for providing aid. Such different approaches among members paralyzed the EU's efforts to address the crisis.

With its current structure, the European Council risks being paralysed as the Polish-Lithuanian Commonwealth, a council that ruled over both Poland and Lithuania in the sixteenth and seventeenth centuries, in which any member could block any decision. The commonwealth ended with economic decline, political turmoil, and eventual partition among the Austrian, Prussian, and Russian empires. So how should the eurozone avoid such a fate? There are three components to strengthening the EU's capacity to make collective decisions: first, drop the requirements for unanimity for some cases; second, strengthen the rules that constrain national decisionmaking; and third, enforce all of the EU's rules better.

Strengthening collective decisionmaking would require the EU to modify the rules of the European Financial Stability Facility, so that bailout decisions can be made by a qualified majority (as is the case in the IMF, for example) instead of a unanimity. This may not happen in the short run, but the risk of paralysis and worsening of the crisis might prompt some rethinking on the issue.

The second component—strengthening the rules to constrain national decisionmaking-- is already underway. This year's EU governance reform package includes proposals are to streamline procedures for economic surveillance and allow for sanctions to kick in automatically whenever a eurozone country breaks the

Stability and Growth Pact's rules. But these plans do not go far enough. In particular, the Stability and Growth Pact, signed by all eurozone members to avoid excessive budget deficits, should be modified to ensure compliance among all countries. In any event, the European Parliament has made progress by taking on the issue. It remains to be seen how successful its efforts will be.

Even if the structure of the EU remained unchanged, individual governments could do more to abide by common fiscal rules. For instance, they could introduce their own debt ceilings consistent with the EU's stability programs. Such measures would halt excessive debt growth even before EU procedures were initiated. Rather like neighborhood watch programs, national debt ceilings would spread policing responsibilities and involve national parliaments and fiscal institutions in enforcing them.

Debt ceilings, however, contain an inherent "good times" bias—most include no mechanisms to prevent governments from busting through them in times of emergency. One way to police debt ceilings (and to ensure that decisions are in the collective interest) would be to give the EU responsibility for issuing public debt in the eurozone. Member states would no longer have the ability to issue debt to cover expenses over the limit.

Had such measures, known as debt breaks, been in place all along, Greece would neither have been able to expand its debt in 2009 nor hide it. By refusing to issue more debt to Greece, the EU would have forced the country to take corrective measures at a much earlier stage. In that situation, Greece would have had to come up with immediate additional financing on its own—either by sharply cutting expenditures or by raising taxes—or else request the support of the European Stability Mechanism, which finances strict economic adjustment programs. In both scenarios, the damage to the rest of the eurozone would have been more contained than it was this past year.

This is not the same as issuing bonds on behalf of the whole EU in the form of Eurobonds, as some commentators and politicians have proposed. For Eurobonds to work, the eurozone would have to have a federal system of taxation and revenue transfers. Under a debt-brakes system, national treasuries would still be responsible for their own debt, and fiscal instruments would still differ from country to country, but the total amount of debt allowed for each would have to be agreed on at the EU level—and the decision would be binding.

The third component needed for better eurozone policy is stronger enforcement of existing rules. In this respect, the eurozone faces its own version of the old impossible trinity in economics: just as countries cannot have a fixed exchange rate, free capital movement, and an independent monetary policy all at once, the eurozone can't function if the three enforcing institutions of the Stability and Growth Pact (the Council of Ministers, the European Commission, and the IMF) do not operate properly. The eurozone needs an enforcement mechanism that can both monitor domestic policies and ensure that they are compatible with the union.

The second part of that trinity—the European Commission's willingness to police—is probably the readiest for being given a stronger role. The EU could give the Economic and Monetary Affairs Commissioner, one of the commission's 27 members, more power to independently review national budgets, rigorously enforce EU rules, and suggest course corrections for countries with poor fiscal policies. This can be achieved without redrafting the European Commission's charter. If that still does not work, additional institutional changes may be required—for example, the creation of a European finance minister, as Trichet recently proposed. The minister would have special powers to intervene in national fiscal policies when they get out of order.

The EU's current institutional framework cannot manage fiscal problems effectively. This does not mean that it is too late to build one that can. Many European citizens want to know why the EU did not monitor Greece's economy before the crisis—indeed, why the country was even allowed to adopt the euro to begin with if the EU framework could not ensure that its economic practices were sustainable. It is time to turn the monetary union into a stronger political union.

Europe's union has no modern precedent. It demands original thinking, as much as, if not more than, that of the United States' Founding Fathers. It also requires similar political courage and leadership.

# Europe After the Crisis

## How to Sustain a Common Currency

*Andrew Moravcsik*

From the start, the euro has rested on a gamble. When European leaders opted for monetary union in 1992, they wagered that European economies would converge toward one another: the deficit-prone countries of southern Europe would adopt German economic standards—lower price inflation and wage growth, more saving, and less spending—and Germany would become a little more like them, by accepting more government and private spending and higher wage and price inflation. This did not occur. Now, with the euro in crisis, the true implications of this gamble are becoming clear.

Over the past two years, the eurozone members have done a remarkable job managing the short-term symptoms of the crisis, although the costs have been great. Yet the long-term challenge remains: making European economies converge, that is, assuring that their domestic macroeconomic behaviors are sufficiently similar to one another to permit a single monetary policy at a reasonable cost. For this to happen, both creditor countries, such as Germany, and the deficit countries in southern Europe must align their trends in public spending, competitiveness, inflation, and other areas.

Aligning the continent's economies will first require Europe to reject the common misdiagnoses of today's crisis. The problem is

ANDREW MORAVCSIK is Professor of Politics and International Affairs and Director of the European Union Program at Princeton University's Woodrow Wilson School of Public and International Affairs.

not primarily one of profligate public sectors or broken private sectors in debtor countries. It is rather the result of a fundamental disequilibrium within the single currency zone, which applies a single monetary policy and a single exchange rate to a diverse group of countries. Policy proposals for budgetary austerity, the micromanagement of national budgets, fiscal federalism, bailouts, or large funds to stave off speculators are insufficient to solve this problem alone. Instead, Europeans should trust in the essentially democratic nature of the EU, which will encourage them to distribute the costs of convergence more fairly within and among countries. The burden must be shifted from Europe's public sectors and deficit countries to its private sectors and surplus countries. If this does not occur, the survival of the euro will be called into question and Europe will face a long-term economic catastrophe that could drain its wealth and power for the rest of this decade and beyond.

## A RISKY BET

Since Europe began cooperating on monetary issues in the 1970s, nearly every agreement has been negotiated on terms set primarily by Germany. The 1992 Maastricht Treaty, which committed Europeans to the euro, was no exception. Germany's main motivation for a single currency, contrary to popular belief, was neither to aid its reunification nor to realize an idealistic federalist scheme for European political union. It was rather to promote its own economic welfare through open markets, a competitive exchange rate, and anti-inflationary monetary policy. Most German business and government leaders believed then and believe now that the European economy would be best supported by independent central banks that are like their own Bundesbank, which almost always prioritizes low inflation over growth or employment.

In France, Italy, Spain, and other countries that have traditionally had weaker currencies, politicians viewed monetary union in part as a means to emulate Germany's success by committing themselves to low inflation and low interest rates, reforming the structures of their economies, and encouraging cross-border investment.

Yet they also saw the euro as an instrument to bring Germany closer to their own economic models, thereby relaxing external constraints and competitive pressures on their economies. These weak-currency countries had suffered many debt and exchange-rate crises in the 1970s and 1980s that were driven by the gaps in prices, spending, and wages between themselves and Germany. To avoid repeating this, they hoped to encourage Germany to accept a European structure that would allow for higher domestic spending, wage increases, and inflation. The two approaches would meet somewhere in the middle.

It didn't work. Even Jacques Delors, who was president of the European Commission from 1985 to 1995 and who is often considered to be the father of the euro, told me shortly after the Maastricht Treaty was negotiated that he saw the single currency as a failure because he had been unable to persuade the Germans to compromise. Berlin's nonnegotiable demand in exchange for monetary union was a European central bank that would be even more independent in its design and even more anti-inflationary in its mandate than the old Bundesbank. No provision was made for fiscal transfers or bailouts among European states.

From the start, then, the single currency imposed high risks on some European governments. If deficit countries, such as Greece and Italy, could not persuade Germany to change its behavior, then they were betting their future prosperity on their own abilities to adopt German standards of wage discipline, government spending, and international competitiveness. These were ambitious goals, because such standards are deeply embedded in national social compromises and political histories. The eurozone had to become more of what economists call an "optimal currency area," in which economic behavior is similar enough to justify a single monetary policy.

In practice, getting there would be very difficult, because the euro system required governments to surrender the tools that they had traditionally used to offset their gap with Germany. These had included unilateral control over interest rates and the money supply, restrictions on capital flows, and the manipulation of exchange rates. Faced with a debt or competitiveness crisis, a country would have to act directly to push down economic activity through wages, private consumption, business investment, and government spending. This is a risky course for any government, because it imposes immediate and visible costs across the entire society. Yet the creators of the euro apparently thought other European countries would be able to converge on something resembling the German model, or that Germany itself would relent, because they made few provisions to address bank collapses, sovereign debt crises, or other potential consequences of failure.

## GROWING APART

At first, other European economies seemed to bring their policies in line with Germany's, as optimists had expected. Weak-currency governments restrained wages, government spending, and consumption—or presented statistics that made it seem as if they had done so. Adopting the euro reduced interest rates for these countries and encouraged northern European lending to their economies, stimulating growth.

Yet underneath the surface, the eurozone was a ticking time bomb. Europe's economies once again grew apart, the consequences of which were made clear after the U.S. and British financial collapses in 2008. Deficit governments immediately came under pressure from international markets: speculative domestic markets crashed, interest rates rose, external debts ballooned, and growth plummeted. By contrast, Germany, after a short hiccup, has enjoyed an unprecedented economic boom. These disparate trajectories have called into question the viability of the euro.

According to conventional wisdom and the official rhetoric in Germany and elsewhere, the crisis was caused primarily by excessive public spending in a few extravagant eurozone countries. Solving the crisis, and preventing future ones, would therefore simply require imposing tight restraints on government budgets in deficit countries. To this end, the so-called fiscal compact recently negotiated by EU members would, if ratified, enforce budgetary austerity across the continent. Some economists, including Mario Draghi, who now heads the European Central Bank, also believe that cutting budgets is good for growth.

Yet this is a misleading diagnosis. Although some southern European countries, like many Western democracies, might do well to cut government deficits, public profligacy was not the main cause of the crisis. The eurozone countries have relatively prudent fiscal policies; most have run up smaller deficits than Japan, the United Kingdom, and the United States. Greece is the only eurozone country with an average deficit above three percent of GDP, the maximum level permitted by the Maastricht Treaty, and Portugal was the only other one plagued by major public-sector deficits before the crisis. Spain was actually running a surplus. Far more important in causing the crisis was shortsightedness in and lax regulation of the private sector, which bred imprudent banking policies in Ireland, insufficient competition in markets in Italy, and a housing boom gone bad in Spain. Nor is there any reason to blame the crisis on the bankruptcy of the continental social model. The recent solvency and competitiveness of northern European economies suggest that prudent welfare and labor-market reforms can keep the European model viable.

A chorus of German critics, from the tabloid *Bild* to Josef Joffe, the editor of the respectable *Die Zeit*, have blamed the crisis on a unique southern European culture of corruption and inefficiency, which they contrast with northern sobriety. Yet this dichotomy is also misleading. Severe housing and banking crises are hardly specific to southern Europe; they have recently occurred across the Western world. Between 1999 and 2008, despite tough competition from emerging markets and central and eastern Europe, the Greek economy grew by almost a third. All the countries in crisis have nearly matched or surpassed Germany in some combination of growth in gross national product, labor productivity, and hours worked. This explains why ill-fated investment in southern Europe did not come solely from domestic sources; those sober French and

German bankers and bondholders helped finance it with low-interest loans.

Although big deficits and broken private sectors may have been part of the problem, the deeper cause of today's crisis lies in contradictions within the euro system itself. Ten years after adopting a common currency, Europe is still not an optimal currency area. Instead, the single currency exaggerates existing differences and eliminated the policy instruments required to overcome them. Bankruptcy in southern Europe and prosperity in Germany are two sides of the same coin.

Greece, Italy, Portugal, and Spain have spent the last decade accumulating large and increasing current account deficits, and so they are accused of inefficiency and overspending. But German policies are equally to blame for the deficits. At the founding of the euro in 1999, the European Central Bank set a continent-wide two percent target for inflation, based on trends in Germany's labor market. Yet Germany subsequently moved the goalposts by dampening its price and wage growth below that level. To see how this helped cause the crisis, consider the most important component in measuring an economy's external competitiveness: the cost of labor per unit produced, also called unit labor costs, which should ideally rise at the same rate as inflation. Between 1999 and 2008, the average unit labor costs in Greece, Italy, Portugal, and Spain rose by one percent per year over the target, slowly rendering their economies uncompetitive and signaling the need for reform. During the same period in Germany, by contrast, sluggish wage growth, weak domestic consumption, labor-market reforms, and cuts in government spending meant that unit labor costs rose by an average of less than one percent per year, well below the European target. Over a decade, this combination of excessive rises in unit labor costs in some places and wage suppression elsewhere generated a 25 percent overall gap in competitiveness between Germany and its European partners. This chiefly benefited Germany's export sector—the only part of its economy to enjoy net growth over the decade—at the expense not just of foreigners but also of German workers and taxpayers, whose wages were not keeping pace with inflation.

Many observers, and not just in Germany, view Germany's competitiveness as the well-deserved fruit of a decade of domestic reform and restraint, during which the government and unions worked together to deregulate labor markets and dampen wages. Southern European countries, they maintain, should simply emulate Germany's success. There is some truth to this view, but it misses the fact that Germany's wage suppression was excessive, fueling both trade imbalances and imprudent international lending. Because Germany is in the eurozone, its external competitiveness was not offset by a rising currency. Germany's real exchange rate today, under the single currency, is roughly 40 percent below where it would be if the deutsche mark still existed. The result: Germany's trade surplus, at $200 billion a year, is the world's largest, even greater than China's. Forty percent of the surplus comes from Germany's trade within the eurozone—a total roughly equal to the combined deficits of the crisis countries.

Accumulating export surpluses and suppressing domestic consumption, moreover, generated a surplus of capital. German banks and investors lent their extra cash to southern Europe at historically low interest rates, ignoring the longer-term risk. So southern Europe's deficits are as much the fault of northern European lenders as they are the fault of southern European borrowers. In using an undervalued currency to accumulate trade surpluses, Germany is acting like the China of Europe. Yet its eurozone membership spares it from the kind of criticism that China regularly suffers.

This euro-induced disequilibrium helps explains why Germany's export-driven economy has recently been growing at three to four percent per year, while neighboring economies remain mired in crisis. Such large imbalances have historically been more than enough to trigger severe crises in debtor economies. Yet in trying to catch up to Germany, southern European governments are further hampered by the euro system, which stripped them of the main tool they had traditionally employed to keep up with their economically competitive neighbors: currency devaluation. Devaluation reduces the price of exports and increases the price of imports, shifting some of the burden of adjusting to deficits to foreigners whose products have become relatively less competitive. The euro has also forced southern European governments to surrender unilateral control over interest rates and inflation as instruments to tweak prices or reduce their debt burdens. The only remaining policy option deficit countries have to make up for the 25 percent competitiveness gap is to drastically cut wages, private economic activity, and government spending, leading to a reduced level of aggregate consumption. In any country, such direct cuts tend to be controversial, politically costly, and difficult to carry out. Germany, meanwhile, although it bears a large part of the blame for the gap, faces no immediate market pressure to share the cost of adjustment.

## MONEY IN THE BANK

In the face of these tensions, keeping the eurozone together requires European governments first to address the crisis of liquidity by stabilizing debt-ridden countries and shoring up European banks and then, in the long term, to bring about the fundamental convergence of European economies. The eurozone countries appear to have successfully, if perhaps only temporarily, addressed the first challenge. After two years, bank balance sheets have stabilized, stock and bond markets have rebounded, and the immediate pressure on debtor countries has been relieved. To achieve these goals, the EU, reputed to be slow and cautious, has acted with remarkable flexibility.

Starting in May 2010, European leaders created a series of funds that totaled nearly 800 billion euros, including commitments from the International Monetary Fund (IMF) and agreements reached between individual countries, aimed at preventing uncontrolled defaults. A permanent European stability mechanism is slated to take over the function of many of these funds in July of this year, potentially with even more money. The European Central Bank bought bonds from the distressed countries, which were subsequently discounted, although doing so may have violated clauses of the Maastricht Treaty that ban bailouts and monetary financing of budget deficits. In February, European governments forced Greek bondholders to accept a 53 percent loss and lowered the interest rates on the country's remaining debt.

The EU has also stabilized its financial sector. In recent months, the European Central Bank shored up the continent's banking system by offering banks 600 billion euros in three-year loans at the very low interest rate of one percent. It has hinted that it might supply more such loans, if necessary. The EU has passed important new banking regulations, which increase the amount of capital banks must keep on hand, and has clarified its responsibility in regulating banks.

Berlin has exceeded most expectations by consistently supporting such bold actions, in the process taking on great costs and risks. But it has not done so out of idealism or charity, despite Chancellor Angela Merkel's well-timed inspirational calls for greater European political union. Germany is the greatest beneficiary of financial stability and the common currency. A sudden default by a eurozone country or the collapse of the currency itself would devastate the German economy, particularly its export industry. Moreover, because bailouts are unpopular in Germany, EU support for deficit countries has so far offered the most cost-effective and politically expedient way for Berlin to ensure that German banks and bondholders get paid back for their imprudent international loans. It is no surprise, then, that strong support from German businesses has been decisive in ensuring a multiparty majority in the Bundestag behind committing resources to defend the euro.

It is less clear whether the euro serves the long-term interests of the deficit countries. In these countries, the strongest argument for staying in the eurozone has been that the costs of pulling out would be prohibitive. Were Greece to abandon the euro, for example, the costs imposed by the rapid outward flow of capital, the mass bankruptcy of banks and businesses, and the adjustment to a national currency would likely total one trillion euros. And the risks of a

Greek collapse pale in comparison to those of the contagion reaching Italy or Spain.

The American and European media have criticized Merkel for her indecisive leadership, which they say has produced a slow European response focused more on imposing austerity than on rekindling growth. It is true that facing unrealistic expectations for recovery, Germany initially opposed bailouts and debt restructuring and then organized loans at punishing interest rates. Only in October 2011, and largely at the insistence of the IMF, did Europe begin to trim Greek sovereign debt. The best technocratic solution might instead have been for Germany to back a swifter and more generous restructuring of Greek debt, with private bondholders in northern Europe taking their share of the losses, and for the EU to provide more generous funding to pull distressed economies through the recession. This might have prevented those economies from accumulating debt, leaving better prospects for tighter budgets and structural reforms in the long term.

Yet expectations for that kind of outcome underestimate the inherent political difficulty of debt negotiations, which involve bargaining with deficit and creditor governments while worrying about the responses of financial markets and taxpayers. Had Greek debt been forgiven sooner, or had a larger "firewall" been created to protect Italy and Spain from collapse, the incentives for the debtor countries to reform would have diminished. Germany is rightly committed to squeezing significant domestic change out of the process, particularly given its willingness to risk funding other countries without a firm guarantee of repayment. In coping with the short-term consequences of the debt crisis, and in saving a system from which they benefit, German leaders have displayed bolder political leadership than at any other time in the history of European monetary integration.

## WHEN IN ROME, DO AS THE GERMANS DO

Unfortunately, managing the short-term symptoms of the crisis is not enough. Resolving the immediate liquidity crisis has bought

European governments several years to address the deeper challenge: how to encourage fundamental economic convergence. For as long as the eurozone countries continue to take such radically different trajectories regarding labor costs, government spending, private-sector behavior, and competitiveness, Europe will remain no more of an optimal currency area than it was when the euro entered circulation.

Now that they know this, most member states today would probably not opt for a common currency. At the eurozone's founding, proponents justified the currency with the claim that painful short-term adjustments would generate long-term economic health. Now, the argument has been flipped: it may have been ill advised to create the euro, but now that it exists, the short-term benefits of sticking with it (compared with the catastrophic alternative) outweigh the long-term costs.

New reform-minded governments have taken office across Europe, led by Mario Monti in Rome, Mariano Rajoy in Madrid, Pedro Passos Coelho in Lisbon, Lucas Papademos in Athens, and Enda Kenny in Dublin. These governments are committed to making the euro work, but they face tough choices. Opposition politicians in Greece and elsewhere increasingly advocate leaving the eurozone rather than enduring austerity. Meanwhile, prominent German business and economic leaders have suggested that Germany could survive in a smaller northern eurozone or with its own currency, as Sweden has. These issues will be resolved not in Brussels or Frankfurt but in national capitals. Preserving the euro in its current form depends on crafting a politically sustainable compromise on which countries and which groups within those countries will shoulder the burden of getting Europe's disparate economies to converge.

The German view—that the future of the euro rests on countries' making tough reforms and cutting public spending—is partially correct. It would be foolhardy for Germany to assume liabilities for deficit countries without such reforms. That is why Berlin has insisted that the EU fiscal compact require governments to incorporate balanced-budget provisions into their national constitutions. Yet this still leaves unresolved two crucial questions about how to distribute the costs of Europe's adjustment, both within countries and among them.

First, how will Europe's private sectors be reformed? Different private-sector wage and business practices are a greater obstacle to economic convergence than different public-sector spending. Yet it is often unclear exactly how national governments can encourage reforms of wage and business practices or how the EU can assure that such reforms are actually implemented. It is often easier for governments to slash public spending than to impose solutions on powerful banks, corporations, or unions. As a result, even if a crisis originates in the private sector, the cost of stabilization often falls disproportionately on public-sector beneficiaries.

Second, which countries will need to chart new economic paths? Germany benefits greatly from the current system, in which deficit countries must do nearly all the adjusting by cutting spending and Germany provides the funding to assure that they repay their loans, which also serves to bail out northern European banks and bondholders. The new fiscal compact would institutionalize this. Yet imposing the primary cost of recovery on deficit countries in the form of austerity is likely to fail both pragmatically and politically. Economies without growth cannot support or sustain debt reduction or structural reform. Even official EU and IMF reports do not project that the current policies will generate sustainable competitiveness and convergence. This is why even Monti, the technocratic Italian prime minister, recently made clear that the deficit countries could embrace austerity and reform only if Germany changed its policies to accept a greater adjustment burden.

The economist Paul Krugman and others argue that such a burden could come in the form of a more centralized European fiscal federalism. If only Europe possessed a common political identity that supported fiscal transfers among governments—not unlike the transfers among U.S. states carried out through the federal government—the eurozone countries could bring their economies into alignment. This analogy is not entirely persuasive; Europe is not America. Washington allows U.S. states to function under a single currency not through fiscal federalism and orderly bailouts but through local balanced-budget rules backed by the often brutal departure of firms, capital, and people to more economically buoyant regions. When traditional manufacturing collapsed in Michigan, federal intervention did not save the state from suffering a decade of a shrinking population and shrinking incomes; Michiganders and their money simply moved south. (The intense controversy over the auto-industry bailout proves what an exception it was.) Moreover, northern Europeans are even less willing to support large direct transfers to their foreign neighbors than Americans in southern states are willing to bail out Michigan. Although northern Europeans have accepted European financial bailouts for the time being, such funds are insufficient to salvage large countries, such as Italy and Spain, and so they have not supplanted the need for a more fundamental convergence.

Since austerity and fiscal federalism cannot bear the entire burden of adjustment, particularly for large debtors, Europe's convergence will also require a shift in the domestic policies of Germany and other surplus countries. Berlin must move to increase its public spending, wages, and consumption at a faster rate. This would help bridge the competitiveness gap between surplus and deficit countries, encourage the deficit countries to grow and export more, and reduce current account deficits across southern Europe. A fall in the value of the euro would have a complementary, if weaker, effect. Within Germany, such a shift might well earn support from unions, service industries, the public sector, and left-wing parties, all of which would benefit directly from the policies. The trick is to convince Germany's export industry, its inflation hawks, and Merkel's own conservative coalition that the long-term benefits of a stable currency outweigh the risks of inflation and of the country's commitments to bail out its neighbors. German chancellors have historically been more willing than neoliberal economists and central bankers to contemplate increases in spending and wages, especially around election time.

There is some evidence that Germany is moving in this direction, despite what its politicians and diplomats sometimes say; the costs of inaction in the short term are too high. But absent a deeper convergence, the eurozone's long-term economic fundamentals are stacked against success. Whether or not Germany will ultimately make the tough political decisions required to save the euro will likely depend on the contours of the next financial crisis.

## DEMOCRATIC SURPLUS

Many Europeans complain that the crisis has revealed the EU to be undemocratic. European institutions can appear distant, technocratic, and unfair to the common people, as the scholars Timothy Garton Ash and Larry Siedentop, among many others, have argued. In most cases, such claims contain little truth. The EU remains tightly controlled by elected national politicians. True, each country surrenders some unilateral control over its domestic policy, but in exchange it secures influence over the policies of other countries that affect it. In the EU, concurrent decision-making by national officials and directly elected European parliamentarians amounts to a form of limited government that would make John Locke and James Madison proud. No one's democratic rights are restricted as long as the people of every member state freely choose to act in union, and cooperation preserves the same public input and transparency that Europeans expect in domestic policymaking.

Judged by this standard of democracy, however, the single currency has always come up short. The problem is not the role of technocratic central banks, or even temporary technocratic governments. Nearly every modern country accepts that a credible commitment to monetary stability requires that national central banks be more autonomous than parliaments or presidents. The problem is rather that the European Central Bank is more independent than any comparable national bank—without any obvious technocratic or democratic justification. The reason is instead political; it was Germany's price for creating the euro. The result is a system tilted toward German priorities: low inflation, austerity, and the repayment of creditors.

The political and social costs of adjusting to a common currency, meanwhile, have fallen disproportionately on the poor and the powerless. Over the past two years, the EU has called for cuts in the minimum wage and government spending, but it has asked less of wealthy citizens, bankers, and the citizens of surplus countries. A fairer system would demand better enforcement of income tax collection (on average, rich Greeks illegally withhold one-quarter of what they owe), as well as reforms to housing and business practices. Watching technocratic governments in Greece, Italy, and elsewhere agree to impose what appear to be one-sided policies, backed by European authorities, naturally makes many citizens nervous.

This problem makes clear that a more balanced eurozone, in which as much is required of Germany as of debtor countries, is not just a pragmatic necessity; it is a democratic imperative. Still, despite its serious structural biases, at the end of the day, if the eurozone collapses, it will be because of an abundance of democracy as much as a lack of it. Divergence among European states reflects local priorities and preferences. No long-term solution to Europe's woes can be imposed on a member state without the consent of its government, and any government—even the technocratic governments that now sit in Athens and Rome—requires an electoral mandate. (Ireland went even further to secure democratic consent when, in February, it announced that it would put the EU fiscal compact to a referendum later this year.) Democratic governments often find it difficult to commit to the types of long-term reforms that both northern and southern Europe require today. In this case, if they cannot, then the euro will not remain viable.

## THE END OF THE AFFAIR?

The euro crisis will shape not just the fate of the single currency but also the future of the whole continent. The recent turmoil has made clear that the alignment of European domestic policies is a prerequisite for mutually beneficial cooperation. This is typical of the EU. Where basic national interests and regulatory styles have converged, as in the area of trade, governments have developed strong rules to coordinate their policies, and these policies have remained stable through the crisis. In the areas where countries have not brought their policies in line, regulation remains voluntary and largely national. So the outcome to the euro crisis will depend on how well northern and southern Europe can close the gaps in their macroeconomic behavior. But the difficulties in getting European countries to adopt similar monetary policies suggest that the EU's leaders may have pushed integration as far as it will go.

In this regard, the euro crisis is only the latest development in a two-decade-long trend toward the leveling off of European integration. At the time the Maastricht Treaty was ratified, many observers expected the EU to start regulating more and more policies, including those on social welfare, health care, pensions, criminal justice, education, issues of culture and language, local infrastructure, national politics, and, above all, taxation and fiscal priorities. Little of this has occurred, and Europe now puts forward few policies that open up new areas to centralized regulation. Today, European states retain far more control than Brussels over justice and home affairs, immigration, intellectual property, and social policy. And when the EU does launch a new centralized policy, it is rare for every government to sign on or implement it entirely. Not every EU member uses the euro, just as not every EU member adheres to the Schengen agreement, which eliminated border controls, or participates in all EU foreign policy and defense actions.

Yet none of this vindicates the Euro-pessimists. No country has issued a serious challenge to any of the EU's core activities. Nor has a single prominent European politician advocated withdrawal from the EU, as that would amount to economic suicide. Brussels continues to manage about ten percent of national policies, from business regulation to European migration, under a unified legal system. The union has recently expanded, from 12 members at the time of the Maastricht Treaty to 27 today, leaving lasting movement toward open markets, democracy, and the rule of law in its wake. Countries have not responded to the euro crisis by turning to protectionism or refusing to enforce EU policies, because cooperation in these areas is firmly grounded in common interests. The euro crisis itself has even allowed European policy to intensify in existing areas, such as monetary and banking regulation. And even a collapse of the euro would not jeopardize the existence of the EU, despite what such commentators as Walter Laqueur and Wolfgang Münchau have at times suggested. Whatever the outcome of the crisis, the EU will remain without rival the most ambitious and successful example of voluntary international cooperation in world history.

Still, the crisis does signal that the process of European integration is reaching a natural plateau, at least for the foreseeable future, based on a pragmatic division between national policy and supranational policy. The movement toward the "ever-closer union" of which the EU's founding fathers dreamed when they signed the Treaty of Rome in 1957 will have to stop at some point; there will never be an all-encompassing European federal state. But within the increasingly clear mandate of a stable constitutional settlement, Europe will continue to respond to the challenges of an increasingly interdependent world.

# Europe's New Normal

## It's Here, It's Unclear, Get Used to It

### R. Daniel Kelemen

The eurozone's troubles no longer qualify as a crisis, an unstable situation that could either quickly improve or take a dramatic turn for the worse. They are, instead, a new normal—a painful situation, to be sure, but one that will last for years to come. Citizens, investors, and policymakers should let go of the idea that there is some magic bullet that could quickly kill off Europe's ailments. By the same token, despite the real possibility of Greek exit, the eurozone is not on the brink of collapse. The European Union and its common currency will hold together, but the road to recovery will be long.

It has been nearly two and a half years since the incoming socialist government in Greece revealed the extent to which its predecessor had accumulated debt, precipitating an economic storm that has left slashed budgets, collapsed governments, and record unemployment in its wake. With each dramatic turn, observers have anticipated the story's denouement. But again and again, a definitive resolution—either a policy fix or a total collapse—has failed to emerge.

The truth is that there are no quick escapes from the eurozone's predicament. Divorce is no solution. Although some economists suggest that struggling countries on the periphery could

R. DANIEL KELEMEN is Professor of Political Science and Director of the Center for European Studies at Rutgers University. He is the author of *Eurolegalism: The Transformation of Law and Regulation in the European Union* (Harvard University Press, 2011).

leave the euro and return to a national currency in order to regain competitiveness and restore growth, no country would willingly leave the eurozone; doing so would amount to economic suicide. Its financial system would collapse, and ensuing bank runs and riots would make today's social unrest seem quaint by comparison. What is more, even after a partial default, the country's government and financial firms would still be burdened by debt denominated largely in euros. As the value of the new national currency plummeted, the debt would become unbearable, and the government, now outside the club, would not be able to turn to the eurozone for help.

Some economists go further and argue that countries on Europe's periphery could thrive outside the euro straitjacket. This is equally unconvincing. Southern European countries' economies suffer from deep structural problems that predate the euro. Spanish unemployment rates fluctuated between 15 and 22 percent throughout most of the 1990s; Greece has been in default for nearly half of its history as an independent state. These countries are far more likely to tackle their underlying problems and thrive inside the eurozone than outside it.

Others have suggested that Germany and other core countries—weary of funding endless bailouts—might abandon the euro. That is even less plausible. Germany has been the greatest beneficiary of European integration and the common currency. Forty percent of German exports go to eurozone countries, and the common currency has reduced transaction costs and boosted German growth. An unraveling of the eurozone would devastate German banks, and any new German currency would appreciate rapidly, damaging the country's export-led economic model.

A number of policy reforms may improve economic conditions in the eurozone, but none offers a panacea. Eurobonds, increased investment in struggling economies through the European Investment Bank and other funds, stricter regulations of banks, a common deposit insurance system, a shift from budget cuts to structural reforms that enhance productivity and encourage private-sector job creation—all of these could improve Europe's economic situation and should be implemented.

But none of these measures would quickly restore growth or bring employment back to pre-crisis levels. That is because they do not address Europe's central economic problem: the massive debt accumulated by the periphery countries during last decade's credit boom. The 2000s saw a tremendous amount of capital flow from the northern European countries to private- and public-sector borrowers in Greece, Ireland, Portugal, and Spain. Germany and other countries with current account surpluses flooded the periphery with easy credit, and the periphery gobbled it up. This boosted domestic demand and generated growth in the periphery but also encouraged wage inflation that undermined competitiveness and left massive debt behind. As the economists Carmen Reinhart and Kenneth Rogoff have pointed out, when countries suffer a recession caused by a financial crisis and debt overhang, they take many years to recover.

With both breakup and immediate solutions off the table, then, the eurozone is settling into a new normal. As the union slowly digs itself out of the economic pit, it is important to recognize that its system of economic governance has already been fundamentally transformed over the past two years.

First, the eurozone has, at least in practice, done away with its founding documents. In any monetary union in which states retain the autonomy to tax, spend, and borrow, there is a risk that some countries' excessive borrowing could threaten the value of the common currency. Recognizing this, the euro's creators drafted the Stability and Growth Pact and the "no bailout" clause in the Maastricht Treaty. The SGP placed legal restrictions on member-state deficit and debt levels, and the no-bailout clause forbade the European Union or individual member states from bailing out over-indebted states to avoid moral hazard.

The Maastricht governance regime is dead. The SGP was never strictly enforced, and when the crisis hit, the European Union tossed aside the no-bailout clause. Fearing contagion, it extended emergency loans to Greece, Ireland, and Portugal and set up a permanent bailout fund—the European Stability Mechanism (ESM)—which will be up and running this summer.

Having broken the taboo on bailouts, Europe had to find a way to limit the moral hazard of states turning again and again to the European Union for aid. EU lawmakers introduced the so-called six-pack legislation, which strengthened the European Commission's ability to monitor member states' fiscal policies and enforce debt limits. Twenty-five EU member states signed a fiscal compact treaty, which committed them to enshrining deficit limits into national law. Only those states that eventually ratify the treaty will be eligible for loans from the ESM.

Such legal provisions alone will not overcome the moral hazard, but they have been accompanied by evolution in bond markets, which now distinguish between the debt of healthy governments in the core and weak ones on the periphery. For the first decade of the euro's young life, bond markets priced the risk associated with the peripheral economies' bonds nearly the same as that associated with German ones. Today, the yield spreads are substantial and increase at the first sign of heightened risk. And by forcing private investors to take a nearly 75 percent loss on Greek bonds in conjunction with the second Greek bailout in February 2012, European leaders made clear that private bondholders should not expect bailouts to cover their losses, too. Now, more vigilant bond markets will police governments that run up unsustainable deficits or whose banking sectors grow fragile.

The second major structural change is that the European Central Bank—legally prohibited from purchasing any member state's debt—has thrown its rules aside and directly purchased billions in Greek, Irish, Italian, Portuguese, and Spanish bonds. Moreover, the ECB has indirectly financed billions more loans through its long-term refinancing operation, which extended over a trillion euros in low-interest loans to commercial banks.

ECB President Mario Draghi has repeatedly insisted that the bank is not engaging in "monetary financing" of member-state debts. If I were an Italian president of a central bank located in Frankfurt with a mandate designed by German inflation hawks, I would say that, too. But in practice, the ECB has shown itself to be far more flexible than many had anticipated. It has revealed, quite simply, that it will not oversee the demise of the currency that justifies its existence.

This new system of eurozone governance is more sustainable than the pre-crisis regime set in place by the Maastricht Treaty. It will withstand a Greek exit, for example. If Greece refuses to adhere to the terms of its bailout package and is forced out of the eurozone in the coming weeks, the ECB will likely scramble to stop contagion, but it will not be faced with the entire system's collapse. Meanwhile, by standing firm on Greece, the European Union will have further demonstrated that the conditions attached to its bailouts are serious, motivating other states to stick to their reform programs.

Greece's exit from the eurozone would be a catastrophe for Greece and a trauma for Europe, but it would not change the fundamentals of the post-2008 eurozone governance regime, which will still be based on stronger fiscal surveillance, more robust enforcement procedures, more vigilant bond markets, and a more activist central bank. With such a system in place, and with their commitment to fiscal discipline established, EU leaders will now face the slow, difficult tasks of adjustment and structural reform. And those burdens must be shared by all. It is understandable that Germany and the ECB initially demanded austerity as the condition for bailouts, but this one-sided approach has driven peripheral economies deeper into recession. Moving forward, austerity, wage reductions, and structural reform on the periphery must be coupled with public spending and wage increases in Germany, which will boost demand. There will be no quick fix, but the eurozone will recover, slowly but surely.

# So Long, Austerity?

## Syriza's Victory and the Future of the Eurozone

*Stathis N. Kalyvas*

T wo and half years after Greeks voted into power a coalition government led by Antonis Samaras, the head of the center-right New Democracy party, they returned to the polls this weekend.

The elections, which were forced because the Greek parliament was unable to select a new president, have propelled Greece back into the world's headlines. The Coalition of Radical Left, known by its Greek acronym Syriza, won a decisive victory, polling at 36.3 percent of the vote compared to 27.8 percent for New Democracy, 6.3 percent for the neo-Nazi party Golden Dawn, and six percent for To Potami, a centrist party. Those results hand Syriza 149 seats out of 300, and it will form a coalition government with the far-right, anti-austerity party of Independent Greeks (which won 4.7 percent of the vote). Syriza's 40-year old leader, Alexis Tsipras, who ran a successful anti-austerity campaign, will be the next prime minister of Greece.

Until 2010, Syriza was a small fringe party on the far left. Its transformation to electoral powerhouse is commonly explained as a reaction to the devastating effects of the economic depression that has racked Greece for about eight years now. Since 2007, Greece has lost one fourth of its GDP, and its unemployment rate

STATHIS N. KALYVAS is Arnold Wolfers Professor of Political Science and Director of the Program on Order, Conflict, and Violence at Yale University.

has surpassed 25 percent. It is, in other words, natural for Greek voters to turn toward a party that is promising them a different economic recipe.

In particular, Syriza has promised to do away with austerity, which was imposed on Greece in 2010 by the European Union, the European Central Bank (ECB), and the IMF (collectively known as the Troika), after Greece's reckless economic policies caused it to over-borrow and subsequently lose its ability to finance its huge debt. To eliminate its deficits, Greece had to cut spending and raise revenues, a combination that caused widespread economic pain. It certainly didn't help Greece's self-esteem that the bitter medicine was administered from abroad.

In addition to austerity, Greece was supposed to launch a full reform of its dysfunctional administrative machinery and economy so that it could begin to regain lost ground. But vigorous resistance by powerful interest groups undermined many of the structural reforms, while the slowing of the European economy and political uncertainty in Greece made a bad economic situation worse. Things began to look up in 2014, when the Greek economy grew for the first time since 2007. But this proved too little, too late to benefit the governing coalition, made up of New Democracy and PASOK, the socialist party that has towered over Greece since 1981.

Indeed, the biggest loser of the Greek crisis was PASOK, which initially emerged in the 1970s as a radical alternative to the political status quo. In its years in power, PASOK relied on a combination of fiscal expansion and low taxation, which translated into widespread prosperity for most Greeks. The party's main rival, the right-of-center New Democracy, proved able to copy this winning recipe thanks to low-interest borrowing afforded by Greece's euro membership. But it was PASOK that got most of the blame when Greece had to be bailed out in 2010; the economy had imploded under PASOK's watch. The party's leader, George Papandreou, thought he could manage the situation with economic stimulus, but his Keynesian experiment turned sour when financial markets turned their backs on the country, forcing it to seek a bailout. As a result, PASOK went from regularly polling over 40 percent to polling around five percent.

Among the many anti-austerity parties that sought to capitalize on the Greek voters' disenchantment after 2010, Syriza was most successful because it was best able to imitate PASOK's early radical style—a mix of populist language and grand promises of change through the expansion of the public sector—which many voters had come to associate with the good times. But this parallel doesn't mean that Syriza will be as successful as PASOK was back in the day. To do that, Syriza will need to generate positive economic results. It has full confidence that it can renegotiate Greece's bailout deal to get rid of most fiscal conditions attached to it. But is that possible?

For many in Europe, especially in the debtor countries of the eurozone, a Syriza victory does offer a renewed opportunity to call for the relaxation of austerity measures, which Germany has supported. So far, however, the discussion has focused on the narrower issue of the renegotiation of Greece's foreign debt. The debt is unusual in that it is primarily held by the member states of the eurozone (along with the IMF and ECB) rather than private investors. Despite a substantial haircut in 2011, Greece's debt has exploded (since the country's GDP has collapsed) reaching a nominal value of close to 170 percent of GDP.

In practice, however, servicing the debt is less onerous than its size would suggest because the debt's real present value is much lower and it carries long maturities and low interest rates. The interest is likely to be further lowered—and the maturities extended—in the coming negotiations, although more extensive debt forgiveness appears premature. At most, Greece could perhaps expect an additional relaxation of some of its most stringent fiscal targets, including the requirement that it produce a large (4.5 percent of GDP) primary surplus.

Such measures, however, are unlikely to prove sufficient to finance Syriza's economic program, particularly in light of a combined revenue shortfall and bank deposit outflow caused by creeping political uncertainty. Given that Syriza is also opposed to many of the structural reforms that are necessary to overhaul Greece's economy and that Greece still lacks access to international financial markets, the implementation of its program requires nothing less than a commitment by the EU to permanently finance Greece's growing deficits. That just isn't realistic.

Tsipras thus faces the following choice: He could take whatever adjustments the Troika offers and execute a U-turn, betting that the Greek economy will benefit from the ensuing political stability, the fall of oil prices and the euro, and new quantitative easing policies that the ECB recently announced. If, on top of this, Tsipras proves able to reform Greece's notoriously dysfunctional administration, fix the pension system, and cut down on corruption and tax evasion, he will be hailed as a great reformer and will dominate Greek politics for the next decade. Needless to say, such a strategy requires considerable vision, political skill, and expert maneuvering both in the European and Greek arenas. Tsipras and his team, however, are inexperienced when it comes to the former. Furthermore, if these adjustments fail to improve Greece's economic outlook, Tsipras could face the same fate as Samaras, who, like him, began as a critic of austerity, or his predecessor, Papandreou, whose 2009 fiscal expansion program blew up in his face.

Alternatively, Tsipras could turn down the Troika's offer. He may be unwilling to execute such a significant U-turn and renege on his promises because of his ideological opposition to market-oriented structural reforms. Or, he may be willing to do a U-turn but fail to convince the substantial chunk of his party that is made up of unreformed die-hard Marxists to follow him. Greece is still subject to the conditions of the bailout program and needs the last 7.2 billion euro installment to cover its financing gap. Hence, for the time being, the new government will need to abide by the program's requirements—that is, the very combination of austerity and reforms that Syriza has pledged to overturn. This may be enough to break the party. Such a development would usher in a political crisis, possibly leading to another round of elections that would further undermine Greece's fragile economic situation. At that point, Greece could see anything from a grand coalition between New Democracy and Syriza moderates to a full-fledged economic collapse and Greece's exit from the euro.

There is no doubt that a Greek collapse and exit from the euro would be a negative development for the European Union and the eurozone alike. On the one hand, Germany prefers to avoid such an outcome, even if it is widely considered to be manageable and unlikely to cause a financial contagion. It must also deal with the widespread disenchantment with austerity and the rise of populist parties in many European countries. On the other hand, the Greek voters, despite their economic suffering, still support the country's membership in the euro by a large margin and would steeply penalize any government that takes the country in that direction. Even if the worst can be avoided, however, the road ahead will be bumpy.

# Austerity vs. Democracy in Greece

## Europe Crosses the Rubicon

*Mark Blyth and Cornel Ban*

It may be odd to use a Roman metaphor to describe a Greek political event, but in this case, it's apt. Just as Julius Caesar crossed the Rubicon river because he could, in spite of the warnings of the Roman Senate not to, so Alex Tsipras, leader of the anti-austerity party, Syriza, has decided to try to end austerity in Greece, in spite of Europe's leaders saying he shouldn't. Whether Tsipras will succeed is still unclear, but whatever happens, his victory represents a crucial turning point for Europe—a signal that time has run out on austerity policies.

A "Tsipras" had to happen somewhere eventually, because there's only so long you can ask people to vote for impoverishment today based on promises of a better tomorrow that never arrives. If voting for impoverishment brings only more impoverishment, eventually people will stop voting for it—and the timing of "eventually" will depend on when people's assets run out. In the Greek case, backers of the incumbent New Democracy party and its austerity policies constitute that quarter of the electorate who still have assets (pensions, paper, and portfolios) after five years of depression and who want to preserve what they have. The 36 percent

MARK BLYTH is the Eastman Professor of Political Economy at Brown University.

CORNEL BAN is Assistant Professor of Political Science in the Frederick C. Pardee School of Global Studies at Boston University.

that voted for Syriza were the young, the asset-less, and the unemployed—people who either lost what they once had or never had much to begin with. Greece's 1.9 percent of growth last year means essentially nothing to a society that has lost nearly 30 percent of GDP in a little over half a decade; on the current course, it would take, by latest estimates, two generations for the country to get back above water.

Syriza's victory presents two lessons for the rest of Europe. First, no one votes for a 15-year-long recession. Second, you can't run a gold standard in a democracy. Either the gold standard goes, or democracy goes, and that is the choice Europe may face sooner than it thinks.

The Euro is the gold standard that pretends that it's not one—and therein lies the rub. While Europe has a plethora of national parliaments and free and fair elections, as well as a European parliament and multiple institutions with delegated power to represent the interests of citizens, once a country is a member of the eurozone, certain things happen that bypass any possible democratic checks. On the upside, its credit history gets rewritten. Greece and Italy get to borrow like Germany (with predictable results). On the downside, when a eurozone country is hit with an economic shock, it cannot respond to it through the exchange rate (devaluation) or by using the printing press (inflation). It must choose between default, which is not allowed, and balancing its books through internal devaluation (austerity). And if that means a couple of constitutional coups d'état have to happen in the heart of democracy to get the policies through, as happened in Italy and Greece in 2011, then so be it.

So austerity becomes the only game in town. Although it may be rational for any one country to be austere, when multiple countries that share the same currency with no common fiscal policy do so, the result can only be a massive contraction of GDP and a corresponding increase in debt—which is exactly what has happened in Europe in recent years. The boost in consumer and investor confidence that austerity was supposed to provide never materialized, and the eurozone as a whole slid into recession, and then, in the periphery, into depression and deflation. Now that all of this has occurred, however, the politics of sustaining the euro have changed, and changed utterly.

Until now, Eurozone policymakers' obsession with fighting inflation has given them a one-sided understanding of politics. In fact, Europe has not had an inflation problem of any magnitude since the 1970s. What it now faces is deflation—and since the politics of inflation and deflation are very different, the wrong policy choices produce Syrizas.

Inflation, after all, is not a general malaise that hurts all members of society equally, but a class-specific tax. Those with assets, particularly paper assets, lose harder and faster than other groups that can pressure the state to accommodate them, which is why under inflation creditors suffer and debtors prosper. Consequently, periods of inflation produce a type of politics where creditor interests come to the fore and the state is forced to retreat. The 1920s were one such period and the 1970s another—which is when Europe, and the euro, began to take their current form.

Deflation is different. Rather than creditors losing and debtors benefitting, in a deflation almost everyone loses, regardless of asset class. Consider the choice of whether to work. A worker who decides to take a pay cut to price herself into a job is individually rational. But collectively, if all workers try this, the result is a collapse in consumption. Employers get cheaper labor, to be sure, but also less demand for their products. Their logical individual responses are to cut prices to spur sales—but once again, the aggregate effect of such responses is to lower prices further. This increases real wages at a time when the economy is shrinking, which leads to more layoffs. In such a world, with practically everyone losing, calls ring out for state intervention to stop the bleeding, and eventually, they are heard. It happened in the 1930s, and it is happening once again today.

This is what Tsipras and Syriza represent: the moment Europe drifted from ever-deeper and ever-wider open capital markets and institutionalized neoliberalism to a system in which the state comes back to reassert sovereignty over markets. At that point, either democracy trumps markets (which need not be a progressive move, as Syriza's immediate choice of coalition partners demonstrates) or markets undermine democracy to protect their asset values. Which course European countries choose will be determined in the next few years, but a glance around the continent suggests that such a choice is indeed coming.

Greece may have crossed the Rubicon first, but due to its size in the European economy, Spain may be the game changer. In Spain, Podemos is likely to form a winning left-wing coalition after that country's general elections this fall, especially after the demonstration effect of Syriza. In Ireland, Sinn Fein is cut from the same anti-austerity cloth and has risen substantially in the polls. Although such parties are often called extreme, it is important to stress that their support bases, regardless of their leader's dodgy connections, are democratic political forces whose core claims—an end to self-defeating austerity and impoverishing wage policies— echo mainstream social democracy and the recommendations of many prominent economists on both sides of the Atlantic. With regard to debt relief, these parties are merely restating the standard economic case that their countries' debt overhangs are too big for investment to be resuscitated to levels that would permit high growth. Maturities can be extended indefinitely, but unless growth is restored, the game is over, and not just for Greece.

For those who fear Syriza and its left-wing counterparts, it is worth looking at the alternatives on the radical right. From Britain to Hungary, political parties—whose ideology spans the spectrum from the explicitly Nazi (the Golden Dawn in Greece) to the nationalist–populist (the United Kingdom Independence Party and the French National Front)—are busy working to channel public anger in a different direction. Harkening back to Europe's darkest days, they translate negotiable conflicts over economic policy into non-negotiable conflicts over ethnic identity. They attack European integration even more than the left-wing parties, question the democratic rights of existing citizens, and fan the flames of xenophobia toward ethnic minorities and immigrants. If Europe's ruling elites want to save the European project, and the Euro at the heart of it, they need to start actively engaging with democratic left-wing parties such as Syriza and Podemos rather than shunning them. If they don't, they will drive some of these parties into volatile left–right alliances, or, if they fail in their mandates, leave the stage open to political forces whose goals will be far more radical than mere debt restructuring and opposition to austerity.

What is at stake now is not simply Syriza's next moves or even a possible "Grexit." These are symptoms, not causes. The problem is that European authorities, driven by Germany, are enforcing a politics of deflation under a pseudo-gold standard, expecting citizens to vote indefinitely for their own impoverishment in order to save the asset values of creditors. In such a world, both radical left- and right-wing forces can only stand to gain ground across many supposedly stable countries, and quicker than we think. To avoid that fate, the continent's powerbrokers should make some sort of deal with Syriza now—because what may follow it may be far worse.

# Why Greece Will Cave-and How

## Alexis Tsipras and the Debt Negotiations

*George Tsebelis*

S ince the January 2015 election of a coalition government made up of the left-wing SYRIZA party and the right-wing ANEL (Independent Greeks) party, Greece has been in constant negotiation with the EU about reformulating the Greek bailout. Although Athens has often (but not always) denied it, any new deal will come with serious restrictions on the Greek people.

The negotiations are secret, but there are plenty of leaks on both sides. They traffic not in facts but in the impressions of people participating in, or close to, the talks. It is clear that the Greek government is relentlessly optimistic—it has been expecting an agreement "any day now" ever since the removal of Yanis Varoufakis, the Greek finance minister, from the chief negotiating position last month—whereas the rest of the EU cannot see striking a deal anytime soon.

In other words, the leaks and conflicting daily statements from participants offer little clarity about the real state of affairs. Beneath them, though, lie structural issues that imply the EU has the upper hand. In the negotiating game, the deck is stacked in the EU's favor. In the Greek domestic game, it favors Greek Prime Minister Alexis Tsipras, who wants a compromise.

GEORGE TSEBELIS is Anatol Rapoport Collegiate Professor of Political Science at the University of Michigan.

*A protester wearing a carnival mask depicting Greek Prime Minister Alexis Tsipras takes part in an anti-austerity and pro-government demonstration in Athens, February 15, 2015. (Yannis Behrakis / Reuters)*

## WAITING GAME

In any negotiation, the two parties have "reservation prices" (that is, the point at which a negotiator would rather forgo any agreement). Reservation prices depend on how beneficial the deal on the table is and how disruptive the alternative would be. Understanding that Greece represents only three percent of the EU's GDP, an outside observer might believe that the EU's reservation price is quite low—it would be willing to walk away from the talks much sooner than the Greeks. In turn, any agreement will be weighted this way. Yet there are some additional factors—one institutional and one substantive—that are important to note.

The EU's institutional advantage is that decisions (in the Eurogroup and in the council) are made unanimously, which implies that it is very difficult for any proposal to be accepted. For example, the Treaty of Lisbon, which is the functional equivalent of an EU constitution, took a decade to be negotiated and adopted. In the negotiations game, unanimous decision-making works against the Greek government, given the difficulty of getting any of its proposals accepted.

The Greek government does not seem to understand this institutional feature of the EU. The government maintains that its position expresses the will of the Greek people and that it is thus entitled to impose its preferences ("tear up the memorandums") on the EU or demand that the EU make at least 30 percent of the concessions to reach a compromise. Tsipras has repeatedly asked for private meetings with European leaders (German Chancellor Angela Merkel, European Commission President Jean-Claude Juncker, and European Central Bank [ECB] President Mario Draghi) to talk about a political solution. Yet time and time again, he is pushed back politely with the argument that the decision will be made by institutions—namely, the Eurogroup, or the "troika" of the International Monetary Fund (IMF), the European Commission, and the ECB.

The EU's substantive advantage is that it has control over liquidity. In all bargaining situations, the most impatient player has to make the most concessions. The Greek government points out that a failure in negotiations would be detrimental to the EU as well as to Greece. That might be true, but not over the same time frame.

Time extracts a price during negotiation games, and an early agreement is better than a later one. In this particular case, delays diminish Greek liquidity: Greece is running out of cash for payments on salaries, pensions, and debts to the IMF. Several government officials have announced that they may decide to pay salaries over creditors, which has resulted in capital flight from Greece. Delays in the talks are also hurting the tourism industry, Greece's major source of income. Foreign travel agencies are asking for contracts in which the Greek side assumes the risks of a change in currency (in case of Grexit) or an increase in the value-added tax (one of the major negotiation issues for the payment of the debt). Finally, delays have hurt the Greek government's standing with the public. Although Greek popular support for SYRIZA has remained

*A Greek national flag in Athens, May 28, 2015. (Alkis Konstantinidis / Reuters)*

more or less stable since the election, government policies have recently lost backing in the polls.

Although SYRIZA leadership seems to be aiming for a compromise, some 40 percent of the members of the party's central committee recently voted for a draft for decision that promoted exit from the EU. Perhaps understanding that the negotiating deck is stacked in the EU's favor, the leadership of SYRIZA has stopped promising to tear up the old debt memorandums and started to talk of a mutually beneficial compromise. Some are even starting to speak about a "painful compromise" and a postponement of key portions of SYRIZA's election platform. Whether there will be a compromise or not—whether Merkel will try to intervene at the last minute or not, as some expect her to do—the outcome of the negotiations will be a far cry from what SYRIZA promised in January.

## PARTY POLITICS

If there is an agreement in Brussels, it will still have to be approved by the Greek parliament. To understand coming events (the current extension agreement expires at the end of June, and Greek cash could run out before that deadline), it is worth examining an important feature of Greek institutions: any elections held within 18 months of a previous vote take place under a list voting system. This means that party headquarters determine the sequence of candidates on the ballot. Put simply, party leaders decide who gets elected.

This particular provision gives exceptional power to the Greek prime minister, power much greater than that granted to counterparts in any other country in the world. Almost all prime ministers of countries with parliamentary systems have the power to call for a vote of confidence, forcing members of parliament to decide not only whether they are in favor of a particular bill but also whether they are willing to defend their choice by standing for a new election (the result of a negative vote). This is a serious weapon in the hands of a prime minister. Yet the Greek prime minister has an even bigger gun: not only can he threaten to call an election, he can control the future members of parliament (given that he can threaten not to place dissidents on the party's lists). Many party officials, including the ones closest to Tsipras, have claimed that they will whip the vote and that if the government loses the vote, there should be an election.

Working backward, it is easy to see the effects of these rules on the negotiation game.

In all polls, SYRIZA is at least 20 points ahead of the second party, New Democracy (ND). The reason is that the head of ND is the previous prime minister, who wants to have his own policies recognized and approved by the Greek people. As long as there is no change in the leadership of ND or the creation of a wide coalition of all other parties, Tsipras (assuming he brings negotiations to a conclusion) will be the winner. Out of the dissidents of his party, very few will actually oppose him, and most of them will not have the name recognition to be elected in opposition to him.

So here are the strategic calculations of the actors: Tsipras is the median voter among the left wing of his party and of the Greek

*People make their way past a closed Alpha Bank branch in Athens, May 29, 2015. (Alkis Konstantinidis / Reuters)*

people. The left wing of his party has become louder and stronger over the last four months. The Greek people have become more confused and ambivalent. Any agreement that Tsipras signs with the EU and brings in front of the parliament is sure to be approved. (Even if he loses some of the 163 parliamentarians that support his government, he will gain many more from the current pro-EU opposition.) The question is, does he want to strike a deal that will violate all (or most) of the principles he has advocated and the redlines he has drawn?

Assuming he is undecided or does not want to bring such a deal in front of his party, he is likely to get one more chance: if he dramatizes the situation—defaults on one of the debt payments and restricts currency movements—the public (projecting the current trend of polls) will likely grow more decisively in favor of staying in the eurozone. Such an outcome will tilt the balance of power more in his favor within SYRIZA. This, of course, is a risky gamble because predictions under such unprecedented circumstances cannot be precise. But more to the point, it is a significantly more costly solution for the Greek people, who will suffer as the economy freezes.

## DONE DEAL?

As of early June, it looks as if any compromise that Greece negotiates with the EU will indeed violate SYRIZA's redlines. It will come to parliament and will be approved without the need for elections (elections may become necessary for the adoption of a new package). There is a possibility that Merkel will step in to sweeten the deal (after all, she cares about having a positive outcome, although she has to pass it in her own parliament) or that some proportion of SYRIZA parliamentarians (a small one may be enough) will vote down the deal (after all, they may be more ideological than ordinary members of parliament from other Greek or EU parties). But neither is very likely.

# No Exit

## Why Greece and Europe Will Still Stay Attached

*David Gordon and Thomas Wright*

G reek Prime Minister Alexis Tsipras' decision to call a referendum on the latest plan for handling Greek debt—to which his government is urging the public to vote "no"— brought to a shocking end a week that started with high hopes of a compromise agreement between Greece and the European Commission, the European Central Bank (ECB), and the International Monetary Fund (IMF). Many observers had long seen a referendum in the cards, but they expected Tsipras to call one in order to seek public approval for an agreement that he actually backed in order to outflank the far left within his own Syriza party. Instead, the man who argued for months that an agreement with Europe was the only possible path forward appears to be declaring "game over" with time left on the clock.

The odds of Greece leaving the eurozone have now substantially increased. Throughout the talks, Greece and its creditors have been desperately seeking ways around the political roadblocks in front of them. Syriza has promised that Greeks won't have to choose between ending austerity and remaining in the eurozone. That, the politicians reassured voters, was Greece's "democratic choice." But

DAVID GORDON, a former Policy Planning Director at the U.S. Department, is affiliated with the Center for a New American Security.

THOMAS WRIGHT is Fellow and Director of the Project on International Order and Strategy at the Brookings Institution.

the country's principal creditors—other European governments— also face political pressures, and Syriza has done little to assuage concerns in Europe's parliaments about throwing good money after bad and creating a moral hazard for future debtors.

With those two positions fundamentally at odds, and neither side willing to budge, a clean break between Greece and the eurozone might seem like the best option for Syriza and for many eurozone finance ministries. But the possibility of a clean break is an illusion.

Geography is particularly important. Greece lies at the heart of southeastern Europe, Europe's least stable neighborhood. There are already signs that Bulgaria and Serbia are vulnerable to contagion from the failure of Greek banks. Instability in the Balkans was part of the rationale for Greece joining the eurozone in the first place. Full integration into the European Union, it was believed, would stabilize Greece and, in turn, have positive geopolitical

*Riot policemen stand guard next to a small flag with the word "Yes" in Greek during a rally in front of the parliament building, in Athens, Greece, June 30, 2015. (Marko Djurica / Reuters)*

effects on the region. The converse remains true as well—failure in Greece will exacerbate growing tensions in southeastern Europe. Thus, the ties that bind Greece to Europe, and vice versa, are unlikely to break.

No one understands this better than German Chancellor Angela Merkel, who has been resolute in her commitment to keeping the eurozone intact and coming to an agreement with Tsipras. She remains acutely aware of Greece's long flirtation with Russia and of Russian President Vladimir Putin's continuing efforts to sow discord in the EU. As the dominant political figure in the EU's preeminent country, Merkel (not ECB President Mario Draghi, IMF head Christine Lagarde, German Finance Minister Wolfgang Schäuble, or Eurogroup chief Jeroen Dijsselbloem) remains the most important decision-maker on the creditor side, and she will try to prevent a quick Grexit after what looks like an inevitable default by Greece on its 1.5 billion euro ($1.6 billion) payment due to the IMF this week.

Merkel's task will not be easy. During a talk at Brookings Institution last week, Emmanuel Macron, France's minister of the economy, described Europe as being in a religious war. On the one side, he said, are Calvinists, led by Germany, who want those who made bad economic decisions to suffer. On the other are Catholics, who want to go to church and start off with a blank slate. There is truth to Macron's analogy. And the thing about religious wars is that they tend to last a long time. Europe's economic conflict is no different.

## TACTLESS TACTICS

Ultimately, hard negotiating lines on both sides will lead to a long and drawn-out economic conflict, sustained by religious-like certainty, in which European integration will be the biggest loser. As we described in an earlier article for *Foreign Affairs,* the Syriza government started with a strong negotiating position but squandered it early on. It chose the wrong coalition partner; alienated its allies in Europe, which played into Germany's hands; and made serious economic mistakes that weakened it at home.

Add Tsipras' referendum stunner, and it becomes hard to think of a recent democratically elected government that has blundered more.

However, the eurozone has also pursued a risky strategy—one that can only be described as regime change. Eurozone financial leaders find Syriza impossible to deal with, and so they have (almost openly) hoped that a deteriorating economic situation in Greece, including the near collapse of the banks and the drying up of the money supply, would cause the Greek people to turn on their government. The result would be either full capitulation by the Greek government, new elections (which Syriza would lose), or a new coalition with the pro-European party Potami.

European leaders' decision on Friday to put the weekend negotiations in the hands of finance ministers (rather than in the heads of government) may well have been the straw that broke Tsipras' back, because he knew full well that significant new compromises were unlikely.

There is little doubt that some eurozone leaders and finance ministers will be secretly hoping for a "no" in next weekend's referendum. They must expect that the eurozone can simply cut Greece loose with great cost to Greece but with little or no contagion to others. The rest of Europe can then move on without the distraction of the Greek drama. In fact, the euro should be stronger without its main delinquent, or so the argument goes.

Based on recent interviews one of us conducted in Berlin recently, this argument has apparently come to dominate the German Finance Ministry. Schäuble probably holds it, too, as evidenced by reports that he believes policymakers should prepare for an orderly Greek exit from the euro. One German newspaper, *Bild,* even suggested he was on the verge of resigning over differences about how to handle Greece. Now, Tsipras' decision to call a referendum will probably reinforce that line of thinking, making it even harder to grant Athens any new concessions.

Those in favor of regime change forget, though, that financial crises are notoriously unpredictable, especially in their political effects. A Greek collapse and large-scale default would result in unprecedented financial losses for the IMF and European governments, which could have a significant knock on effect. Moreover, those outcomes would poison the well between Greece and the rest of Europe, even though the two sides will have to cooperate with each other in the years ahead.

Moreover, if the world has learned one thing from financial crises over the past two decades, it is that governments must stop thinking in terms of moral right and wrongs. Sometimes, to save the system, they must help the irresponsible banks and financial institutions at the heart of the crisis. If they don't, as happened in the 1930s, the crisis will deepen, contagion will spread rapidly, and democracy itself will come under serious strain.

## END OF THE LINE?

Tsipras' strategy of scheduling a referendum after the deadline for Greece to repay the IMF is similarly risky. In anticipation of a very turbulent week in Greek politics, the government has already declared a bank holiday and the onset of capital controls.

Should the "no" vote win, it is unlikely that Tsipras has any plan for the day after, not only because the deal upon which Greeks were voting would no longer exist but also because, even if it did, it is very unlikely that creditors would be willing to reopen discussions of its terms. And even if they were, within Greece, Syriza's far left would be emboldened and Tsipras would have even less room to make any additional concessions. In this scenario, Greece would default on its ECB payment and would be forced to quickly issue some form of pseudo-currency to finance the banks and internal obligations.

A "yes" vote appears to be the more likely outcome of next weekend's referendum, not least because recent public opinion polls have showed increasing support for staying in the eurozone. That doesn't mean that Tsipras (or Greece) will be out of the woods, though. Should there be a "yes" vote, Syriza's standing within Greece would be diminished, hurting its legitimacy in

*A chalk drawing depicting German Chancellor Angela Merkel saying
"No" in Greek is pictured during a demonstration at the new European
Central Bank (ECB) headquarters in Frankfurt, Germany, June 30,
2015. (Ralph Orlowski / Reuters)*

negotiations with creditors. It isn't at all clear whether or how a
new coalition government would form.

Should Tsipras resign following a "yes" vote, the path would
open to some form of national unity government, either political or
technocratic. This government would immediately restart negotiations with the creditors in the hope of closing a deal before Greece's
3.5 billion euro ($3.92 billion) repayment to the ECB comes due
on July 20, and it would probably succeed.

But if Tsipras chose not to resign, which looks equally likely, the
path to a deal with creditors would be much more challenging.
With Syriza on its heels, Tsipras could opt to walk back Syriza's
previous demands by pointing to the referendum mandate to reach
an agreement with creditors. Should that scenario come to pass,
Tsipras would restore his reputation for craftiness, call new elections, and likely remain the dominant political force in Greece.

By far the most welcome outcome for the rest of the eurozone would be for Tsipras to form a new coalition with pro-European parties, such as Potami, but it is unclear that Syriza has the will, or the ability, to follow through on a deal with Europe by getting serious about structural reform.

## AVOIDING "NO"

At the end of the day, it is in Europe's best interest not to push Greece out the eurozone door. Should Greece vote "no," Europe's negotiators could double down on the regime change strategy in the hope that a deepening financial crisis will shift the Greek political dynamics. This strategy could very well succeed, especially given that any pseudo-currency would likely rapidly depreciate against the euro and erode the Syriza government's credibility. But should Syriza not fall even then, Europe would be faced with the worst-case scenario of a weak and alienated Greece becoming a "free radical" in Europe's least stable region. So, just as a "yes" vote would focus pressure on Tsipras, a "no" vote could become Merkel's most serious challenge yet.

Ultimately, hard negotiating lines on both sides will lead to a long and drawn-out economic conflict, sustained by religious-like certainty, in which European integration will be the biggest loser. The only way out is what the IMF, the United States, and many Europeans have long known—debt relief for Greece in exchange for unprecedented and far-reaching structural reform. This appears unlikely, though, as long as the theocratic Tsipras and Schäuble remain in place.

# G(reece)2K

## How to Contain Athens' Economic Problems

### Brendan Simms

In the late 1990s, the Western world became concerned with a phenomenon known as Y2K (Year 2000), or the Millennium Bug—that is, a mass collapse of all computer systems in the seconds after the clock struck 12:00 on New Year's Eve 2000. Most early computer programmers had entered dates only according to their last digits, rendering 1976, for example, as "76." They did so mainly to save memory space, which was very expensive in those days, and also because they assumed that their programs would have a limited shelf life. Now it was feared that some computers would not recognize the new date in 2000 and assume instead that they were back in 1900. Some worst-case scenarios envisaged hospital machines breaking down, banking chaos, and even airplanes falling out of the sky.

The threat was taken extremely seriously both by governments and by the private sector, which spent billions of dollars checking and updating computer programs in the years leading up to 2000. In the end, the bug did not bite. There were some system failures—for example, in Japan, radiation-monitoring equipment at Ishikawa failed for a while; in the United Kingdom, falsely positive pregnancy tests were sent to some women; and in some countries, various ticketing machines gave a little trouble—but that was about it.

BRENDAN SIMMS is President of the Project for Democratic Union and author of *Europe: The struggle for supremacy, 1453 to the present* (Basic Books).

*A "No" supporter flashes a victory sign before a Greek flag atop the parliament in Athens, Greece July 5, 2015. (Yannis Behrakis / Reuters)*

All this calls to mind the long Greek agony over the euro. When the crisis first blew in 2010, there were widespread fears that if Greece defaulted on its public debts, contagion would bring down banks across the eurozone and destroy the market for government bonds in the next-in-line states, such as Italy, Spain, Portugal, and perhaps even Ireland. The fears seemed somewhat justified: nobody quite knew how markets would react, and the complex interconnections between Greek debt and bank solvency elsewhere were not clear to even seasoned experts. It was precisely this sense of uncertainty on which Greek governments traded from the start of the crisis and upon which Syriza's "game theorists" based their ultraconfrontational stance starting in January this year.

For this reason, the European Union provided emergency bailouts for Greece, writing down a substantial proportion of the debt in return for commitments to reform state and economy. To be on the safe side, though, European officials and banks have spent the last five years conducting the financial equivalent of what the Y2K teams did, quarantining Greece so that any fallout could be safely contained and a G2K avoided. Recently, German Chancellor Angela Merkel claimed that this had been achieved and that Europe was now "much stronger" than when the Greek crisis had first exploded in 2010.

The announcement greatly increased the willingness of Brussels and the other European capitals to confront what they perceived as repeated Greek backsliding on the implementation of agreed reforms. The showdown between EU and Syriza last weekend was the result, and yesterday's "no" vote in the referendum on the bailout terms seems to suggest that the country is about to exit the euro. So we will now see whether fears of G2K will be realized or whether the mechanisms put in place by the rest of the EU since 2010 have worked—although, as with Y2K, we will never be sure if the threat was all imaginary in the first place.

In some sense, contagion will probably be contained. Sunday's referendum was framed by the Greek government as a vote against austerity, not against Europe or even the euro. We don't yet have reliable polling data, but it is clear that many of those who voted "no" on Sunday were young professionals—or educated but un- or underemployed Greeks—who would be natural Europeanists in any other country and who in fact remain committed to the European idea but have been worn down by five years of austerity. Their ballot was a rejection not just of the harsh bailout terms, but also of stark warnings from Brussels that a "no" vote would result in Greece's automatic departure from the eurozone. Observers must thus deal with the paradox that some of the most pro-European Greeks (along with many extreme leftist and rightist anti-Europeans) voted against the bailout deal. Greek Prime Minister Alexis Tsipras and his Syriza party want a return to the drachma. They know that most of Greece wants to stay in the euro, so they will not be in any hurry to leave it. Much better to wait until Brussels forces them out. Athens will play this game, in which the resignation of Yanis Varoufakis as finance minister is only the latest move, to the bitter end.

*German Chancellor Angela Merkel arrives at the Chancellery in Berlin, Germany, July 6, 2015. France and Germany called for an emergency summit of euro zone leaders to discuss Greece's stunning referendum vote on Sunday to reject bailout terms, as calls mounted in Berlin to cut Athens loose from Europe's common currency. (Fabrizio Bensch / Reuters)*

It may be that the financial contagion in Europe can be contained, but the strategic and political contagion will be immense. Unless it also leaves the EU, Greece may become an open door, as some Syriza ministers have already threatened, through which migrants pour in. The country will drift even more into the Russian orbit, with potentially fatal consequences to the EU's common foreign policy, especially its sanctions over Ukraine. Above all, the irreversibility of monetary union will be called into question, with huge implications for all kinds of political and economic bets placed over the past three decades. No amount of modeling can quantify the likely damage to the union, but it will be colossal and perhaps fatal to deeper integration.

Either way, the Greeks are faced with an impossible choice: either to agree to an austerity program that is crushing the life out of its young people and its weakest or to return to the failed national politics that got the country into this mess. The world will soon know the answer on G2K, but whatever it is, as we contemplate the ruin of one of Europe's nations, we should remember that Europe is neither a system nor a game, but a common destiny, and we should wish a plague on all those in Brussels and Athens who have brought us to this pass.

# A Pain in the Athens

## Why Greece Isn't to Blame for the Crisis

*Mark Blyth*

When the anti-austerity party Syriza came to power in Greece in January 2015, Cornel Ban and I wrote in a *Foreign Affairs* article that, at some point, Europe was bound to face an Alexis Tsipras, the party's leader and Greek prime minister, "because there's only so long you can ask people to vote for impoverishment today based on promises of a better tomorrow that never arrives." Despite attempts by the eurogroup, the European Central Bank, and the International Monetary Fund since February 2015 to harangue Greece into ever more austerity, the Greeks voted by an even bigger margin than they voted for Syriza to say "no" once more. So the score is now democracy 2, austerity 0. But now what? To answer that question, we need to be clear about what this crisis is and what it is not. Surprisingly, despite endless lazy moralizing commentary to the contrary, Greece has very little to do with the crisis that bears its name. To see why, it is best to follow the money—and those who bank it.

The roots of the crisis lie far away from Greece; they lie in the architecture of European banking. When the euro came into existence in 1999, not only did the Greeks get to borrow like the Germans, everyone's banks got to borrow and lend in what was effectively a cheap foreign currency. And with super-low rates,

MARK BLYTH is Eastman Professor of Political Economy at Brown University.

countries clamoring to get into the euro, and a continent-wide credit boom underway, it made sense for national banks to expand private lending as far as the euro could reach.

So European banks' asset footprints (loans and other assets) expanded massively throughout the first decade of the euro, especially into the European periphery. Indeed, according the Bank of International Settlements, by 2010 when the crisis hit, French banks held the equivalent of nearly 465 billion euros in so-called impaired periphery assets, while German banks had 493 billion on their books. Only a small part of those impaired assets were Greek, and here's the rub: Greece made up two percent of the eurozone in 2010, and Greece's revised budget deficit that year was 15 percent of the country's GDP—that's 0.3 percent of the eurozone's economy. In other words, the Greek deficit was a rounding error, not a reason to panic. Unless, of course, the folks holding Greek debts, those big banks in the eurozone core, had, over the prior decade,

*Greece's Prime Minister Alexis Tsipras arrives at an emergency eurozone summit in Brussels, Belgium, July 7, 2015. (Francois Lenoir / Reuters)*

grown to twice the size (in terms of assets) of—and with operational leverage ratios (assets divided by liabilities) twice as high as—their "too big to fail" American counterparts, which they had done. In such an over-levered world, if Greece defaulted, those banks would need to sell other similar sovereign assets to cover the losses. But all those sell contracts hitting the market at once would trigger a bank run throughout the bond markets of the eurozone that could wipe out core European banks.

Clearly something had to be done to stop the rot, and that something was the troika program for Greece, which succeeded in stopping the bond market bank run—keeping the Greeks in and the yields down—at the cost of making a quarter of Greeks unemployed and destroying nearly a third of the country's GDP. Consequently, Greece is now just 1.7 percent of the eurozone, and the standoff of the past few months has been over tax and spending mixes of a few billion euros. Why, then, was there no deal for Greece, especially when the IMF's own research has said that these policies are at best counterproductive, and how has such a small economy managed to generate such a mortal threat to the euro?

Part of the story, as we wrote in January, was the political risk that Syriza presented, which threatened to embolden other anti-creditor coalitions across Europe, such as Podemos in Spain. But another part lay in what the European elites buried deep within their supposed bailouts for Greece. Namely, the bailouts weren't for Greece at all. They were bailouts-on-the-quiet for Europe's big banks, and taxpayers in core countries are now being stuck with the bill since the Greeks have refused to pay. It is this hidden game that lies at the heart of Greece's decision to say "no" and Europe's inability to solve the problem.

Greece was given two bailouts. The first lasted from May 2010 through June 2013 and consisted of a 30 billion euro–Stand By Agreement from the IMF and 80 billion euro in bilateral loans from other EU governments. The second lasted from 2012 until the end of 2014 (in practice, it lasted until a few days ago) and comprised another 19.8 billion euro from the IMF and another

144.7 billion euro disbursed from an entity set up in late 2010 called the European Financial Stability Facility (EFSF, now the European Stability Mechanism, ESM). Not all of these funds were disbursed. The final figure "loaned" to Greece was around 230 billion euro.

The EFSF was a company the EU set up in Luxemburg "to preserve financial stability in Europe's economic and monetary union" by issuing bonds to the tune of 440 billion euro that would generate loans to countries in trouble. So what did they do with that funding? They raised bonds to bail Greece's creditors—the banks of France and Germany mainly—via loans to Greece. Greece was thus a mere conduit for a bailout. It was not a recipient in any significant way, despite what is constantly repeated in the media. Of the roughly 230 billion euro disbursed to Greece, it is estimated that only 27 billion went toward keeping the Greek state running. Indeed, by 2013 Greece was running a surplus and did not need such financing. Accordingly, 65 percent of the loans to Greece went straight through Greece to core banks for interest payments,

*A worker cleans graffiti outside the central Bank of Greece building in Athens, Greece, July 7, 2015. (Yannis Behrakis / Reuters)*

maturing debt, and for domestic bank recapitalization demanded by the lenders. By another accounting, 90 percent of the "loans to Greece" bypassed Greece entirely.

Telling though those numbers are, they still miss the fact that, after Mario Draghi took over from Jean Claude Trichet at the ECB in late 2011, Draghi dumped around 1.2 trillion euro of public money into the European banking system to bring down yields in the Long Term Refinancing Operations (LTROs). Bond yields went down and bond prices soon went up. This delighted bond-holders, who got to sell their now LTRO-boosted bonds back to the governments that had just bailed them out. In March 2012, the Greek government, under the auspices of the troika, launched a buy-back scheme that bought out creditors, private and national central banks, at a 53.4 percent discount to the face value of the bond. In doing so, 164 billion euro of debt was handed over from the private sector to the EFSF. That debt now sits in the successor facility to the EFSF, the European Stability Mechanism, where it causes much instability. So if we want to understand why the combined powers of the eurozone can't deal with a problem the size of a U.S. defense contract overrun, it's probably wise to start here and not with corrupt Greeks or Swabian housewives' financial wisdom. As former Bundesbank Chief Karl Otto Pöhl admitted, the whole shebang "was about protecting German banks, but especially the French banks, from debt write-offs."

To fix the problem, someone in core Europe is going to have to own up to all of the above and admit that their money wasn't given to lazy Greeks but to already-bailed bankers who, despite a face-value haircut, ended up making a profit on the deal. Think about it this way. If 230 billion euro had been given to Greece, it would have amounted to just under 21,000 euros per person. Given such largess, it would have been impossible to generate a 25 percent unemployment rate among adults, over 50 percent unemployment among youth, a sharp increase in elderly poverty, and a near collapse of the banking system—even with the troika's austerity package in place.

Doing so would, however, also entail admitting that by shifting, quite deliberately, responsibility from reckless lenders to irresponsible (national) borrowers, Europe regenerated exactly the type of petty nationalism, in which moral Germans face off against corrupt Greeks, that the EU was designed to eliminate. And owning up to that, especially when mainstream parties' vote shares are dwindling and parties such as Syriza are ascendant, simply isn't going to happen. So what is?

Despite Germany being a serial defaulter that received debt relief four times in the twentieth century, Chancellor Angela Merkel is not about to cop to bailing out D-Bank and pinning it on the Greeks. Neither is French President Francois Hollande or anyone else. In short, the possibilities for a sensible solution are fading by the day, and the inevitability of Grexit looms large. It is telling that Tsipras and his colleagues repeatedly used the phrase "48 hours"—sometimes "72 hours"—as the deadline for getting a new deal with creditors once the vote was in. This number referred to how long Greek banks could probably stay solvent once the score went to 2–0.

At the time of writing, the ECB is not only violating its own statutes by limiting emergency liquidity assistance to Greek banks, but is also raising the haircuts on Greek collateral offered for new cash. In other words, the ECB, far from being an independent central bank, is acting as the eurogroup's enforcer, despite the risk that doing so poses to the European project as a whole. We've never understood Greece because we have refused to see the crisis for what it was—a continuation of a series of bailouts for the financial sector that started in 2008 and that rumbles on today. It's so much easier to blame the Greeks and then be surprised when they refuse to play along with the script.

# The Agreekment That Could Break Europe

## Euroskeptics, Eurocritics, and Life After the Bailout

*Harris Mylonas*

As the Greek negotiating team was preparing its latest reform proposal for the country's creditors, I was walking to the Montparnasse metro station in Paris on my way to the Council for European Studies conference held at Sciences Po. At the station, a woman my age was standing behind the ticket booth. In her attempt to help me buy the most appropriate tickets for the next three days, I (apologetically) revealed to her that I am Greek and that I do not speak French. When she heard the word "Greek," she put her hand close to her heart and repeated the word in French with compassion and solidarity. She asked me to wait for a second. In 30, she came back with her own credit card, swiped it, and handed over to me the first of the three tickets saying: "This is from me. For Greece."

It is besides the point that I did not personally need this form of solidarity. It was also of little matter that many of my compatriots would find this story depressing. What resonated in the moment was that this exchange was exactly what the founders of the European Union envisaged: a solidary group of European citizens living in peace and prosperity.

HARRIS MYLONAS is Assistant Professor of Political Science and International Affairs at the Elliott School of International Affairs at George Washington University.

*An anti-EU protester holds a banner in front of the parliament building during a demonstration of about five hundred people in Athens, July 13, 2015. (Christian Hartmann / Reuters)*

Instead, many EU bureaucrats, ministers of finance, and heads of state saw—and some still see—the Greek crisis as a case study in moral hazards. Greece, the thinking goes, needs to fail now in order to discipline other unruly countries. Its governing party, Syriza, needs to fall in order to dampen the European public's support for parties that are challenging the EU status quo. From this point of view, a hard line toward Greece is a necessary evil.

This logic, however, fails to understand the real problem in Greece and the psychology of the European public. Indeed, from the periphery, it is the European core, mainstream elites, officials, and institutions that all look rather euroskeptic—that is, skeptical of the very idea of unity, prosperity, democracy, solidarity, and mutual respect for which EU founders worked so hard to nurture. As of this writing, it appears that these elites have reached a deal with Greece, but the way they manage the relationship from here on out remains crucial. To avoid fueling the very euroskepticism and sovereigntist tendencies they want to quell, they have to abandon all ideas of vindictiveness and, instead, foster a spirit of cooperation among equal partners.

## FROM GREFERENDUM TO AGREEKMENT

The forces supporting Europe's status quo, namely the euro-establishment spearheaded by the German government, found an opportunity in the Greek financial crisis to reaffirm their commitment to austerity as the main way to guarantee Europe's continued economic competitiveness. But there are plenty of people who oppose those forces. In fact, at the moment, the deepest divide within European societies is between those who want to leave the EU—in the Greek case this camp is represented mainly by the Communist Party, Golden Dawn, along with some of the more radical members of Greece's coalition government—and those who want to stay in the union but reform it.

In the first camp are euroskeptics of both the right- and left-wing varieties. They range from the United Kingdom Independence Party's Nigel Farage to Jobbik's leader Gábor Vona in Hungary, and they have found in the Greek crisis an opportunity to intensify their rhetoric and accuse the EU for operating as a "prison of nations." It is no accident that during Greek Prime Minister Alexis Tsipras' address to the European Parliament last week, euroskeptic parliamentarians of all stripes held up "no" (όχι) signs—in support of Greeks' recent "no" vote on the June 25 plan proposed to the Greek government by the creditors.

It is not only euroskeptics that sided with the "no" vote, though, but also eurocritics who don't want to leave the union but want to reform it. In this camp are a number of parties and figures, including the Podemos party in Spain and Lega Nord in Italy. Some in this camp prefer merely an inter-governmental union. Others envision a federal Europe. Tsipras himself is a eurocritic; he is not against the European Union project as a whole, but would like to see less austerity, more democratic EU institutions, and more redistribution of wealth.

Core Europeans might have interpreted Greece's "no" as a vote against the euro or even Europe. But, in fact, the Greek people tried to send multiple messages with their vote. For his part, Tsipras interpreted the vote as a "yes" to a different type of Europe. It is questionable whether the referendum led to a better deal, but it gave Tsipras more power at home to get his way. He isolated domestic opposition, turned Syriza into a more cohesive party, and avoided becoming a "Left Parenthesis"—a phrase that refers to a short-lived government of the Left in Greece that some had predicted or wished for.

The vote also deepened cleavages in Greek society, particularly between the young in poor neighborhoods, who tended to vote "no," and those over 65 and in wealthy neighborhoods, who tended to vote "yes." Young Greeks, who rightly feel that they had no part in the system that led Greece to financial ruin, are less tolerant of the current deal and status quo European institutions. The Greek youth, who are experiencing 60 percent unemployment rates, have very little patience. They bristle at the humiliating way in which the euro-establishment treated Tsipras and the Greek people. With deep feelings of marginalization, many eurocritics have been pushed into becoming euroskeptics.

How far this process has gone is hard to quantify. In Greece, it is indicative that many Syriza parliamentarians, as well as the head of the Greek government's minor coalition partner, Panos Kammenos, openly opposed the latest deal as the product of blackmail by the EU. Elsewhere in Europe, Britain's upcoming "in/out" referendum to decide its own EU membership will be a critical test. For Europe to survive such trials without significant—if not irreparable—damage, the euro-establishment camp needs to demonstrate that it understands where the legitimacy of the European Union project lies: building an ever closer union of peace, prosperity, respect for human rights, and democratic governance. The deal struck on July 13 is far from a promising first step toward this goal.

Namely, the agreement, which was reached after a marathon summit, could lead to a third bailout for Greece, which would come with the transfer of 50 billion euros ($55 billion) worth of Greek assets to a new fund for the recapitalization of Greek banks, immediate pension and tax reforms, and the reversal of many of the economic measures the Greek government has passed since its election in late January. Not surprisingly, when the newest demands became publicly known, Twitter exploded with hashtags such as #ThisIsACoup.

## EUROPEAN DREAMIN

During several decades of economic growth and expansion of the welfare state, EU polities managed to downplay the frictions among and within them. Then the financial crisis hit. The alliances that formed as a result—and the ensuing debates over austerity— cut across the traditional Left-Center-Right ideological axis. In fact, the social cleavages currently dividing EU member states and the populations within them are the product of a dual integration crisis: European and national. The European integration crisis was brought on by the challenges emerging from the recent financial crisis coupled with tensions surrounding the eurozone's eurozone's uneven economic and political development. Meanwhile, the demographic decline across the continent and the inability of European societies to successfully integrate immigrants brought to the fore national integration problems.

The social cleavages currently dividing EU member states and the populations within them are the product of a dual integration crisis: European and national. Greece was not the only country that faced a financial debt crisis. Cyprus, Ireland, Portugal, and Spain did as well. In all cases, democratically-elected governments no longer had the ability, due to their participation in the eurozone, to devalue their currency or inflate their economies by printing money. As I wrote in *Perspectives on Politics*, "they were faced with two suboptimal options: to default or to implement austerity measures (internal devaluation)." Meanwhile, the European institutions opted for policies that would punish the already-suffering countries as a way to prevent further contagion. "These developments have since given rise to Euroscepticism throughout the EU, leading to a growing public dissatisfaction in the crisis-stricken countries with their own governments but also with the European Commission and the European Central Bank, and reminding everyone of the democratic deficit problem that has long existed within the European Union."

It is perhaps bad luck that all this happened while the region's poorest were hit with other economic and social challenges. Migration from outside of Europe and from within it, coupled with the governments' failures to successfully integrate the new arrivals, left some Europeans jobless or fearful for their jobs and uncertain about their place in the continent's social fabric. In turn, they believed that both their national governments and the EU had let them down, and their euroskepticism took on a decidedly nationalist and populist tinge.

In Greece, most—if not all—citizens agree that the policies of the past five years have utterly failed; they also agree that the "patronage social contract" that underwrote political rule for the past four decades is bankrupt. Meanwhile, even those who supported the "no" vote in the recent referendum—those who consider Greece a "colony of debt"—are internally divided on quintessential questions such as whether one is born Greek or can become Greek. France, Germany, Italy, Spain, and others are all facing similar identity crises, which is only exacerbated by the economic situation and the pressures on the welfare state.

All this is happening while austerity—chosen as the main way to keep the euro strong and the EU competitive—has undermined popular support for the union across Europe, not just in Greece. These developments constitute the dual integration crisis: EU and national. The safest way out of this predicament is an ever closer union, a political Europe with a fiscal union and democratically elected institutions that would redistribute more wealth and would achieve competitiveness through innovation, not austerity and internal devaluation. The hope for such a Europe is still alive. The woman I met in the Montparnasse metro station is a testament to this.

Printed in Great Britain
by Amazon.co.uk, Ltd.,
Marston Gate.